Alaska
Climbing

Alaska Climbing

By Joseph Puryear

Foreword

As a kid I was inspired by the tales of Jack London. His depiction of Alaska and the hardy souls pitting themselves against a boundless and unforgiving wilderness struck a chord in my dreamy adolescent mind. The heck with Klingons and transporters—Alaska, in my impressionable young mind, was the final frontier. I just had to go there. The call of the wild was strong and irresistible.

In 1987, at the tutelage of my mentor Mugs, Seth, Bob and I departed Salt Lake City in a destitute Econonoline van, bound for the Alaska Range. We were on a mission to find adventure. Driving to Alaska is a rite of passage, one that we as aspiring alpinists, had to do. Fixing the van with salvaged parts and driving in white-out conditions on dirt roads were small lessons in adaptability and perseverance that were part of the upcoming adventure. When we finally saw the rosy ramparts of the Denali massif at dawn from the Talkeetna hill, we knew we had arrived. We tried to mask our fear and trepidation with bravado and moxie. We knew only too well that the high mountains of Alaska were a very unforgiving and harsh place. The Alaska Range is unique with its near arctic setting, Himalayan proportions and wild mix of geology. It is the place for alpine climbing in North America.

In Alaska I found the spirit that inspired Jack London a century earlier. With modern novelties making life much easier, the challenge wasn't merely to build a fire; rather it was to test oneself on the hidden ridges and facets of the peaks that define the crown of North America. From the international atmosphere of Denali's West Buttress to the forbidding north wall of Mt. Hunter, climbers are able to find a route that matches their ambition and ability. The SuperTopo guidebook you are holding will motivate you and help select a climb. Use this book as a tool to inspire and plan. It is not a replacement for experience, nor will it be able to provide any when the going gets tough.

In 1995, after helping with several rescues on Denali, my partner Alex and I decided to give the Moonflower Buttress on Mt. Hunter a go. We skied to the base of the wall, roped up and started climbing. We never made the summit, yet the climb was the quintessential Alaska experience. We climbed through the night in the twilight that seamlessly blends into dawn, warmed our hands at belays and felt hunger as the few candy bars we brought were no match for the effort we exerted. Suffering strips away pretensions and our raw souls grew closer as friends. We had to trust each other, we had to believe in our intuition about the weather and, finally, we realized that although climbing is a frivolous pursuit, it does provide those who choose to explore it a great sense of self fulfillment.

May the following pages allow you to unleash your inner quest for adventure. It is all there. Go find it.

Be good, be kind, and be safe,

Conrad Anker

Warning!

Climbing is an inherently dangerous sport in which severe injuries or death may occur. Relying on the information in this book may increase the danger.

When climbing you can only rely on your skill, training, experience, and conditioning. **If you have any doubts as to your ability to safely climb any route in this guide, do not try it.**

This book is neither a professional climbing instructor nor a substitute for one. **It is not an instructional book. Do not use it as one.** It contains information that is nothing more than a compilation of opinions about climbing in Alaska. **These opinions are neither facts nor promises.** Treat the information as opinions and nothing more. Do not substitute these opinions for your own common sense and experience.

Assumption of Risk

There may be errors in this book resulting from the mistakes of the author and/or the people with whom they consulted. The information was gathered from a variety of sources, which may not have been independently verified. Those who provided the information may have made mistakes in their descriptions. The author may have made mistakes in histheir conveyance of the information in this book. **The author cannot, therefore, guarantee the correctness of any of the information contained in this book.** The topographical maps, photo-diagrams, difficulty ratings, protection ratings, approach and/or descent information, suggestions about equipment, and other matters may be incorrect or misleading. Fixed protection may be absent, unreliable, or misplaced. **You must keep in mind that the information in this book may be erroneous, so use your own judgement when choosing, approaching, climbing, or descending from a route described in this book.**

DO NOT USE THIS BOOK UNLESS YOU [AND YOUR ESTATE] PROMISE NEVER TO TRY TO SUE US IF YOU GET HURT OR KILLED.

Disclaimer of Warranties

THE AUTHOR AND PUBLISHER WARN THAT THIS BOOK CONTAINS ONLY THE AUTHOR'S OPINIONS ON THE SUBJECTS DISCUSSED. WE MAKE NO OTHER WARRANTIES, EXPRESSED OR IMPLIED, OF MERCHANTABILITY, FITNESS FOR PURPOSE, OR OTHERWISE, AND IN ANY EVENT, OUR LIABILITY FOR BREACH OF ANY WARRANTY OR CONTRACT WITH RESPECT TO THE CONTENT OF THIS BOOK IS LIMITED TO THE PURCHASE PRICE OF THE BOOK. WE FURTHER LIMIT TO SUCH PURCHASE PRICE OUR LIABILITY ON ACCOUNT OF ANY KIND OF NEGLIGENT BEHAVIOR WHATSOEVER ON OUR PART WITH RESPECT TO THE CONTENTS OF THIS BOOK.

Dedication

To Mom and Dad
Thanks for your everlasting support
and understanding.

Acknowledgements

Foremost thanks go to Chris McNamara for seeing the vision and going for it. I'd also like to thank Conrad Anker, Jim Litch, and Joe Reichert for contributing their thoughts and expertise to help enhance this guide.

Much gratitude is owed to the following people who contributed crucial beta, history, and photos: Dave Anderson, John Burcham, Kelly Cordes, Jim Donini, John 'Jedi' Fitzgerald, Dan Gambino, David Gottlieb, Chad Kellogg, Gordy Kito, Roy Leggett, Brian McCullough, Rob Newsom, Jared Ogden, Andi Orgler, Steve Quinlan, Paul Roderick, Roger Robinson, Kristian Sieling, Ben and Natasha Summit, Karl Swanson, Dylan Taylor, Chris Turiano, Jesse Williams, Jeff and Lori Yanuchi, and Daniel Zimmermann. And to Mike Gauthier for providing advice and outstanding aerial photography. And to Mark Westman for additional suggestions, critiques, and access to his extensive image collection.

I'd like to give much praise to those friends and family that have supported me through my Alaskan adventure: Thanks to my wife Michelle for her encouragement and support through this process. Thanks to Natasha and Ben Summit for endless rides to Talkeetna and letting me crash their pad with my stinky climbing friends. And to Mel and Don Roller for also providing a place to stay. Thanks to Base Camp Manager and friend Lisa Roderick for taking good care of me. Thanks to Paul Roderick, David Lee, and the staff and pilots at Talkeetna Air Taxi over the years for providing the absolute best air service support. Thanks to Tony Martin and his plane the Pegasus, and Todd Burleson (owner of Alpine Ascents International) for additional aerial photography sessions. And additional appreciation goes to Chris Bowman, Trisha Costello (owner of the Talkeetna Roadhouse), Bill Rodwell, Sandra White, and Dieter Zeph.

The Denali Climbing Rangers and staff are to be commended for their excellent stewardship to these mountains.

Thanks go to the production crew: David Safanda Design Solutions for the design, Chris McNamara for editing and layout, Clair Nicholas for assistance with the maps, and Steve McNamara for his copy editing work.

And of course none of this would have been possible without my climbing partners in Alaska and around the world. Thanks for the great times and I look forward to many more: Mike Gauthier, David Gottlieb, Chad Kellogg, Chris McNamara, Stoney Richards, Mark Westman, and Daniel Zimmermann.

Published by
SuperTopo
2 Bradford Way
Mill Valley, CA 94941
www.supertopo.com

Layout and editing by Chris McNamara and Joseph Puryear
Topo and map artistry by Joseph Puryear
Assistant layout by Clair Nicholas
Copyedited by Steve McNamara

Cover Photography
Top: Sunset over Mt. Foraker. *Photo by Joe Puryear*
**Main: David Gottlieb climbing along the Southwest Ridge of Peak
11,300.** *Photo by Joe Puryear*

Cover Design
by David Safanda, www.safanda.com

**Page 2 Photo: Daniel Zimmermann leading steep ice on the North
Couloir of the Mini-Moonflower.** *Photo by Joe Puryear*
Page 6 Photo: Joe Puryear on Pitch 2 of Goldfinger, The Stump. *Photo
by Chris McNamara*
Contents Page: The north face of Mt. Foraker. *Photo by Joe Puryear*

All uncredited photos by Joe Puryear.

Puryear, Joseph
Alaska Climbing

ISBN 0-9765235-0-7

Contents

Introduction

Alaska is huge. At over 586,400 square miles it is 1/5 the size of the entire United States and larger than the next four largest states combined. It is no surprise that Alaska has one of the greatest climbing arenas on earth. The Alaska Range is one of the world's finest mountain environments and North America's premier alpine climbing destination. At 20,320 feet, the continent's highest peak, Denali is the central focus of the range. Because of the lure of climbing to this lofty point, a network of easy access has been created to allow climbers to explore the magnificent peaks surrounding Denali as well. This area, referred to as the Central Alaska Range, contains some of the biggest, baddest, and steepest peaks to be found anywhere. Expert climbers from around the world come here year after year to put their skills to the test. But the range is certainly not limited to the elite. An array of easier peaks and "back-side" routes makes it just as appealing to novice and intermediate climbers. Climbing amongst the splendor of these mountains is a delight for all.

The mountains of the Central Alaska Range contain incredibly diverse types of climbing all in a relatively close area. On the same day only 15 miles apart, climbers in the Ruth Gorge may be cruising up 10-pitch rock routes in shirt sleeves, while climbers high on Denali may be struggling up difficult ice and mixed terrain in desperate conditions. In these mountains there is something for everyone: high-altitude mountaineering, technical ice and mixed climbing, big wall climbing, alpine rock climbing, cragging, and ski touring. It is common for climbers to show up on the glacier with rock shoes and a chalk bag in addition to their ice tools and ice screws.

While it is true that the Alaska Range has a reputation for having poor weather and brutal storms, when the weather is good, the rewards of being here are immeasurable. The expansive glaciers, rugged summits, and pristine ridge lines will forever be impressed in your memory. And the huge Alaskan scale of these mountains continually astounds all that visit.

Getting There

Anchorage
The path to climbing in Alaska has changed immensely since the days of Belmore Browne who mushed dogs from Seward to reach the Muldrow Glacier months later. These days simply hop on a jet-liner to the booming metropolis of Anchorage, Alaska. A few adventuresome folk prefer to drive to Alaska each season. Pick up **The Milepost** magazine for the best driving beta available.

If you've purchased all of your food prior to the trip and do not need anything in Anchorage, it is possible to have a shuttle van pick you up at the airport and deliver you directly to Talkeetna. Make sure your flight schedule matches your shuttle company's pick-up schedule. The driver may be able to make a few short stops, but this should be arranged with the company in advance. Check the appendix for a complete list of shuttle services.

Another option is to take the **Alaska Railway** directly to Talkeetna or Denali Park. The train is definitely a pricey option, but it is a neat way to experience Alaska. Although the train goes directly to the Anchorage International Airport, this service is reserved for tourist groups only. To catch the train it is necessary to travel 20 minutes by bus or taxi to the Anchorage Depot. The **People Mover** bus is a good way to get around town.

With airline baggage limits so restrictive these days, many climbers (especially international climbers) find it easier to take a day in Anchorage to complete their expedition food and gear shopping before heading up to Talkeetna. A good option is to rent a car at the airport for a day and complete all your necessary shopping, then have the shuttle service come and pick you

The east face of Mt. Barrill with Denali in the background. Photo by Joe Puryear

up. An overnight stay at one of the youth or climbing hostels can also be arranged. Check out **Earth Bed and Breakfast** for the best climber friendly accommodations. Lori and Angel go out of their way to welcome climbers from all over the world.

While there are numerous locations to get supplies around Anchorage, the following combination of businesses will carry everything you need for an Alaskan expedition.

Costco: $45 membership required. Good cheap source for staple foods needed in large quantities. Bulk batteries and cheap calling cards also available.

Fred Meyer: General grocery outlet and multi-department store. The Brown Jug liquor store is attached as well as a bank and ATM.

Natural Pantry: Health food and bulk food store.

New Seguya: Excellent source for specialty and gourmet foods.

Alaska Mountaineering and Hiking (AMH): Local dealer of climbing and outdoor gear and clothing.

Recreational Equipment Incorporated (REI): Climbing and outdoor gear and clothing.

If in search of some good food and entertainment in Anchorage, stop by either the **Moose's Tooth Pub and Pizzeria** or the **Bear Tooth Theatrepub & Grill**. Both are

The Talkeetna Roadhouse

fun and popular spots with great food and variety. Also the **Middle Way Café** (right next to REI) and the **Organic Oasis** both serve excellent vegetarian and vegan cuisine.

Talkeetna

From Anchorage, follow Alaska Highway 1 north 35 miles to the junction of Highway 3 just east of the town of Wasilla. Turn on Highway 3 north (the George Parks Highway) and follow it another 64 miles to the Talkeetna Spur Road junction. Take a right and follow the Spur Road 14 more miles to Talkeetna. The drive takes about 2.5 hours. Talkeetna is a wonderful little community with a rich Alaskan history. Originally a railroad supply depot on the way to gold mining claims farther north, the Talkeetna townsite was established in 1919. The economy nowadays is largely tourist driven with many activities such as fishing, hunting, river-rafting, flight-seeing, and of course mountaineering. Talkeetna is a Den'aina Indian word meaning "place where food is stored by the river", or more poetically translated, "river of plenty".

Once in Talkeetna, there are a few more businesses for last minute shopping. Prices in Talkeetna are generally higher but supporting the local businesses helps the local small-town economy. Two very small grocery stores and a health food store may have some last minute goodies, but don't count on being able to buy food for a three week expedition. Climbing gear stores come and go in town, so it's best to check with your air service beforehand to see what the current situation is. Some of the air services may have some gear for sale or for rent as well. White gas or Coleman fuel can be purchased from the air services.

For eats, the **Talkeetna Roadhouse** is by far the best bet for breakfast, and they also serve fresh pastries, homemade soup, and sandwiches for lunch. Bring your laptop for a free wireless connection. **Mountain High Pizza Pie** serves gourmet pizzas and calzones. The **West Rib Pub and Grill** is a favorite climbers' hangout, with great beer and burgers. **Sparky's** is the old standby for a variety of take-out meals. The **Latitude**

62 is a nice alternative for breakfast, lunch, and dinner.

After dinner, the **Historic Fairview Inn** is the local drinking establishment, often featuring live music. Much to the dismay of everyone, the Fairview was closed for the 2005 season, and its fate remains to be seen. **The West Rib** is also a great place to tie one on after (or before) a hard climb.

For overnight accommodations, check with your air service to see if they have a bunk-house or other lodging facility. Often, climbers are allowed to camp on the air service grounds, but be sure to check with your company beforehand. The **Talkeetna Hostel International** is located near the airport and is a good deal for climbers. **The Talkeetna Roadhouse** has convenient and comfortable rooms. **The Fairview** offers nice rooms, but can be very loud at night. **The Swiss Alaska Inn** and the **Latitude 62** also have rooms.

There is a bank located at the Talkeetna Spur Road junction (The 'Y'). There are no banks in Talkeetna, but there is currently at least one local ATM. Laundry can be done at **Tanner's Trading Post**. Public showers can be found here as well. A small public library offers free internet access. Several other establishments around town offer internet for a fee. Some air services offer internet access for their customers.

Other local attractions include the Talkeetna Historical Society Museum, which features an intriguing 12-by-12-foot raised relief wood model based on Bradford Washburn's Mt. McKinley map.

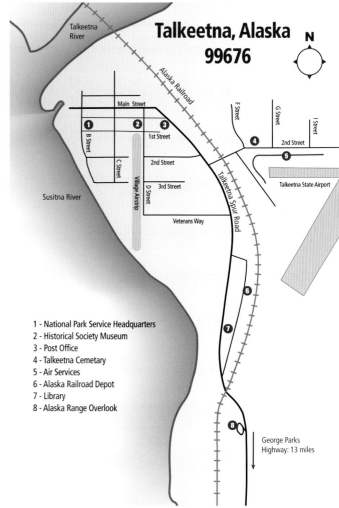

Talkeetna, Alaska
99676

Talkeetna River
Alaska Railroad
Main Street
B Street
C Street
Village Airstrip
D Street
1st Street
2nd Street
3rd Street
Veterans Way
Susitna River
F Street
G Street
I Street
2nd Street
Talkeetna Spur Road
Talkeetna State Airport
George Parks Highway: 13 miles

1 - National Park Service Headquarters
2 - Historical Society Museum
3 - Post Office
4 - Talkeetna Cemetary
5 - Air Services
6 - Alaska Railroad Depot
7 - Library
8 - Alaska Range Overlook

The Talkeetna Cemetery has a climber's memorial as a tribute to all that have died while in the Alaska Range. **The Talkeetna Ranger Station** is the single largest source of Alaska Range climbing information with their somewhat organized binders with route info and pictures. To really get your blood pumping, several gigantic Washburn photographs line their walls. An excellent indoor climbing wall can be found at the **Alaska Mountaineering School**. For a great view of the Alaska Range, follow Main Street west out to the river.

*** Bold faced businesses are listed in the Appendix.

The National Park Service

All of the climbs in this book are located within Denali National Park. The Mt. McKinley National Park was created on February 26, 1917 for the protection and preservation of this unique natural resource. In 1980, the original park was designated a wilderness area and the much larger Denali National Park and Preserve was formed. Currently, all climbers attempting to climb Denali and Mount Foraker must pre-register with the National Park Service and pay a special use fee. Each member of the team is obligated to visit the Talkeetna Ranger Station in person at the time of their climb to pay the fee and have a pre-climb briefing with a climbing ranger. Climbers on other peaks in the range are encouraged to voluntarily register with the Park Service at the ranger station. In addition, all users of the park must pay the standard National Park entrance fee. Please refer to NPS Climbing Ranger Joe Reichert's article on page 28 for more details.

The Mountains

In Talkeetna there are five licensed air services that can land climbers and their gear on the glaciers within the National Park. All of the air services are located at the Talkeetna State Airport east of town, although several of them have offices downtown. The air services use ski-wheel aircraft that can land and take off on both pavement and snow by protracting and retracting large skis. These small airplanes typically hold 3 to 5 climbers and their gear, although larger aircraft being used can hold over 10 people. Contact your chosen air services well in advance of your trip for more information and reservations. A list of these services can be found in the appendices.

Glacier landing locations and information is given at the beginning of each climbing area section. Air services may be able to shuttle parties between climbing areas. Check with your air service for availability. The North Side routes are not accessible by airplane and must all be approached overland. See the North Side section for further details.

Seasons and Weather

"In Alaska there are two types of clouds: Serious and Accumulating."
  - Karl Swanson, Alaskan resident and climber

The Central Alaska Range is the middle section of a great 500-mile arc of mountains that sweeps across southern Alaska. The mountains sit unobstructed some 130 miles from Cook Inlet and about 430 miles from the Bering Sea, where weather systems form. It's no wonder that the range gets some of the biggest and most feared storms on the planet. Combined with its proximity to the ocean, the huge uplift off the lowlands is a major factor to the brutalness of the weather. The mountains rise steeply from the 1,000-foot elevation lowlands on the south and the 2,000-foot tundra on the north. Denali itself has an abrupt uplift of about 15,000 feet from the head of the Ruth and Peters Glaciers.

The Central Alaska Range mountains are also sub-arctic. Denali is located at 63° 04' 10.5" latitude; 35-degress or 2,400 miles farther north than Mount Everest. This attributes to not only much colder temperatures than more equatorial ranges, but also a thinner atmosphere and lower pressures. Twenty thousand feet on Denali feels much higher and colder than 20,000 feet in the Himalaya or Andes.

It should be noted that the range creates a rain-shadow effect to its north side. Talkeetna, 60 miles south of Denali, averages 30-35 inches of rainfall per year. Lake Minchumina, 60 miles north of Denali, averages just 12 inches of rainfall per year. The north side glaciers and tundra generally receive much less snowfall and it tends to be drier and the snow less consolidated in the early season.

Planning

The overall climbing season in Alaska is March through September, with most ascents occurring in May and June. Winter and off-season ascents are rare but not unheard of. If there is one thing I've learned, it's that there is not a particular month that has better weather than others. Over the last ten years I have seen no discernable difference between the average number of good climbing days in March, April, May, June, or July. People try to predict monthly trends in the weather but every year is different. So how does this help? Instead of planning your trip around when you think the weather is best, plan your trip on when the temperatures are best for your climbing objective.

For Denali, it is no secret that the highest success rate is in June. This is a result of warmer temperatures rather than better weather. April and May can provide for great experiences on Denali, with fewer crowds, cleaner snow, and a generally more pristine environment, but chances of success go down because of the extreme cold at altitude. There have been years where there have been no summits in May until the last two days. July certainly has warm weather but the glaciers become so broken up that traveling on and even landing on the Kahiltna becomes problematic.

On the other hand, April and May are generally the best time to do the lower elevation technical snow and ice routes, such as Ham and Eggs, Mount Dan Beard, Kahiltna Queen, and Mount Hunter's North Buttress. These routes typically fall apart and become very dangerous by June. Snow mushroom and cornice collapses are a clear and present danger. In general, early season ascents may have unconsolidated snow, more snow over rock, and brittle ice. As the season progresses, snow and ice conditions generally improve but natural rock and icefall become a problem.

Another consideration when planning a trip is the available amount of light versus dark. The joys of climbing in Alaska come when you are able to climb at all hours of the day and night without a headlamp. This usually comes in early May for non-technical snow routes where there is enough radiant light from the snow. By late May it becomes possible to climb technical routes and see to place gear at the darkest hours. As Alaska veteran Dave Anderson puts it, "The endless days of the Alaskan summer are the alpinist's ace in the hole."

For rock routes in the Ruth Gorge and Little Switzerland, the season typically starts early June when temperatures have warmed up enough to melt much of the seasonal snow off the rock and it is light and warm

enough to climb 24 hours a day.

Match your objectives within the suitable time frame. Your best bet is to come with lots of time and lots of objectives. Be prepared to take whatever the weather dishes out. Remember, storms create the unique environment in which we climb.

Predicting

There are a few key weather observations that will help in predicting and preparing for storms and climbing days. The following are the typical storm events and weather systems that occur in the range.

General Storms:

Southwesters:
The typical storm starts in the western Aleutian Islands and tracks up the south side of the islands into the Gulf of Alaska. These storms tend to give at least 12 hours of warning, first by a sequence of high cirrus clouds approaching from the southwest. Winds increase and the sky will often turn a solid white color with a prominent ring around the sun. Eventually cumulus clouds will form and precipitation is imminent. One of the major warning signs of bad weather in general is a warming in temperature. These storms characteristically last about four days.

Bering Storms:
These storms originate in the Bering Sea to the west and are pushed north of the Aleutian Islands by high barometric pressure over Hawaii. They can be the fastest and most violent of all storms. Black clouds quickly appear due west, and it may be snowing within four hours. Although not always fast and terrible, a few of these have been the worst storms I've ever experienced, with up to eight feet of snow within 36 hours and sustained winds of 60+ miles per hour. The longest of these storms can last up to eight days.

The Eastern Flow:
The bane of the technical climbers wanting to get on a hard route, this weather pattern is the hardest to come to grips with. The forecast will generally call for precipitation everyday, and evil looking clouds will be constantly streaming in from the east, but long dry periods occur. The weather is never really stable, but is never usually violent either. Lenticular clouds will form and dissipate frequently. There normally will be long enough weather breaks to summit Denali or sneak up the Mini-Moonflower, but climbers waiting for that perfect forecast to get on the Infinite Spur

or Hunter's North Buttress will be sitting in base camp, watching much good weather go to waste. This weather pattern can last from one to three weeks.

North Flow:
If there is to be a flow of weather, the best is from the north. An arctic high that forms north of the range brings very cold temperatures but generally clear weather. Conditions up high can be extremely windy and frigid for the first couple of days. Look for plumes of snow blowing off the high peaks from the north to signify a possible couple days of clear weather. If the plumes change direction, watch out for a southwesterly.

High Pressure:
A high pressure system in the Gulf of Alaska and/or the Bering Sea generally brings clear weather and moderate temperatures. It lasts from one day to a week or more. Long weather windows also tend to occur when high pressure develops over the western Yukon or northeast and north central Alaska, holding back moisture from the sea.

The big peaks and localized storms:
Mount Hunter, Mount Foraker, Denali, and occasionally some of the smaller peaks, suffer from the infamous lenticular cloud cap formation. These airfoil-like clouds are created by the mountain itself and the prevailing winds aloft. The air around a mountain tends to be warmer than the mountain. Depending on its humidity or moistness, as winds collide with this air mass, it forces it over and around the mountain to create a lenticular cloud. It can be completely clear and cloudless everywhere else, except for this cloud. These clouds can form and dissipate within minutes and can be either quite violent or mild. Whiteout conditions normally exist within the cloud, and precipitation and winds can be intense. The caps usually form during the day but disappear in the evening when the air temperature around the mountain cools down.

Climbing (using the weather to your advantage)
The weather is by far the most talked about subject when climbing in the Alaska Range. Don't always trust the forecast given to you. It may be valuable for predicting general weather trends, but on a day-to-day basis it can be unreliable. This really comes in to play when climbing the smaller peaks in the range, or when making the summit push on a big route.

For the smaller peaks, the unpredictableness of the weather means that the climber must always be ready. Even though the forecast may call for snow the next four days, there just may be a 12-16 hour window of opportunity in there somewhere. This may be your one shot at the Southwest Ridge of Frances or Shaken, Not Stirred. (Remember to allow for snow conditions to settle out after a big dump.) Have your gear packed and check the weather, especially at night. For rock climbing in the summer, a weather window may come in the middle of the night.

For the larger less technical routes on Denali and Foraker, it is best to try and move on the lower sections of the route in periods of marginal to bad weather. Do not wait for perfect weather all the time or you will not get very far. Work on maneuvering your team into the highest possible position, then wait for the good weather to make a summit bid. On the flip side, don't push too high in bad weather or you may become demoralized and destroyed and at the first sign of good weather, you may find yourself going down. For big long routes such as the Cassin or the West Ridge of Hunter, climbers generally wait and sit tight for a big high-pressure system to be forecasted, and then move as fast as possible to utilize it.

Also be sure to consider and prepare for the range of temperatures that will be encountered. It can be downright broiling on the Kahiltna Glacier or in the Ruth Amphitheatre in mid-June on a sunny calm day. During hot days down low, the best strategy is to move during the cooler nights and sleep during the day. This assures better snow conditions, safer crevasse crossings, and less risk of heat related illnesses. As you ascend higher in elevation, the schedule will eventually be reversed as nighttime temperatures become frigid.

Check the **National Weather Service Alaska** website for more information and current weather conditions: www.arh. noaa.gov. Check out the **Alaska Mountain Forum** climbers' bulletin board for current conditions and trip reports: www. alaskamountainforum.com.

Equipment

This book covers a wide selection of climbs and types of climbing. Packing gear for a three-week trip up the West Buttress in May will be substantially different than a one-week trip to Little Switzerland in July. Alaska in general requires high-quality pre-tested gear to combat the extreme winter conditions, temperatures, and winds. For late spring and summer ascents on snow and ice routes in Alaska, come prepared as if you were going to make a foul-weather winter ascent of Mount Rainier or an extended winter climb in the Canadian Rockies. Earlier season climbs in Alaska require an extra level of preparedness. For technical rock routes later in the season, come prepared at base camp for cold weather, but the gear taken on the climbs can be tailored to the current temperature and weather.

Listed with each climb are gear suggestions related to protection selection, rope recommendations, and other climb specific items. More equipment suggestions can be found below. A full equipment list can be found in the appendix.

Glacier Travel:

Every route in this book requires climbers to carry standard glacier travel and crevasse rescue gear and be proficient at using it. Travel on Alaskan glaciers can be much more serious than on lower-48 glaciers and elsewhere around the world. High winds and heavy snowfall allow gigantic crevasses to be bridged with thin layers of snow. This combined with a lack of the freeze-

thaw cycle makes these unconsolidated snow bridges exceptionally dangerous. With the increased scale of the glaciers comes increased crevasse sizes. It is not uncommon for crevasse bridges to be 30 feet wide or more.

Either skis or snowshoes are obligatory. Skis are by far the safest and fastest means of glacier travel, but they can be difficult to use when roped up and handling a sled. It is best if each member of the rope team uses the same method of travel. Plastic sleds are commonly used to haul gear around. It's helpful to practice rigging and dragging a sled before arriving on an Alaskan glacier. Sleds are generally provided for free by your air service.

Personal Gear:

Boots:

For all of the snow and ice routes in this book it is recommended to use expedition-style plastic double-boots with warm high-altitude liners. For elevations higher than 14,000 feet or for early season climbs, fully insulated overboots should be available for use. Footwear is a bigger concern for climbers on technical routes. Overboots can make rock and mixed climbing difficult. Test your footwear thoroughly before getting on a big climb. For a route like the Cassin in June, I find I can get by with just good plastic boots and supergaiters. Luckily on this route, the more technical climbing ends at 16,700 feet. If you need to take overboots with you, they can be donned here for the summit bid. Make sure you can easily adjust your crampons to fit with or without your overboots.

For the summer rock climbing areas such as the Ruth Gorge and Little Switzerland, insulated leather boots are generally sufficient to get around on the glaciers and are easier to take up routes. Depending on the temperatures, rock shoes may need to be able to accommodate socks.

Clothing:

For non-technical routes, a standard layering system works fine. Bring a high-quality down parka with attached hood. Water-proof breathable shell fabrics are great for cutting out the wind and snow. For technical routes, I prefer the layer-over-the-top system. Over your synthetic base layer, a micro-fiber shell is worn. When conditions worsen, insulated synthetic layers are put on over existing layers. With this method it is much easier to regulate body temperature and your clothing tends to fit better and stay drier.

Sleeping Gear:

For routes up the big peaks and base camps, a sleeping bag rated to -20 to -30-degrees is necessary. Sleeping bag ratings are highly subjective. Ask around and test your bag out to make sure it is right for you. Most people use down bags which are lighter and more compressible but require more care and effort to keep dry. A -30-degree synthetic bag is just plain huge, but it will always keep you warm. Make sure it is roomy enough to accommodate boot liners, water bottles, camera, sunscreen, etc.

Two full-length sleeping pads are a necessity. Be aware that the inflatable type can be prone to popping, rendering them practically useless.

For more technical routes on smaller peaks, live by the adage "light is right." I often use a 10 to 20-degree down bag. If I get cold, extra clothes and a hot water bottle help me through the night. To keep the pack size small, sleep on only one sleeping pad, often cut small, in addition to your pack, ropes, and other items.

Group Gear:

Tent:

A strong four-season dome tent for two or three people should be used for base camps and all non-technical snow and ice routes. A floorless circus-style tent makes a great cooking shelter. For technical routes requiring an overnight camp, a small foot-print single-wall tent is best. If just out a single night and the weather is good, a bivy sack may be adequate.

Shovels:

Leave your plastic shovels at home. A sturdy aluminum shovel with a flat blade is the best for all-around use and building snow structures. A steel pointy garden blade can be useful for breaking up ice layers at the higher camps. Bring at least two shovels per tent. At least one snow saw is also a handy addition for building snow walls and igloos.

Stove:

A good, field-tested stove is mandatory. Your stove is your life. I recommend using a white gas model over a fuel canister model. They melt water faster, create less waste, and work better in the cold. White gas (Coleman fuel) is widely available and used in Alaska and on the glaciers. The MSR XGK model is an excellent all-around choice. Be sure to bring a good stove board to insulate the stove from the snow.

Fuel:

White gas fuel can be purchased at any department, hardware, or climbing store. Other forms of fuel, such as propane or butane canisters, are available at most of the climbing shops. Each season white gas is flown up separately to Kahiltna Base Camp by the air services. Climbers going here must buy their fuel from the air service in Talkeetna and acquire it at Base Camp. For other landing areas or if using canisters, check with your air service for current regulations for flying with fuel. Fuel canisters generally have tighter government restrictions and are more difficult to fly with.

Bring a minimum 8 oz. of white gas per person per day. White gas is typically sold by the gallon. This comes out to 16 person-days per gallon. A two-person West Buttress trip would do well with 2.5 to 3 gallons. When traveling by plane to Alaska with fuel bottles, separate the pumps or lids, rinse out the bottles, and put them in a stuff-sack with the lid off.

Communication:

Citizen Band (CB) radios:

CBs have limited functionality throughout the range, except in the Kahiltna Glacier area where they are commonly used. They provide only line of sight transmissions. Channel 19 is the most commonly used frequency and Channel 7 on the north side of the range. Airplanes generally do not monitor either frequency. Several air services will rent a CB radio or you can buy one for about $65 at an electronics or large multi-department store. Check with your

air service for availability. Be sure to keep the batteries warm and carry a spare set.

Aircraft radios:

Although a federal license is technically required to use one, these are far more reliable than CB radios, allowing you to communicate directly with pilots. Aircraft radios should only be used in emergency situations or when scheduling a pick-up. They should not be used to check the weather or talk to other climbers. You will be talking on the same frequency the pilots use to relay their positions to other planes. Interfering with this vital communication, compromises their safety. Check with your air service for rental availability.

Cell Phones:

Cell phones have limited functionality with spotty coverage in the Alaska Range. They generally work above 14,000 feet on the south side of Denali or Foraker, and from the summits of more southern peaks that are closer to the road system. Do not rely on your cell phone for your only means of communication.

Satellite phones:

Sat. phones have slowly been decreasing in size and price over the years. This is by far the most reliable and useful form of communication in any remote region. Satellite phones can be rented from the following retailers:

Globalstar Satellite Phones: 866.728.7368, www.spiritwireless.com

Satellite Communications of Alaska: 907.677.9699, www.phonehome.tv

Photo by Joe Puryear

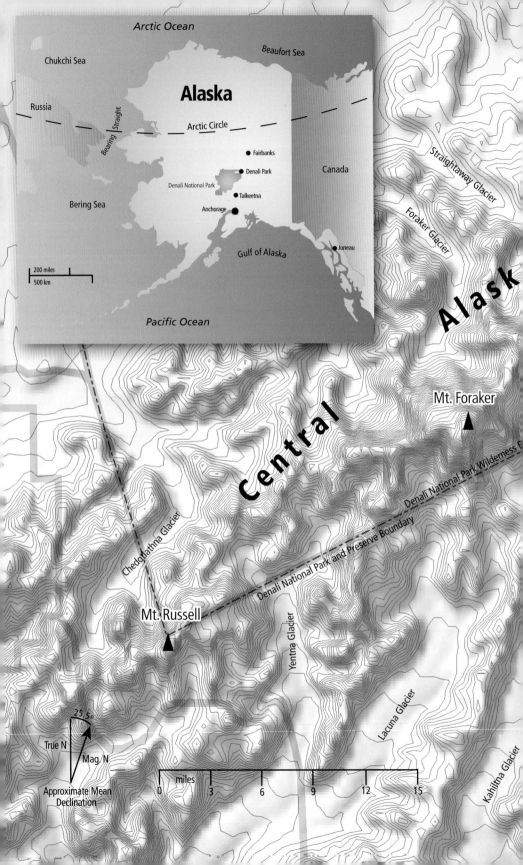

Arctic Ocean

Chukchi Sea

Beaufort Sea

Russia

Bering Straight

Arctic Circle

Alaska

Fairbanks

Denali Park

Denali National Park

Talkeetna

Bering Sea

Anchorage

Canada

Juneau

Gulf of Alaska

200 miles
500 km

Pacific Ocean

Straightaway Glacier

Foraker Glacier

Alask

Mt. Foraker

Central

Chedotlathna Glacier

Denali National Park Wilderness

Denali National Park and Preserve Boundary

Mt. Russell

Yentna Glacier

Lacuna Glacier

Kahiltna Glacier

25.5°

True N

Mag. N

Approximate Mean
Declination

miles

0   3   6   9   12   15

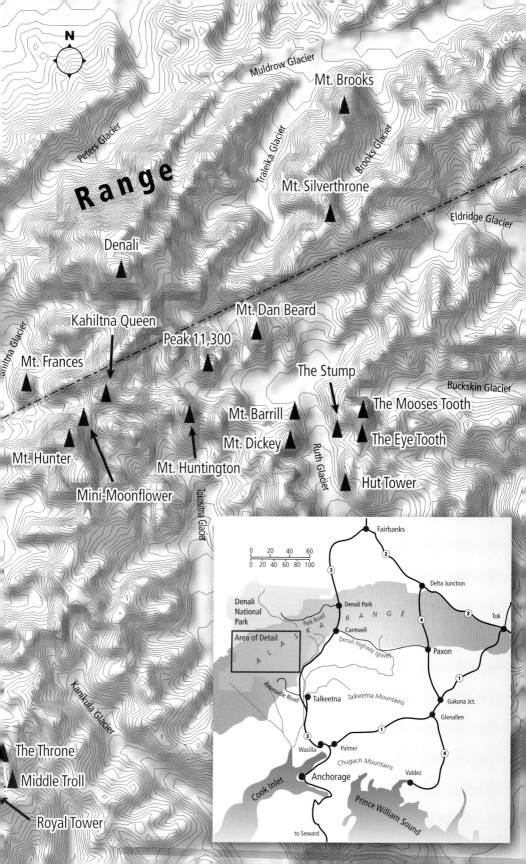

How to use this guidebook

This guidebook contains a selection of 30 routes of all different grades and types of climbing. The routes are grouped into six different sections, based on similar approach locations. Every climb in each section can be accessed from a common airstrip or approach. In addition to the 30 selected climbs, there are additional recommendations for other routes in each area, as well as proposals for new climbs.

How these routes were selected

In choosing these climbs, I focused on routes that climbers actually climb or talk about climbing. Many of them are not only very popular routes, but important historically to the development of the range. None of these routes are sick horror-shows with no second ascents. These are all classic, repeatable routes by "mortal" climbers of all abilities. I've combined mostly first-hand information along with reports from contemporary Alaskan climbers to create these extensive route profiles.

Choosing a route

As with any mountain range, it is certainly a good idea to start small and work your way up. Remember that even though a route may look doable on the topo, this is a big and remote climbing venue and there are many other factors to be considered. You may have climbed a big wall or two in Yosemite, but coming right up here to get on the Cobra Pillar might be ambitious. Remember, El Cap doesn't require crossing a bad crevasse field to get to the base or descending 2,000 feet of serac-strewn, avalanche prone slopes to get off. But don't let this necessarily deter you. With a few basic snow skills, routes like this can be accessible to anyone.

The two major climbing arenas are the Kahiltna Glacier and the Ruth Glacier. This is where over 95 percent of all of the climbers are found. Luckily, within each area there are many different climbs available to test your mettle and see what it's going to take to try harder routes. In the Ruth, try doing the Japanese Couloir on Barrill, and Mount Dan Beard, before trying Peak 11,300. Or warm up on the Stump and the Eye Tooth before attempting the Cobra Pillar. On the Kahiltna, try doing the West Rib of Denali, the Southwest Ridge of Frances, and the Mini-Moonflower, before attempting the Cassin. By starting on easier climbs, you will be able to ease into the rigors of Alaskan climbing. Study the route profiles and talk to other climbers to see if you have what it takes to attempt your chosen routes.

Guided climbing

Climbing with a guide can be a very rewarding and enriching way of experiencing the range for a novice or intermediate climber. Climbers can worry less about the logistical preparations and focus more on learning and climbing. About a quarter of climbers attempting Denali use a guide service. Guides also commonly lead trips on Mount Foraker's Sultana Ridge as well. Although not as common, small guided groups have been seen on nearly all of the peaks in this book. Several companies offer skills classes and multi-day seminars in the Kahiltna, Ruth, and Little Switzerland. Only six companies are authorized to guide on Denali and Forkaer. These and other companies are also allowed to guide elsewhere in the range. A complete list of guides can be found in the appendices.

Route Profile Overview

History and First Ascent Information:
The detailed first ascent history (if known) is given, along with unique or important repeats.

Difficulty:
Each climb is assigned an overall commitment or seriousness grade in addition to individual difficulty ratings. See below for a discussion of the route ratings.

Cornice dangers exist on nearly all the routes. However, if a route has extensive cornice traveling, this is noted here.

Elevation Gain:
The elevation gain is given from different points for reference and to give an idea of the overall effort required. Elevations gains given are absolute and do not take into consideration ups and downs on the route.

Season:
The recommended months for climbing the route are given, in addition to the best time that has the highest success rate. If a best time is not given, the route is doable throughout the season given.

Time:
A "total time" is given to suggest the minimum range of time that should be allowed to complete the climb round trip from Talkeetna. Average approach times are given from different locations, depending on where a team may start. Times for both the ascent and descent of the route are given. All times given are based on an average party with good conditions.

Strategy:
This section includes general hints and tips on how to go about approaching and climbing the route.

Specific Hazards:
Besides the general hazards of crevasses and weather, this section tells of objective dangers specific to the route and where they occur. As mentioned above, cornices are a hazard on nearly all the routes and are not mentioned here unless they are a specific threat.

Gear:
Listed with each climb are gear suggestions related to protection selection, rope recommendations, and other climb specific items.

Camps:
At the beginning of each climbing area section is a recommendation for base camps for the area. Listed with each climb are camps and bivy sites specific to the route and its approach.

Approach, Route, Descent, and Topo:
Because of the non-technical nature of many of the climbs in this book, a route topo is not needed. Directions for these climbs, such as the West Buttress of Denali or the North Ridge of Mount Brooks, are based on a pictorial overview, map, and a detailed route description. This is also the case for a few of the straightforward technical routes, such as the West Face of Kahiltna Queen. On the rest of the technical routes, where a route description is necessary one is given. Otherwise, the detailed SuperTopo has all the information necessary.

Route Ratings:
For the overall commitment grade, Alaska Grades are only used for Denali, Mount Foraker, and Mount Hunter. Here it seems to apply well because of the high-altitude, cold weather, remoteness, and extensive length of the routes. Other peaks in the range can generally be compared to other peaks throughout North America, and the more standard overall seriousness grade originated by the UIAA is used, using roman numerals I through VII. Other common climbing ratings used include: YDS (5.0-5.14) for rock, A or C (A1-A5 or C1-C5) for aid or clean aid, and M (M4-M12) for mixed. Ice ratings are either given as Alpine Ice ratings (AI2-AI6) or as the degrees steepness of a pitch. Snow ratings are given as degrees steepness.

The following is a brief description of the **Alaska Rating System**. For a more detailed reference, read *The Organization of an Alaskan Expedition* by Boyd N. Everett Jr.

Grade 1: An easy glacier route that can be climbed in a day from base camp. Altitude is generally not a concern.

Grade 2: A moderate glacier route with little to no technical difficulties that takes several days to complete. The West Buttress of Denali and the Muldrow Glacier are a Grade 2.

Grade 3: A climb with moderate technical difficulties that takes several days. The climb may have extensive cornicing and knife-edge ridges. The Sultana Ridge on Mount Foraker is a Grade 3.

Grade 4: A climb with more sustained moderate to hard technical difficulties and higher commitment. The climb will take several days to complete. The climb may have extensive cornicing and knife-edge ridges. The West Ridge on Mount Hunter and the West Rib of Denali are Grade 4.

Grade 5: A climb with sustained hard climbing and a high level of commitment. Technical portions of the route may take several days. Bivy sites may be difficult to find. The climb may have extensive cornicing and knife-edge ridges. The Cassin Ridge on Denali is a Grade 5.

Grade 6: A climb with sustained hard technical climbing and the highest level of commitment. Technical portions of the route exceed 4,000 feet and will take several days. Bivy sites are infrequent and hanging bivies may be required. The climb may have severe cornicing and knife-edge ridges and retreat options may be poor. The Infinite Spur on Mount Foraker and the North Buttress of Mount Hunter are Grade 6.

Topo Symbols

right-facing corner		face climbing or route to follow	direction of route or route instructions
left-facing corner		hooking	off-route or other variation
straight-in crack		belay station ❺	snow or ice ridge
groove/ dihedral		pitch length ❺ 170'	technical ice and mixed terrain
arête		optional belay	snow and ice
chimney		rappel	
		pitch or rappel length 200'	rock
slab		degrees steepness of a pitch 65°	
roof		camp or bivy ▲	
ledge		summit	

Topo Abbreviations

ow = offwidth
lb = lieback
p = fixed piton
R = runout (dangerous fall)
x = bolt

Metric System Conversions

1 inch = 2.54 centimeters
1 foot = 0.305 meters
100 feet = 30.5 meters
50 yards = 45.7 meters
To convert fahrenheit (F) to celcius (C):
$C=(5/9)*(F-32)$

Safety, Survival, and the National Park Service

by Joe Reichert

In your hands are the most accurate route descriptions ever published for routes in these mountains. Having read this information you may approach one of these climbs with the same casual preparation that you might for a similarly rated challenge where the car is a 10-minute walk from the base. Please read on to understand some of the potentially deadly differences between a grade IV 5.10 A1 in the Alaska Range and one anywhere else (except possibly Antarctica).

Time in the mountains represents some of my most enjoyable and rewarding outings. The energy I feel through the excitement of a pending climb is beyond description; it is almost as refreshing to me to feel this energy exuded by so many of the climbers whom I speak with in Talkeetna at the start of their adventure. I encourage you to harness this ambition and use it, but use it wisely. Unbridled motivation is probably the leading cause of injuries and fatalities in the mountains. Be aware of the risks you are taking all of the time. Sometimes the approach or the descent will prove to be the "crux" of your technical route. Pay attention to conditions. These mountains are always changing and "bomber" conditions are the exception not the norm on many of the routes. Crevasses are everywhere! (And probably not very common at your home climbing venues). There is not a single route in this book that you could climb and not have the possibility of dying in a crevasse. Weather is a universal consideration. Just remember that you are much closer to the Arctic Circle up here and therefore, even though you will enjoy warmth in the sun, the possibility of debilitating cold is always present. Let's

take a break from the touchy-feely stuff and read some of the facts about climbing in the Park and Preserve.

All users touching snow, ice or ground in Denali National Park and Preserve (DNPP) must pay a $10 entrance fee. For folks attempting Denali or Foraker this is in addition to the $200 special use fee required for a permit to climb on those peaks (so go break your piggy bank). Denali and Foraker aspirants must also register with the Park Service 60 days prior to departure from Talkeetna. I encourage climbers who know they want to attempt one of these two peaks (or both) to get your deposit in as early as possible, say January. The small deposit and early registration allows you greater flexibility to change dates, partners and mountains, assuming you are still 60 days out and your partners are all pre-registered. Call the Talkeetna Ranger Station for the most up-to-date information and to ask any questions you may have about registration and climbs in the Alaska Range (907-733-2231) e-mail to DENA_Talkeetna_Office@nps.gov and look at our web site at http://www.nps.gov/dena/home/mountaineering/index.htm.

Once in the park the old adage that you should "leave the area as you would like to find it" is no longer strong enough. I have been amazed by the trashy conditions some climbers are willing to endure as well as, subject others to. Whether it is Camp VI on El Capitan or the South Col of Everest, we all need to do our best to leave camps in cleaner conditions than we find them. In DNPP we are constantly experimenting with different techniques to maintain clean climber camps. All items packed in with you need to be packed out when you leave. Human waste needs to be off the surface of the glaciers so it does not contaminate drinking water. At high camp on Denali and all fly-in base camps, the NPS now requires you to pack your human waste out and dispose of it in Talkeetna. (Currently, the NPS provides Clean Mountain Cans (CMCs) for this purpose. Sign them out at the ranger station.)

Enough of the rules and regulations—lets get back to the more abstract. Through

Photo by Joe Puryear

education the rangers in Talkeetna hope to prevent as many accidents as possible. Regardless of a person's technical climbing abilities, the first trip into the Alaska Range will always incur a large learning curve. From packing sleds to gauging the "Alaskan scale" of your surroundings, every returnee I have spoken with has reported being far better prepared for subsequent trips than they were for their first adventure in the range. Even with preparation and prudent judgment, accidents will happen. Therefore another goal of the Talkeetna rangers is to be proficient at mountain rescue. If your leader takes a whipper, bonks her/his head and is unconscious 103 feet above your belay, you will be able to call us on your satellite phone. If it is a clear blue day between April 20 and July 10 the NPS Lama rescue helicopter COULD be at your location the same day. This is a best-case scenario; there are many factors that could delay this timeline such as environmental delays, aircraft being used elsewhere, pilot down time, and mechanical problems. Remember that your partner is hanging and will most likely expire in

less than 30 minutes if his/her breathing is compromised. Self-rescue needs to be the first line of action for any team in distress. Your goal is to get the injured person stabilized and to a location from which they can be extracted, assuming that you have communication with the outside world. Technology for communication is developing rapidly. At the time of printing, satellite phones appear to offer the greatest chance for successful communication. Do your homework and decide what will work for you. Realize that if you choose not to carry the technology, search and rescue will not be initiated until you are overdue or another party makes a report. The NPS will help in any way that it can during an emergency, but remember that your emergency is not always the number one emergency for the NPS. Ultimately, it is your responsibility to make safe decisions and leave detailed written information with family, friends, and other climbers in the area when you depart for a climb.

The Washburn Route (aka West Buttress) on Denali deserves its own brief introduction because most Alaska

Range climbers will make this pilgrimage at one point or another. Deservedly, this spectacular route is the most visited in the range. While its technical difficulties are limited and the wilderness character compromised in May and June by human population, the West Buttress is never a disappointment. The intensity of the weather on Denali does not care which route you choose. When the winds are howling you can feel as isolated from the 50-plus tents around you as if you were climbing Mount Igikpak. Traveling the Washburn Route is a spectacular mountain experience whether your goal is the summit or to acclimatize for another line. While this is a good route to learn the ropes of expedition mountaineering, even it should be a later step in an apprenticeship that includes multi day 14,000-plus foot mountains such as Mount Rainier (especially Rainier in winter). The NPS has a ranger presence at base camp and the 14,200-foot camp in order to enforce the stewardship rules of the National Park as well as maintain an acclimatized team that can respond to emergencies higher on the mountain. Rangers are there to be of assistance. Do not hesitate to visit the camp and ask questions.

Allow several weeks for your Alaskan adventure and have several objectives. One objective should be to return with a satisfied memory of your mountain experience. This will be achieved even if all climbing attempts are thwarted by conditions. Use the information here to assist with your adventure. By no means fully rely on it for your safety. Just as a hand jam is a technique used in rock climbing, route-finding is a skill required for mountaineering. This skill is honed by looking at the entire portion of the mountain on which the route you want to climb lies. Your collective knowledge based on reading, photos, maps, reconnaissance from the air as you fly in, and observations on the approach will prove more beneficial to you on the climb than relying solely on written descriptions. You can not drop your memory. I have experienced a team

returning from a climb, proud of their success, yet bad mouthing the authors of a guidebook. They had photocopied and laminated the published topo and their interpretation of the terrain did not match that of the authors. Fortunately the climbers mistake in route-finding only cost them time and energy. The possibility haunts me that such a mistake could be fatal. Routes change; one person's "rising traverse" may be another's "ascend the left leaning gully" so study your route and treat every ascent with the preparation that you would make for a first ascent. Not only will this aid you with the climb at hand it will train you for the time in the future when you return to attempt that line that you spotted from you last route. Joe Puryear has climbed almost every route in this book. His fantastic memory, along with thorough research, has contributed to an identification of routes that offer classic lines to a wide spectrum of climbers. Please climb safely and let this book introduce you to the wonderful experiences that await you in the Alaska Range.

Joe Reichert
Mountaineering Ranger
Denali National Park and Preserve

sometimes last 12-18 hours. Photo by Mike Gauthier

Mountaineering Health

by Dr. Jim Litch

There are many factors that isolate us when climbing – vertical technical ground, distance, and unidentified location. Yet in the great ranges there are a number of others that periodically weigh in as well – intense weather, snow load and avalanche conditions, severe cold, darkness, high altitude, poor communication, and remoteness. Simply paging to and reading this health chapter in a route guide suggests awareness on your part that knowledge and preparation can make a difference. As in other remote ranges in the world, when one enters the realm of climbing in the Alaska Range, we are taking a big step toward accepting the heavy responsibility for our independent actions and decisions.

A rescue that we conducted during my time as a Denali mountaineering ranger made a strong impression on many involved. The incident unfolded after a fall when the leader pulled back on a large plate of ice on mixed ground in a long steep couloir along the Ruth Gorge. Some 15 meters out from the belay, the impact resulted in a cracked helmet, head injury and broken hip, though the leader rapidly regained consciousness. The belay anchors held, leaving his partner intact and uninjured. It took six hours for the belayer to lower his injured partner to the base of the snow fan below the couloir. He then dug a trench for the night's bivy in sleeping bags. Before dawn the party was hit by a large powder avalanche, but managed to dig out with the loss of equipment including one of the sleeping bags. They were located above an icefall in a small isolated cirque with nowhere to easily move that was entirely safe from above.

The following morning the climber negotiated the icefall and crevasses alone with the hope to discover a group with a radio. By chance, the climber found a ski group in the Ruth Amphitheatre that afternoon, but they also did not have a radio. Exhausted, the climber spent the night, and returned alone to his injured partner, arriving the following afternoon just as the immobile partner was hit by another powder avalanche. On the fourth day since the accident, they moved further from the debris zone and that evening it began to snow, ending a period with good flyable weather. The two were hit by avalanches for the next three days while several feet of new snowfall accumulated down on the glacier below. On the eighth day the weather improved enough for rescuers to fly into the area and pick up the pair.

A request for rescue was eventually communicated after a string of events. On the fourth day after the initial accident, as the weather set in, a private plane sightseeing in the Ruth Amphitheatre spotted a message of "HELP" stamped in the snow by the ski party, and the pilot decided to investigate. The plane crashed while trying to land on the glacier in flat light. The aircraft ELT signal was received by the authorities and the National Park Service was notified, though the poor weather system had closed in sealing the area. The following day word of the climbing accident was sent, using the downed aircraft radio and picked up by a passing commercial jet and relayed to the National Park Service. Another two days passed before weather cleared enough for rescuers to arrive – on the eighth day after the initial climbing accident.

In the event of injury or illness in a remote setting, the decisions leading up to the incident and the immediate decisions that follow have a great impact on the final outcome. Should we need to evacuate, the difference between a really good day and a bad one ranges from clamoring aboard an aircraft after a several hour wait, to a week-long epic of starvation, dehydration, cold and impending doom from storm and avalanche. Before we begin tripping up a route, an appreciation of the uniqueness of the Alaska Range environment and sensitive preparation are within our sphere

of control. When the health of a teammate or the lives of the entire party are caught in the balance, suddenly dozens of small, seemly inconsequential decisions become fiercely monstrous. If we are going to keep monsters under our bed, my bold and adventurous three yearold son tells me, friendly monsters are better than fierce ones. We do create or chose our own monsters. What kind of monster do we wish to meet while climbing out here?

After periods as mountaineering ranger on Denali and Rainier, guide on 8,000 meter peaks in the Himalaya, rescue coordinator in Antarctica, climber/ physician on some 3 dozen expeditions, and countless forays in my backyard ranges in Washington State and Alaska, I find that the unconventional is the norm. We need to approach new environments with an open mind and maintain our adaptability. There is little we can do in terms of first aid beyond basic steps to maintain the airway that actually can save a life on a remote Alaska Range climb. The opportunities to impact the outcome typically present much sooner—well before the accident actually occurs. Prevention of severe illness and accidents are critically important.

This chapter focuses on the prevention, early recognition and appropriate immediate care of health problems. Maintaining our health and recognizing problems early is where the emphasis is placed. There are plenty of other texts that lead the reader through volumes of first aid techniques. As a climber, it is better to attend to what you can carry with you. In your head. One of the aspects of climbing that I find most unappealing is that it is those that have survived an epic or near epic seem to absorb the attention and resulting praise. However, the lasting personal rewards are gained from being out there moving through the terrain with grace, sensitivity, and skill.

COMMUNICATION

Radio and telephone technologies have a powerful capability to diminish the remoteness that is so much a part of the Alaska Range. Certainly this has a potential negative aspect, given that we often travel to remote areas for a break from technology and revel in the isolation. Yet it is often transportation technology that allows us the privilege to visit remote areas. The potential for communication

technologies to facilitate evacuation after an accident, or obtain weather forecasts to avoid being caught by a storm cycle are not to be undervalued. The outcomes of many accidents in the Alaska Range have been significantly altered or entirely avoided by the availability of radios and cell phones. These devices may well be the most valuable emergency item that we can carry. Admittedly there several obvious limitations regarding this technology and these should not be ignored. However there are creative solutions, such as May Day relays over CB radio via climbers high on Denali. NPS mountaineering rangers are excellent sources of specific up-to-date information on the use of this technology in the Alaska Range.

WORK CAPACITY AT ALTITUDE

Altitude adds another variable to an already complex mountain environment. The Alaska Range includes a wide range of elevation up to the 20,000 foot summit of Denali. At this altitude there is half the oxygen available than at sea level as a result of the lower atmospheric pressure. Even at about 14,000 feet, there is roughly one-third less oxygen available than at sea level. Above about 8,000 feet, any further gain in altitude forces our bodies to contend with a significant decrease in the content of oxygen in our bloodstream, and this stresses our body. In fact, we can expect a functional reduction in our work capacity and performance when climbing at high altitudes. Initially this requires a bit of trial and error to accurately predict our capabilities when climbing at altitude. As we travel higher, the situation continues to change by further eroding our physical capacity. This effect of altitude impacts all sojourners as a normal physiologic reaction, and is outside the scope of altitude illness.

ALTITUDE ILLNESS

Altitude illness can further jeopardize our well being. Altitude illness occurs at altitudes above 8,000 ft and commonly presents with mild symptoms of acute mountain sickness (AMS) that include headache, plus malaise, lassitude, poor appetite, nausea, vomiting, dizziness, and/or irritability. Essentially all climbers on Denali suffer from acute mountain sickness during their summit day if not earlier during the climb, depending on the rate of ascent. On lower peaks in the range, the incident of AMS is much less. Both incidence and severity are influenced by the altitude of the climb, rate of ascent to altitude, degree of excursion, and individual susceptibility.

AMS is not life-threatening, but ignoring it is. The illness may worsen over hours or days as dangerous collections of fluid develop in the brain. Increasing fluid in the brain (high altitude cerebral edema, or HACE) causes loss of balance, confusion, and hallucination. In addition, significant fluid in the lungs (high altitude pulmonary edema, or HAPE) may develop, resulting in shortness of breath while at rest and a further reduction of oxygen transfer to the body. If descent or oxygen supplementation is not accomplished within hours, coma and death may ensue.

AVOIDING ALTITUDE ILLNESS

Gradual ascent to altitude over several days reduces the likelihood of acute mountain sickness because your body has time to adapt. Only rarely do climbers have this luxury of time, however. Many climbers simply accept the symptoms of AMS during a summit climb and factor this into the climbing plan.

If we were willing to be patient enough to achieve the same gain in altitude by gradual ascent over a week or more, our bodies would have time to adjust, and we would perform much better. However, many technical routes do not allow this strategy to be employed. Fortunately the technical routes described in the guide are at only moderately high altitudes below 14,000 feet. If a climber has not pre-acclimatize before tackling a route at very high altitude over 14.000 feet, ultimately a climber's only protection from the effects of a rapid ascent to high altitudes is to descend before these effects of altitude progress to life-threatening illness. Fine enough as long as all goes well and the party can keep moving. However, an unexpected stall, such as a storm system, and severe altitude illness could develop. On a typical high altitude ascent in the Alaska Range without prior acclimatization, we are racing the clock.

Another strategy to consider is pre-acclimatization by first climbing a less committing route and spending several nights at high altitude, before committing to our target climb. This can contribute to our margin of safety in several ways. First, we push the threshold altitude for illness higher so it becomes less significant during the targeted climb. Second, the acclimatization will allow us to perform better physically, and third, the opportunity may present to, cache critical food and survival equipment for the descent of the target climb.

Medications are available to help prevent the symptoms of AMS. The most commonly used medications are acetazolamide (250 milligrams twice a day or 500 milligrams slow-release once a day), acetaminophen (325 milligrams up to four times a day), or aspirin (325 milligrams three times a day) at the start of a demanding climb above the elevation at which we are currently acclimatized. Acetazolamide is particularly useful as it actually improves oxygenation, has a positive impact on the quality of sleep at high altitude, and is very effective for periodic breathing that occurs during sleep. However, these medications do not protect against the development of serious altitude illness: HAPE and HACE.

There are a number of medications that have been suggested for use in preventing altitude illness. Acetazolamide is a weak diuretic, causing us to lose fluid through our renal system, which can become a significant factor during a long climb with limited availability of replacement fluids. Gingko biloba and garlic were both recently studied for use in the prevention of AMS and results have not been impressive (no or limited benefit beyond placebo). Nifedipine has been studied for use in prevention of HAPE and found to have a role only for persons with a history of recurrent HAPE. Such individuals would do far better with gradual ascent rather than relying on a medication with limited effect for a life-threatening condition. Dexamethasone, a potent steroid, is generally best avoided as a prevention measure against AMS during ascent, so it may be utilized, if needed, for treatment of HACE along with descent. Extreme climbers have also used other performance enhancing drugs besides steroids, such as dexamphetamine (or speed), though these are extremely dangerous drugs that can kill.

There are several non-medication measures that in my experience can decrease the symptoms of high-altitude illness and maximize performance. They include the following:

- Begin a high-carbohydrate diet one or two days before the climb, and maintain this diet through the climb.
- Make climbing plans that take into account your decreased work capacity at high altitude.
- Reschedule the climb if you come down with an upper respiratory or other active infection.
- Avoid overexertion on the climb by maintaining a reasonable pace and not overloading yourself with nonessential gear.
- Drink enough fluids on the climb to offset increased fluid loss. Passing urine that is clear is a good sign that you're drinking enough fluids.
- Avoid nonessential medications and remedies. There are no shortcuts or quick fixes; they only make issues more complicated.
- Provide good ventilation for camp stoves used in confined places.
- Preacclimatize to very high altitude on a logistically straightforward training climb by sleeping for a few nights at a similar or higher altitude than the target climb.

IDENTIFICATION AND TREATMENT OF ALTITUDE ILLNESS

Altitude illness is common and when climbing at altitude it is rare to completely avoid it. The critical point about altitude illness is to not let acute mountain sickness progress to life-threatening HACE or to allow life-threatening HAPE to develop. It's not uncommon for climbers to dismiss their symptoms as other maladies and push on. If anyone in your party is experiencing even mild symptoms, hold tight and do not begin a technical climb until they improve. If already on route, do not ascend farther to sleep at a higher camp, and consider descent if your supplies or position are compromised. If the symptoms are worsening, the person should descend. Do not let your team member descend alone. The decision to descend must be made well before the climber's ability to perform work is further impaired or worsens further to lose the ability to walk down.

The red-flag symptoms that indicate the need for immediate descent include shortness of breath at rest; the coughing up of pink, frothy sputum; poor balance; confusion; or a decreased level of consciousness. Improved oxygen availability must not be delayed if any one of these signs is present. The seriousness of these signs cannot be overstated. Without additional oxygen, delivered by descent or supplemental oxygen death may occur within hours. Waiting for a rescue without some form of supplemental oxygen is a desperate option. In HAPE, additional measures include maintaining the climber sitting upright and preventing physical exertion while the descent is conducted by the group.

Medications may help with severe altitude illness, but only rarely do they make a critical difference and thus they cannot be relied on. Each has benefits, but they can also cause harm if not used correctly. They include the following drugs: Acetazolamide is very safe, and is used to treat AMS and HACE. Take 250 milligrams twice a day or 500 milligrams slow-release once a day. The current medical standard is to advise that it should not be taken by people with a known intolerance to sulfa drugs, though the risk of a reaction maybe more theoretical than real. Side effects commonly include increased urine output and tingling of hands, feet and lips. Dexamethasone is safe when used for treatment of HACE while descending. It may also be used to treat patients with HAPE if you suspect HACE may also be present. The dosage is four milligrams every

six hours. The drug is dangerous if given as an aid to ascent. Nifedipine is a potentially dangerous medication in a mountaineering environment that is recommended by health professionals for treatment of HAPE. Severe side effects that bottom out blood pressure in climbers that have fluid depleted from the physical exertion of climbing make this medication dangerous for use by climbers that lack specialized training and supplies. I suggest this medication be applied only in desperate circumstances when expertise and supplies are lacking.

HIGH ALTITUDE COUGH SYNDROME

This is a persistent debilitating cough that develops following exposure to very high altitude usually above 14,000 feet. Not commonly a problem in the Alaska Range, with the exception of Denali.

TEMPERATURE-RELATED HAZARDS

The extreme daily temperature swings encountered during a climb in the Alaska Range require constant vigilance to avoid overheating/sweating and cooling/stress. Climbers can learn to effectively guard against hypothermia/frostbite and heat exhaustion/heat sickness, and be prepared to treat the conditions should they develop. Like altitude illness, prevention of these conditions is critical.

Hypothermia

Hypothermia is a drop in the core body temperature to below 95 degrees Fahrenheit (35 degrees Celsius). Hypothermia can occur rapidly after a sudden event like immersion in cold water or a radical change in weather. It can also develop slowly if the body's

Mark Westman leading out on Mt. Hunter's North Buttress. Photo by Joe Puryear

metabolism isn't adequate to meet ongoing environmental exposure.

Hypothermia occurs both ways in the Alaska Range. A person who falls into a crevasse while lightly dressed for a sunny mid-afternoon glacier crossing will be at risk if not extricated quickly. More slowly but just as surely, hypothermia can affect a climber who has eaten little food while climbing through the day with a heavy pack, leaving the body with lessened ability to produce heat as the sun becomes covered by clouds, a breeze kicks up, and rain begins.

Prevention is a matter of minimizing excessive heat loss and ensuring adequate heat production. This is achieved through:

- proper choice and use of clothing and shelter
- staying dry
- adequate nutrition and hydration
- avoidance of overexertion
- anticipating changes in weather conditions.

Hypothermia is progressive. Symptoms of mild hypothermia include a loss of judgment and of fine-motor coordination. The patient shivers to keep warm. This is readily reversible in the field. Patients can warm themselves once they are protected from further heat loss and are given rapidly absorbed high-energy food. A reasonable initial maneuver is for the patient to huddle with other members of the party behind some form of wind barrier, gaining warmth from the teammates. Early recognition and treatment of mild hypothermia is critical to avoid the progression to profound hypothermia.

As profound hypothermia sets in, shivering ceases and the patient becomes confused, with loss of coordination progressing to apathy, stupor, and coma. People with profound hypothermia cannot warm themselves, and in the field it is very difficult to provide adequate sources of heat. The initial step is to prevent additional heat loss by providing the climber with wind protection, removing wet clothing, and applying pre-warmed

insulation (including a ground layer). It's essential to provide warming by applying heat packs or hot water bottles next to the patient's body, cuddling with the patient inside a sleeping bag or bivy sack, or both. Begin these procedures as soon as possible. If the patient is in a stupor or unconscious because of hypothermia, use gentle handling to avoid triggering an irregular heart beat. Do not assume that a hypothermic (cold) patient has died; continue the rewarming process.

Frostbite

Frostbite is a localized area of frozen tissue. It occurs most commonly at the end of extremities and uncovered areas during exposure to subfreezing temperatures. Especially vulnerable are parts of the body that are in contact with metals or liquids or that have been frostbitten in the past. The risk of frostbite increases with extreme cold, high winds, high altitude, dehydration, and overexertion. Wearing tight clothing or footwear, or using alcohol, tobacco, or other drugs, also increases the risk.

Superficial frostbite results in pale, cold skin with underlying tissue that is pliable and soft. Treat with skin-to-skin contact or by immersion in water that is just warm to the touch of the caregiver's elbow (104 to 108 degrees Fahrenheit). If the frostbite produces blisters, the patient should be evacuated to receive further treatment. If the frostbite is on the foot, the climber shouldn't walk, or at least minimize walking, unless their survival depends on it.

Deep frostbite involves the skin and deep structures that become hard and nonpliable. The decision to thaw deep frostbite depends on the situation. Rewarming requires both proper technique to minimize tissue damage and use of a strong painkiller or narcotic. To prevent further damage, don't use the affected part after thawing. The decision to thaw in the field is a complex one that depends on the availability and timeliness of evacuation.

Corneal frostbite is rare but can occur in extreme cold and high winds. Irreversible damage may occur, requiring a corneal transplant. If you travel in harsh conditions, wear goggles and cover exposed skin.

Heat Sickness, Heat Exhaustion, and Dehydration

These conditions can disable even a strong, fit climber. They are common anywhere climbers face frequent and rapid extreme changes in temperatures during a sustained period of physical activity. The conditions result from a lack of attention to basic nutrition, hydration, and regulation of body heat by adjusting clothing layers. Each of these ailments points to its own cure. Heat sickness (dangerous overheating) requires urgent rapid cooling. Heat exhaustion warrants rest and high-energy food. Dehydration and electrolyte imbalance requires the drinking of water containing reasonable concentrations of salts (sodium and potassium) and sugar.

The symptoms of these temperature related conditions overlap with those of altitude illness. Sorting out these potentially dangerous conditions can be difficult. Carefully evaluate a patient's symptoms and closely follow the responses to initial therapy while maintaining a suspicion that altitude sickness is involved. More than one illness may be occurring at the same time.

SNOW-BLINDNESS AND SUNBURN

Both snow-blindness and sunburn result from direct tissue irritation by ultraviolet (UV) rays of sunlight. The UV dose is dependent on the intensity and duration of exposure to sunlight, which increases with altitude. Although both ailments may occur throughout the year, they are more common in the sun-intense spring and summer.

For sunburn, barrier methods are very effective, such as light clothing to cover extremities. Apply sunscreen (SPF 15 or higher) or zinc oxide paste frequently to sun-exposed areas when you are perspiring. High-quality sunglasses filter out most or all UV light and combined with side shields they offer extremely effective eye protection.

PREEXISITNG VISUAL REFRACTIVE ERRORS

At altitudes found on in the Alaska Range, contact lenses are tolerated without the difficulties that are common with use at extreme altitude. Corrective eye glasses can rapidly become a major hassle in poor weather conditions and may lead to serious problems if required for adequate vision. Prescription goggles are available for those who are dependent on corrective lenses to see adequately.

Surgical corrections of near-sighted refractive errors, radical keratotomy (RK) and laser keratectomy (LASIK and PRK) are popular corrective procedures. Although RK can lead to visual changes at altitudes above 9,000 feet, typically approximately 24 hours of altitude exposure at 14,000 feet are necessary for significant visual problems and are fully reversible at sea level. LASIK and PRK are more stable procedures and do not result in visual changes at high altitude below approximately 17,000 feet, and typically visual problems don't occur until approximately 27,000 feet.

PREEXISTING MEDICAL CONDITIONS

The sustained strenuous climbing in harsh environments can precipitate a variety of medical problems. The related dehydration can seriously impact blood levels of particular medications and limit oxygen delivery in the body. If you have a condition that limits your activity at home or that is managed with essential medications, check with your doctor before venturing into a remote area like the Alaska Range. And bring enough essential medications with some extra, so it may be stored in at least two locations; i.e. some with you during the climb and some left stored at base camp.

ACCIDENTS/AVALANCHE/TRAUMA

It is difficult to generalize about accidents in the Alaska Range. Poor sensitivity regarding varying snow conditions and weather appear to be significant factors.

Avalanches are deadly beasts that must be avoided at all cost. Once caught by an avalanche, survival depends on severity of injuries that occurred during the avalanche and duration of burial resulting in suffocation. Extrication times of less than 15 minutes result in more than a 90 percent survival rate. This drops to less than 30 percent by about 30 minutes. However, even relatively small avalanches can lead to fatal falls. Once again, avoidance is critically important.

Crevasses are persistent threats along glaciers in the range. Injuries result from falls, entrapment, sudden hypothermia, and being struck by falling ice. Snow-covered glaciers in the range are suspect for surface failures that range from punch holes to massive bridge collapse. Skis and snowshoes distribute weight but are not complete protection. Roped travel and probing campsites are routinely employed techniques to minimize the risk of accidents.

Weather in the Alaska Range commonly moves in quickly and dramatically. For climbers, weather can be a critical factor contributing in a severe injury or accident. Think twice before pushing a weather window that could leave you stranded on exposed terrain with limited supplies and protection. Learn the local weather patterns before feeling overly confident on reading the weather signs. This takes time, while most climbers are relatively new to the Alaska Range.

Climb using your brain, not only your legs—this is a real challenge, particularly on long climbs. Maintain an alert rational perspective rather than a mechanical routine. Technical climbing in the Alaska

Chris McNamara leading the first pitch of the Cobra Pillar, starting a 15 hour and 10 minute speed ascent of the route. Photo by Joe Puryear

Range is a continuous cycle of observe, assess, act.

Climb well. May your thermos never empty of warm drink, and enjoy this special place!

Jim Litch is a high-altitude and travel medicine specialist and former Denali Climbing Ranger.

Kahiltna Glacier

The 43-mile long Kahiltna Glacier is the largest glacier in the Alaska Range. Over 1,200 climbers visit this mighty glacier each year. With access to Denali, Mount Foraker, and Mount Hunter, it isn't hard to understand its popularity. In addition to the giants, there are a plethora of smaller peaks, from snow walk-ups to technical test-pieces. Because of the number of people and the presence of the National Park Service, there is a large network and community to assist your climbing experience. While this may turn some climbers off who are looking for a more solitary adventure, for most it is this arrangement that keeps bringing people here to push their own limits. Regardless, the Kahiltna Glacier is one of the most incredible and beautiful climbing venues on the planet.

Getting There

There are two options for reaching the Kahiltna:

Air Travel

Nearly all parties fly into Kahiltna Base Camp with a licensed air service out of Talkeetna. The flight takes about 40 minutes one-way. This is used to access every climb in this section.

Some parties may want to consider landing at the toe of the Southeast Ridge of Mount Foraker, near 6,500 feet, for attempting the Infinite Spur or even Mount Hunter's West Ridge. This is a quiet out-of-the-way spot, but it lacks the support net of the Kahiltna Base Camp and is farther away from good moderate warm up climbs. Not all air services will land or pick-up here so be sure to check with them first.

Petersville Road

One or two parties each year walk into the range from the Petersville Road. The trip is best made in early season (before May 1) when snow is covering much of the brushy terrain on the tundra and the

Photo by Mike Gauthier

rivers are frozen to allow straightforward skiing. In May and June, traveling in these lower regions becomes difficult due to the inherently bad snow conditions and break-up of the rivers. Later in the season, it is easier to stay above the valley floors to avoid the thick brush and raging rivers. Expect to take 7 to 10 days for the trip to Base Camp.

There are two ways to go about doing this. At the town of Trapper Creek on the George Parks Highway (mile 114.5), turn left on Petersville Road. Drive this rough road 40 miles to a parking area at Cache Creek. Descend Cache Creek, then head north to the toe of the Kahiltna Glacier. Follow the Kahiltna to the Southeast Fork and Base Camp.

The other route involves traveling to Little Switzerland, down the Pika Glacier, then up the main Kahiltna Glacier. This avoids many of the difficult icefalls and heavily crevassed sections of the Kahiltna, but is not as straightforward. This may be a better late-season approach. Check the Little Switzerland section for approach suggestions.

Kahiltna Base Camp

Kahiltna Base Camp is located at 7,200 feet on the Southeast Fork of the Kahiltna Glacier. Also referred to as Kahiltna International Airport (or simply KIA), this is the fly-in point for over 90 percent of the people that climb in the Alaska Range. It isn't hard to imagine the veritable circus that can form here. With climbers from all over the world, each with their own agenda and opinion on how things should be done, things can sometimes be a little hectic. At the same time, this is an awesome little glacier community of people and a unique chance to learn and make friends. The camaraderie and experience that can be gained is immeasurable.

This is the main base camp location for all of the climbs in this section. The camping spots are located on the hill just north of the airstrip. During the height of the season, several pre-dug campsites exist. Remember, this is a very busy small airport and the noise pollution can be severe. If planning on staying for a while, it might be preferable to set up camp well away from the busy airstrip. Camp at least 50 feet away from the Park Service and Base Camp Manager's tent.

For any climbing trip here, it is recommended to bring an extra week's worth of food and cache it in the snow at Base Camp. Dig your cache at least three feet deep to the top of the cache. Place a minimum eight-foot wand or flag (above the snow surface) on the cache to mark its location. On the wand should be your issued Park Service permit sticker or a tag noting your team name and your fly-out date. Don't forget to pick up your cache on your way out. All of the caches are placed in one general location in the Base Camp. Check with the NPS Ranger before placing your cache.

Base Camp Essentials

1. The Base Camp Manager is in charge of all of the airport operations. You must obey and follow her/his commands and instructions at all times. She/he is in charge of your safety as well as the safety of the pilots and other glacier tourists.

2. As soon as you land, help your pilot unload your plane and immediately clear your gear and yourself from the runway. Be on the lookout for planes landing and taking off.

3. Check in with the National Park Service and give them your Base Camp Card issued to you by your air service. They will provide you with instructions on where to camp, where to place your Base Camp cache, and how to acquire fuel and sleds.

4. Camp only in the designated area around the Base Camp. Do not camp near or at the end of the runway. Do not walk across the runway unless instructed to do so by the Base Camp Manager.

5. Use only designated latrines and pee-holes for human waste. There are generally two pit toilets located on the far west side of camp.

6. Help keep the runway and the camp clean by removing all of your garbage and any other trash you come across.

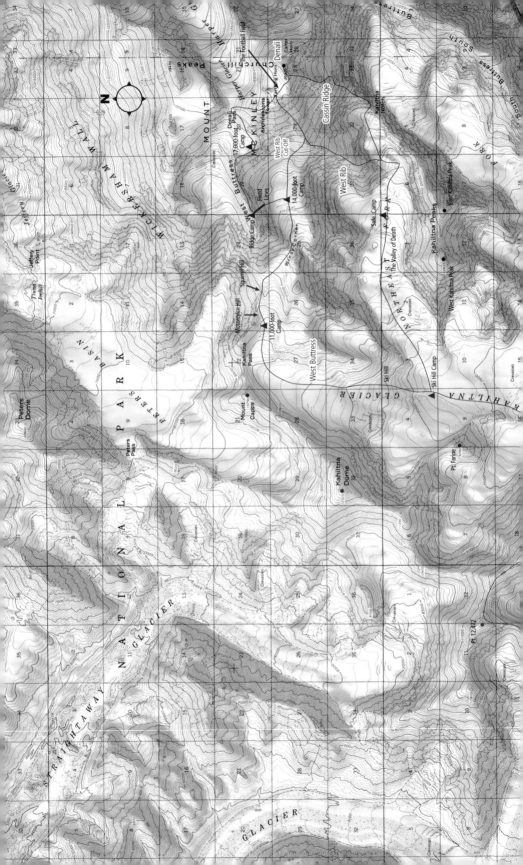

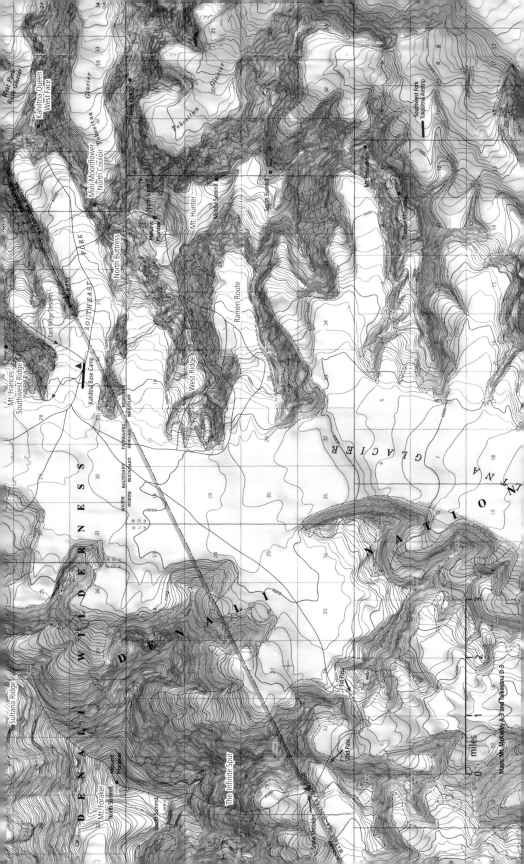

Kahiltna Base Camp and the north face of Mount Hunter. Photo by Joe Puryear

Upon returning from your climb, check back in with the Base Camp Manager. She/he will call your air service and arrange a pickup. Do not expect to be picked up immediately or even that same day or week. Pilots will only fly when the weather and conditions are safe to do so. The Base Camp Manager will inform you at least 30 minutes in advance of your pickup. If you are not ready to go when scheduled, you may forfeit your flight to a team that is ready. Just like any airport, the planes will not wait on the ground for you.

The Base Camp Manager generally gives a weather forecast at 8 P.M. every night on CB channel 19. This forecast is just a repeat of the National Weather Service forecast. Predicting weather in Alaska is difficult at best and this should only be used as a tool in conjunction with your own weather observations to evaluate what you think is going to happen.

Emergency

A CB radio on channel 19 is useful and common in the area of the Kahiltna Glacier. It is monitored by the Base Camp Manager and the Park Service both at Kahiltna Base Camp and at the 14,000-foot Camp on Denali. Because it generally only works line-of-sight, reception can be difficult at times, especially around the 11,000-foot level on the West Buttress. An aircraft radio (for emergencies only) or a satellite phone provides better coverage. A cell phone occasionally works from certain high locations such as the summit of Mount Hunter and above 14,000 feet on Denali and Foraker. Do not rely on a cell phone as reception can be unpredictable. A good plan is to stomp a large (10-foot by 30-foot or larger) SOS into the snow. Enough planes frequent the area that it is bound to be seen. Self-rescue to Kahiltna Base Camp is always the best option if possible.

SUPERTOPO

ALASKA CLIMBING

Denali

Denali (20,320') is the highest mountain in North America, and due to its sheer bulk and extreme vertical relief, it is one of the most stunning features on the Alaskan landscape. It is so huge in fact that the mountain can be seen from up to 250 miles away on a clear day. The mountain has a reputation for being one of the coldest and stormiest peaks in the world. Even summertime temperatures can reach -40-degrees F and winds have been known to gust well over 120 mph. But each year over a thousand climbers from around the world are drawn to its slopes for a chance at standing atop this magnificent peak.

Denali has had many names applied to it throughout the years. The Koyukon and Tenaina tribes, a subset of the Athabascan tribe, were likely the first humans to ever lay eyes on Denali. They labeled it Deenaalee, meaning the "High One". Other native names include Traleika, Tolika, and Doleyka. The Russians referred to it as Tenada and Bulshaia Gora, while early American names included Densmore's Mountain and the Churchill Peaks. It was William Dickey, a 19th century gold prospector, who proposed the name Mount McKinley after 1898 presidential candidate William McKinley. This name stuck and is very commonly used today. In 1917 Mount McKinley National Park came into existence, thanks largely to devoted naturalist Charles Sheldon, but later the Park embraced the name Denali for the name of the Park and its namesake peak.

Denali holds over 30 routes and many more variations. Covered here are the three most popular objectives and the focus of much of the climbing in the Alaska Range. Each route provides unique challenges for all level of mountaineers. The Muldrow Glacier route is included in the North Side section later in the book.

Denali from the summit of Mt. Foraker. Photo by Joe Puryear

West Buttress

Difficulty: **Alaska Grade 2, 50-degree ice**

Elevation gain: **13,100' from Kahiltna Base Camp**

Total time: **14-24 days**

Climbing time: **Up: 12-20 days. Down: 2-4 days**

Season: **April to mid-July, June is best**

The West Buttress of Denali is the most popular big mountain climbing route in all of Alaska. Of the 1,000 to 1,300 climbers that attempt Denali each season, 85 percent head for the West Buttress. Roughly half of them stand on the summit. The route is popular with apprentice and expert climbers alike. Less experienced climbers can test their skills at cold and altitude on a route that is non-technical and straightforward. More experienced climbers will find an excellent chance for acclimatization for harder routes, as well as a myriad of difficult variations should they be so inclined. The route is internationally famous as well. Each year hundreds of climbers come from around the world to attempt this Alaskan giant. Despite the inherent crowds, all climbers will find the West Buttress to be one of the most beautiful and scenic places imaginable. From the wide expanse of the Kahiltna Glacier, to the extensive views of the surrounding peaks and the unending view of the tundra to the north, the West Buttress is an outstanding climb and grand achievement for anyone.

FA: July 10, 13, 14, 1951; Bradford Washburn, William Hackett, Jim Gale, Henry Buchtel, John Ambler, Melvin Griffiths, Jerry More, and Barry Bishop.

History

For many years after Denali's first ascent, the Muldrow Glacier remained the only route attempted and climbed on the mountain. In the days before airplanes could land on glaciers, this was the only reasonable route to approach overland. And even as airplanes started flying onto the slopes around Denali, it was difficult to justify the expense and risk involved in

trying a new route. Bradford Washburn, who had been surveying and capturing aerial photography of the Alaska Range since 1936, spied a route on the western slopes of the mountain that might provide a safe and easy way to the summit. It would also be significantly shorter than the Muldrow route if a team was flown in to the glacier at the base of the route. Washburn published his findings in the 1947 American Alpine Journal.

In 1951, a group of climbers from Colorado teamed up with Washburn and two of his partners to try this new route. Jim Gale and Bill Hackett had climbed with Washburn on earlier Muldrow trips. The Colorado climbers were Dr. John Ambler, Barry Bishop, Dr. Henry Buchtel, Dr. Melvin Griffiths, and Jerry More. Other than to open a new route up Denali, the team hoped to accomplish detailed geological survey work in order to complete the now famous Boston Museum of Science Mount McKinley map.

The team flew in with expert glacier pilot Terris Moore, inventor of the indispensable wheel ski for airplanes. The plan was to have one team flown on to the Kahiltna Glacier, while another team came overland from Wonder Lake, up the Peters Glacier, and over Kahiltna Pass to meet the other party. On June 18, 1951, Washburn, Gale, Buchtel, and Hackett were flown to 7,650 feet on the Kahiltna Glacier. They moved up to 10,000 feet and waited for the other team to meet them here. Meanwhile the military made an airdrop of over 2,500 pounds of food and equipment. Washburn and his team climbed Kahiltna Dome (12,525 feet) for surveying purposes, making its first ascent. The rest of the team, consisting of Ambler, Bishop, Griffiths, and More, slowly made their way up the Peters Glacier. Bishop and More climbed Peters Dome (10,600 feet) and placed surveying equipment on its summit for Washburn. This was a first ascent of this peak as well. Finally on June 30, the team crossed over Kahiltna Pass to meet the rest of the team.

Washburn, Hackett, and Gale continued up new ground on July 4. The rest of the team provided support and continued their

geological surveying. They established a camp at 15,400 feet, underneath the ice headwall that forms the route's crux. From here they fixed ropes all the way to 17,000 feet. The hard ice proved difficult and required chopping steps up 800 feet of 50-degree blue ice. On July 10 they continued up the long traverse to Denali Pass. Having been up the upper section before from prior climbs on the Muldrow, they walked up to the summit in four and a half hours. Bishop, Butchel, Griffiths, and More eventually reached the summit on July 13 and 14.

Thus a new generation of Alaskan climbing was born—one that eliminated the long and grueling approaches to allow climbers to focus more on climbing itself. Washburn's vision had become a reality that will be enjoyed for many generations to come.

In January 1967, three bold Alaskan climbers made the first winter ascent of Denali via the West Buttress. Early in their trip one member, Jacques Batkin, of their team of eight, died in a crevasse fall. Dave Johnston, Art Davidson, and Ray Genet summited on February 28. A vicious

storm enveloped the mountain and they were trapped at Denali Pass for six days. They had little food or fuel to melt water, but with persistence and determination they all endured, creating one of the most renowned survival stories in the history of mountaineering. Art Davidson wrote about the epic in his book *Minus 148°: First Winter Ascent of Mt. McKinley.*

The first solo ascent of the West Buttress and Denali was made in August of 1970 by the heroic Japanese climber Naomi Uemura. Uemura was one of the world's greatest explorers of the time and in January of 1984 he came to Denali to attempt a solo winter climb as training for a solo climb of Mount Vinson in Antarctica. Uemura reached the summit on February 12, but became lost in a storm on the descent and disappeared. His high-camp was found at 17,200 feet and on the summit was found the Japanese and American flags that he carried, but after extensive searches his body was never found.

In more modern times, American climber Chad Kellogg accomplished the first one day round-trip ascent from the Kahiltna Base Camp. In a marathon effort,

Hauling loads on the Kahiltna Glacier. Photo by Jesse Williams

Climbers on the final ridge approaching the summit. Photo by Jesse Williams

Kellogg left Base Camp at 2:15 A.M. on June 17, 2004 and reached the summit 14 hours and 22 minutes later. He returned to Base Camp the next morning at 2:10 A.M.

Strategy

Occasionally climbers who acclimatize well and have unusually good weather are able to make the summit and back in under two weeks. This is the exception, not the norm, and average parties should plan on 18-21 days on the mountain. For a higher probability of success, a longer trip can be planned.

The West Buttress is normally climbed in full expedition style. Double-carrying loads and the "climb high, sleep low" concept are commonly employed. In addition, plastic sleds are used to help ferry gear on the flatter sections of the glacier. When placing a glacier cache, make sure to bury it at least three feet deep and place a 10-foot or longer wand to mark it. Caches on the lower glacier can melt out fast and ravens frequently dig up and destroy poorly buried supplies.

Make sure each campsite is well fortified and protected from the elements. On the Kahiltna Glacier and at the 14,000-foot Camp, it is best to place your tent on the

level of the glacier and build up snow walls around it. Digging a tent-site deep into the glacier will only ensure that you get completely buried during a heavy wind and snow storm, while the snow tries to return your hole to the level of the glacier. Above the 14,000-foot Camp, snow caves are preferable to tents, although they can be much more time-consuming. Make sure your tent-site is completely bomb-proof.

Skis and snowshoes are commonly used along the Kahiltna. It's best if the entire party sticks with one method or the other. Skis are by far better; they are faster and safer over crevasses. Descending between load carries becomes a quick and fun trip, rather than more slogging.

Sample Itinerary

Day 1: Arrive in Anchorage. Complete last minute shopping and drive to Talkeetna. Check in with air service and if you arrive early enough, complete NPS registration at the Ranger Station.

Day 2: Register with NPS and prepare for flight. Fly into Kahiltna Base Camp and obtain fuel and sleds. Cache your emergency gear and food. Motivated parties may be already organized and can ropeup, and take off. Otherwise, relax, acclimatize, and practice your glacier skills.

Day 3: The load carrying schedule for the Kahiltna generally depends on the month and the temperature. Early season climbers will want to travel during the warmth of the day, while June and July climbers will travel at night to beat the intense daytime heat. Leave Base Camp and single-carry the gentle glacier to 7,800 feet. Some parties double-carry this section.

Day 4: Carry a load to the next camp, either 9,800 feet or 11,000 feet.

Day 5: Move up to next camp.

Day 6: Rest Day.

Day 7: Carry a load to either just before or just after Windy Corner (13,000 to 13,500 feet) or all the way to 14,200 feet.

Day 8: Move camp to 14,200 feet.

Day 9: Rest day or pick up cache below.

Day 10: Rest day or pick up cache below.

Day 11: Carry a load to 16,200 feet or 17,200 feet.

Day 12: Move camp to 17,200 feet.

Day 13: Rest day or pick up cache at 16,200 feet.

Days 14-17: Summit days.

Day 18: Return to 14,200 feet or 11,000 feet.

Day 19: Return to Kahiltna Base Camp. Check in with the Base Camp Manager, dig up your emergency cache, and prepare for your flight.

Day 20: Fly to Talkeetna and check out with the NPS.

Day 21: Return to Anchorage and fly home.

Gear

Take standard glacier travel gear. Mechanical ascenders are useful for ascending the fixed lines.

Camps

These are frequently used camping locations. Many more camp locations exist and are used by climbers. The expansive

Kahiltna Glacier provides near infinite camping opportunities, although climbers tend to group together in the following locations.

Ski Hill (7,800 feet): Actually at the base of Ski Hill, some climbers will refer to this as the "Northeast Fork" camp because of the confluence of the Northeast Fork of the Kahiltna. The main camping area is located closer to the 7,700-foot contour of the map. There are some major east-west crevasses that run through the area. Each year climbers must cross huge sagging snow-bridges. It is not unusual to see old snow walls of camps sinking down on these as well. As with every camp, be sure to probe the area well.

Kahiltna Pass Camp (9,800 feet): This broad, relatively crevasse-free area is used as an intermediate camp between Ski Hill and the 11,000-foot Camp.

The 11,000-foot Camp (10,900 feet): This is the last flat area at the end of the main Kahiltna. Beware; this northern part of the Kahiltna Glacier is a sink for bad weather and snow. It can snow six feet here while Base Camp receives less than a foot. Make sure you mark well any caches you leave here. Many parties decide to leave their skis here. If so, plant your skis around your cache and tape your wands atop your skis.

The 14,000-foot Camp (14,200 feet): The location of a seasonal Park Service outpost with several rangers here over the course of the season. This is the best place to rest, acclimatize, and prepare a strategy for the summit attempt. There are two latrines maintained by the Park Service that should be obligatorily used if you camp here.

Ridge Camp (16,200 feet): This is an okay spot to stash gear or make an extra stop in acclimatizing. The back (north) side of the ridge just above the col above the fixed lines affords a small area to dig tent platforms or a good snow-cave (there are actually permanent snow-caves here.) It also allows a quick retreat back down the fixed lines should the weather turn bad. This spot can be exceptionally windy and brutal during a storm.

The West Buttress of Denali from the southwest. Photo by Mike Gauthier

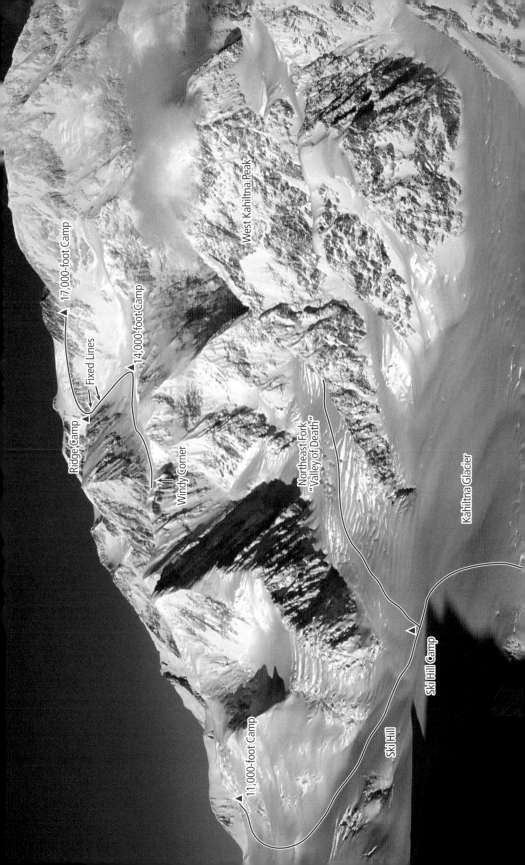

17,000-foot Camp

Fixed Lines

14,000-foot Camp

West Kahiltna Peak

Ridge Camp

Windy Corner

Northeast Fork
"Valley of Death"

Kahiltna Glacier

11,000-foot Camp

Ski Hill Camp

Ski Hill

Climbers heading up Motorcycle Hill out of the 11,000-foot Camp. Photo by Joe Puryear

Route

The route is divided into five sections for a total distance of 16.5 miles.

Kahiltna Base Camp to Ski Hill (junction of Northeast Fork of the Kahiltna) (5.5 miles)

From Kahiltna Base Camp, head west down Heartbreak Hill. The reason for this moniker will become evident on your way back out. Keep to the right and well off the airstrip. At the bottom of the hill (6,750 feet) turn right (north) onto the main fork of the Kahiltna. Below the west face of Mount Frances is a small icefall. This is generally best skirted on its left side. Sometimes parties will take a direct path through it, but this is not recommended. Above the icefall, the best path can vary year to year. Normally, it is best to head northeast staying toward the center of the glacier. Often times, however, there is a good path just right of the southeastern ridge coming down from Pt. Farine (Pt. 9,300 feet). Either way, regain the center of the glacier and head due north to the base of Ski Hill and the junction of the Northeast Fork (7,800 feet).

Ski Hill to 11,000-foot Camp (4 miles)

Ascend Ski Hill, which has two distinct rises. Above, the glacier rises gradually to 10,000 feet. A good side trip can be made here by climbing Mount Capps (Pt. 10,790) above Kahiltna Pass. This easy peak has excellent 360-degree views, including a good overview of the route ahead and an inspiring view into Peter's Basin and the Father and Son's Wall. The main climbing route makes a sharp turn to the east and ascends into a basin below what is referred to as Motorcycle Hill. Just before arriving

The 17,000-foot Camp, a.k.a. The Crow's Nest or High Camp (17,200 feet): This is the main high camp used for summit bids. The broad plateau here is extremely exposed and icy. It is sometimes difficult to construct snow walls or dig snow caves, especially given the high altitude. But digging in good here is an absolute must. Storms this high on the mountain are fierce and unforgiving. Clean Mountain Cans must be used here to control human waste. There is an NPS maintained rescue cache that contains 1,000 feet of rope, oxygen bottles and equipment, a litter, and a Gamow Bag.

On the summit of Denali. Photo: Joseph Puryear Collection

ALASKA CLIMBING

at camp (10,900 feet), there is avalanche danger from a series of seracs up and right.

11,000-foot Camp to 14,000-foot Camp (2.75 miles)

Many parties will leave their snowshoes or skis at the 11,000-foot camp and walk from here in crampons. Some will continue on skis however all the way to the 14,000-foot camp. This is a matter of personal choice. The skiing above here is much more difficult and steeper. Ascend the 700-foot Motorcycle Hill. Every year there are serious crevasses on the hill and near its base. At the top of the hill, the route crosses the crest of the Alaska Range for a brief bit and overlooks the awesome Father and Son's Wall to the north. From the top of the hill, traverse up and under the prominent rocks to the right. Then climb steeply up Squirrel Hill to where the route flattens out below the massive west face of the West Buttress proper. At the top of Squirrel Hill (12,300 feet), insidious crevasses run in several different directions so extra prudence is necessary. Continue by making a long southeasterly traverse underneath the west face of the West Buttress. Be wary of rock-fall from the face above. Climb toward

Windy Corner crossing two large crevasses. One of these crevasses was used as a camp on the first ascent. This spot should be considered more as an emergency camp location. It can provide adequate protection from wind and weather. Windy Corner was named by Bradford Washburn who encountered 90 mile-per-hour winds here. There is a good resting spot in the rocks at the top of the hill (13,200 feet), before continuing around the corner. Another great side-trip is an ascent of Pt. 13,350. This little knoll is a quick 15-minute jaunt and lends an excellent view to the surrounding area.

The east side of Windy Corner has some of the worst crevasse problems on the route. The route makes an exposed side-hill traverse above an icefall and over several crevasses. Be very attentive through this area as it is the site of many accidents. Continue east and drop down slightly into the basin below. Occasionally people will camp here, but due to its proximity to Windy Corner and its exposure to rock-fall, it is not recommended. Continue east up the broad slopes trending left of the major crevasses. Make the final flat traverse to the 14,000-

Denali Pass

17,000-foot Camp

Ridge Camp

West Rib Cut-Off

14,000-foot Camp

Windy Corner

Squirrel Hill

Motorcycle Hill

foot Camp (14,200 feet). This is a good place to rest for a few days and acclimatize while devising a summit strategy. Most parties will carry a load to the 17,000-foot camp and return here to wait for good weather for the final summit bid.

A good side trip here is to go visit the "Edge of the World Rock." Although many people won't, it is highly recommended to rope up to walk out to this amazing overlook. Walk due south from camp heading toward the prominent rock outcrop on the edge of the glacier. Boulder to the exposed top of the rock for hero pictures.

14,000-foot Camp to 17,000-foot Camp (1.75 miles)

The route now turns north up toward the long icy headwall that gains access to the ridge of the West Buttress proper. Climb up 35-degree snow slopes and over a couple large crevasses at the top of the first rise. The angle backs off a little, then becomes steeper as it approaches the ice face and the fixed lines. This hill below the fixed lines is frequently skied. The fixed lines are installed and maintained by the National Park Service each season. Below the fixed lines is a huge bergschrund (15,400 feet) that provides an excellent safe spot to take a break, get ready, and then wait in line for your turn on the fixed lines. It is not totally unheard of for climbers to bypass the fixed lines and climb the 50 to 55-degree ice beside them. Climb or ascend this slope until the col at 16,200 feet is reached. Ascending traffic should use the right fixed line and descending traffic should use the (climber's) left fixed line. It is recommended to clip an ascender onto the fixed line and push it up the line for safety as you climb the ice. A good technique for descending the fixed line is to first clip into the line with an ascender. Wrap the fixed line twice around your back arm and with your other hand, hold your ascender open. Walk down the ice using friction from your arm wrap to control your speed and close the ascender when you need to stop.

The most interesting and scenic part of the route is the climb up the crest of the West Buttress. Start up the ridge looking for a prominent rock prow called Washburn's Thumb. Climb left (north) of the crest to reach the base of this feature. There are often fixed lines here as well that help with safe passage through this section. Above, stay on or near the rocky crest of the ridge until it flattens out at 17,200 feet. Traverse out into the large flat area known as the Crow's Nest and start work on a good protected campsite or snow-cave.

17,000-foot Camp to the Summit (2.5 miles)

The next section of the route is the long and exposed traverse to Denali Pass. Informally known as the "Autobahn," this is the site of numerous accidents. Head up toward a prominent rock outcrop on the slope above. Traverse left underneath this feature and onto the 35 to 40-degree rising traverse to the pass. The National Park Service has installed fixed pickets on this section in recent years. Reach the pass at 18,200 feet. Turn south and climb the right side of the 40-degree slope on the left (east) side of the crest. When the slope becomes less steep, continue up near the ridge crest, heading for the right side of Archdeacon's Tower. A small descent leads to the "Football Field" at 19,500 feet. Traverse southeast across this flat expanse to the final slope heading up to the summit ridge. Climb this short slope to Kahiltna Horn (20,120 feet). Continue east along the sharp and exposed summit ridge to the top.

Descent

Descend the route. Be especially careful when descending from Denali Pass. Climbers tend to be cold, exhausted, and altitude sick. Use prudence and running-belays if necessary. Most parties will spend an additional night at the 17,000-foot Camp to rest before descending to the 14,000-foot Camp. While it is possible to descend all the way to Base Camp from 17,000 in a day for motivated parties, many parties will take a more relaxed two to three day pace. Remember there are still many hazards and difficult sections to reverse on the descent.

West Rib

Difficulty: **Alaska Grade IV, 60-degree ice**

Elevation gain: **On route: 9,200'. From Kahiltna Base Camp: 13,100'**

Total time: **14-24 days**

Approach time: **Alpine style: From the 14,000-foot Camp: 8-15 hours; From Kahiltna Base: 9-17 hours. Expedition style: 4-5 days**

Climbing time: **Up: Alpine style: 3-4 days; Expedition style: 9-12 days. Down: 1-2 days**

Season: **April to mid-July, June is best**

The West Rib is a step down in difficulty from its neighboring Cassin, but it is substantially harder than the West Buttress route. This is a huge direct line for those climbers wishing to push their limits a little more but still stay in proximity to the core climbing area and network of West Buttress route. While the technical difficulties of the route are minimal, the sustained nature and virtue of being on the south face of Denali make the climb daunting. It also requires climbers to enter the dangerous Northeast Fork of the Kahiltna, a.k.a. the Valley of Death, but once this is passed, a pure 9,000-foot ridge-climb awaits.

FA: June 19, 1959; Pete Sinclair, Jake Breitenbach, Barry Corbet, and William Buckingham.

History

Four Dartmouth Mountaineering Club members dreamed up the climb after making the second ascent of the South Buttress of Mount Moran in Wyoming. Bradford Washburn had already made a proposal of the route in an issue of The Mountain World. According to team member William Buckingham, the four were lounging around after their climb "when someone enthusiastically suggested, 'Let's climb the south face of McKinley next summer!'" So it would be that in early June 1959, Jake Breitenbach, Barry Corbet, Pete Sinclair, and Buckingham drove to Alaska to start their fantastic adventure. The young climbers lacked big mountain experience, except for Breitenbach who had climbed

Denali by the West Buttress, but they were technically proficient and very motivated.

By June 8, Don Sheldon had completed transporting the team and gear to the Southeast Fork of the Kahiltna. The team moved up the glacier and turned into what would eventually be known as the Valley of Death. They were fully aware of the great risk of traveling up the Northeast Fork of the Kahiltna and placed their camps accordingly. The western rib of the south face was in full view before them. They initially didn't see the hidden couloir on the east side of the rib that provides access through the rock buttress at the rib's base. After forging a route through the imposing icefall at the base of the rib, things became more apparent. While at their Safe Camp, they received an airdrop or food and supplies, including 1,700 feet of fixed rope.

They split up into two teams to tackle the lower section of the route, each team finding challenging rock climbing and steep rotten ice. Both teams ended up under a huge gendarme that completely blocked their way. After descending back to camp, they decided to explore couloirs farther to the east to find a weakness in the buttress. In 1959, proficiency and technology in ice climbing were still lacking and it was generally easier to stick to the rock. It was decided, however, that anything had to be easier than climbing the buttress crest. So with great determination they started chopping steps up a 55 to 60-degree couloir using rock belays on its left side for safety and placing fixed lines. The team experienced much rock fall; at one point, a "large rock … very nearly wiped out the entire expedition, one by one."

They finally reached the sharp crest of the ridge, only to find that there was no good place for a camp. The next three hours were spent chopping out Concentration Camp, which Buckingham called a "miserable, cramped spot, with nothing to recommend it save a lovely view and excellent garbage disposal facilities." The weather had been holding immaculately, but the way ahead looked difficult and foreboding. Morale was low as they pondered the enormous amount of work

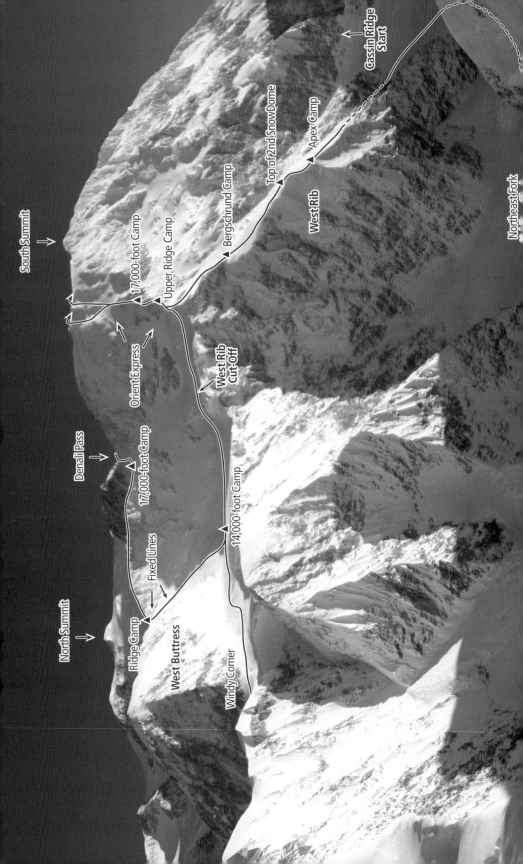

ahead of them. But with three weeks of supplies left there was no reason not to continue, so they pulled their fixed lines and forged ahead. After dispatching the two icy snow domes, they arrived at an excellent campsite they dubbed Camp Paradise.

Things continued to go well as they worked their way up the ridge, eventually making it to their high camp on June 18, a small exposed spot near 16,500 feet they called Balcony Camp. On June 19, the team awoke at 7 A.M. for their final summit push. Unbelievably the weather was still holding strong. They made their way with little difficulty up the final section of the rib and finally stepped onto the huge snow plateau and that joined them with the West Buttress route. They reached the summit between four and five in the afternoon, on a perfect windless day with a complete sea of clouds below. They descended back to Balcony Camp by 10:30 P.M. as the first major storm of their trip began. The next day, in two feet of fresh snow, they blindly worked their way down off the west side of the rib to the 14,200-foot basin of the West Buttress route. They continued down the West Buttress and after toiling with bad weather and crevasses for several days, they finally arrived back at their airstrip and were picked up on June 27 by Don Sheldon.

In 1977, German climber Ruprecht Kammerlander accomplished the first solo of the route. The first winter ascent of the West Rib and the third overall winter ascent of Denali was completed on Febrarary 28, 1983 by Robert Frank and Charlie Sassara, along with Chris Hraback and Steve Teller. Tragically, Frank fell to his death on the descent nearly taking Sassara with him.

Strategy

The route is commonly done both expeditionary and alpine style. Guided parties tend to use expedition style tactics because of the safety net. Most private expeditions that want to travel a little faster will acclimatize first on the West Buttress, and then climb the route alpine style.

Plan for at least a minimum three-week trip on the glacier, whether attempting it expedition or alpine style. For expedition

style, this allows four to five days to reach the base of the route. Then, another six to seven days are used to reach the West Rib Cut-Off. Finally, three days are used in establishing a high camp and summiting. Two more days are necessary for the descent back to the airstrip. This allows three to six storm days or rest days. Typically fixed lines are used and double carry techniques employed.

For an alpine style climb, four to five days are used to reach the 14,000-foot Camp on the West Buttress. Seven days can be spent acclimatizing on this route by making trips to the 17,000-foot Camp, the summit, or moving gear up the West Rib Cut-Off to the proposed high-camp on the rib. The latter is a good way to ensure a successful climb from the base to the summit. Three to six days are used to climb the route and descend to the 14,000-foot Camp. Some parties carry everything over the top and then descend the West Buttress. This is certainly a much safer descent, but requires heavy loads to 19,500 feet. One day will be needed to descend back to the airstrip. This allows one to six unplanned storm days. A longer trip will allow for choosing a good weather window.

Specific Hazards:

The Valley of Death is the biggest hazard for the route. Catastrophic avalanches are common here and climbers must accept a certain level of risk to travel into this area. The initial couloir is prone to rock fall and should be climbed under frozen conditions.

Gear

Take six to eight ice screws, two or three cams, a set of stoppers, and two to four pickets. Substantially more gear should be taken for a group that is planning on fixing ropes. A team traveling very light and fast may only need one 165-foot rope. Two 165 or 200-foot double ropes would allow a good safety margin for leading and retreating. Bring two ice tools per person or one ice axe and one ice tool.

Snowshoes can be very useful up the Northeast Fork for the approach. Use a lightweight pair that you can put on your pack and carry up the route. If conditions are good or a trail is broken, you may be able to walk in. While useful for acclimatizing on the West Buttress, skis are not recommended for the approach because they would be difficult to retrieve after the climb. Some parties purposely break a trail to the Safe Camp or to the base of the icefall with skis, return to the 7,800-foot camp, and then walk back over the broken trail when it is cold and firm.

If you are climbing the route alpine style and acclimatizing on the West Buttress, consider bringing some extra comforts up that route that won't go on the climb itself. Parties climbing alpine style generally leave a cache of gear at the 14,000-foot camp on the West Buttress that includes the heavy amenities that aren't necessary for the route. Another cache at 16,300 feet on the Rib can be used for pre-placing food and fuel for the summit bid. It can also be a good idea to leave the extra climbing gear, climbing food, and fuel for the route in a cache at the Northeast Fork. This allows lighter loads to be carried up the West Buttress. Unfortunately, there has been reported theft

of caches at the Northeast Fork in recent years, so use your best judgment.

Camps

The following is a list of recommended locations to camp specific to this route. See the West Buttress route for other camp locations.

Safe Camp (9,450 feet): Located on the Northeast Fork of the Kahiltna, this is a relatively crevasse-free area. The camp is threatened by only the most catastrophic avalanches. It may not be such a safe place during a storm. The camp sits on a rise in the center of the glacier, set back from the ominous north face of East Kahiltna Peak. Use good judgment when camping here.

Couloir Camp (11,000 feet): Set up camp under the rock buttress just left of the couloir. This is the safest campsite in the area, although it can be exposed to rock-fall and localized avalanches.

Apex Camp (12,900 feet): The first good but exposed campsite on the ridge proper. May require substantial chopping and digging to level out a tent-site.

Overview of the start of the route from the east, showing the access couloir. Photo by Joe Puryear

Climbing up to the 17,000-foot Camp on the West Rib in snowy conditions. Photo by Joe Puryear

Top of Second Snow Dome (13,900 feet):
An exposed but wide spot where the ridge
flattens out after the snow domes.

Bergschrund Camp (14,800 feet): The most
protected camp spot on the ridge. Camp
under the lip of the bergschrund to avoid
sluffs and rock-fall during storms.

Upper Ridge (15,700 to 16,400 feet):
Several very small campsites can be found
tucked in along the crest. A good spot is at
16,300 feet, next to a rock thumb. The first
ascent party originally called their camp
below the rock buttress near 16,500 feet the
Balcony Camp, though many people now
refer to that as the bench above the buttress
at 17,000 feet.

17,000-foot Camp (17,000 feet): What some
people refer to as the Balcony Camp, this
exposed flat area is the last decent campsite
on the ridge. Wind-battered remains of
tents and caches attest to the ferocity of the
elements here. Bad spot in a storm.

Approach

From the Kahiltna Base Camp follow
the West Buttress route 5.5 miles to the
base of Ski Hill (7,800 feet). Here is the

junction of the Northeast Fork (a.k.a.
the Valley of Death). Alternatively, if you
are starting from the 14,000-foot Camp,
descend back down the West Buttress
route to the same spot. The Northeast Fork
will require tenacity and good decision
making to arrive at the base of the West
Rib unscathed. It is extremely inadvisable
to enter the valley until 24 to 48 hours
after any snowfall—more if it was a big
storm. The valley is flanked on both sides
with hanging glaciers and seracs. In places,
the seracs are higher up one side than the
width of the valley. Avalanches can sweep
the entire valley floor and up the other side.
While you can mitigate the amount of time
you are in supreme danger, you must accept
the unavoidable risk of traveling into this
awesome and rewarding place. Many parties
travel though the valley at night to reduce
avalanche danger. However, serac fall can
happen at any time day or night.

Turn northeast and ascend into the
valley. The first three miles are not
exceedingly dangerous or crevassed. Take
the best path through the center of the
glacier. At 9,000 feet there is a spot between
two buttresses on either side of the valley

that provides a relatively safe place to take a long break. The best place to rest or camp on the glacier, dubbed Safe Camp, is reached at 9,450 feet, in the middle of the glacier.

Keep ascending east toward the big icefall and crevasses that split the glacier end to end. The valley starts to narrow and the danger is perceived to increase. The icefall can be quite difficult and has turned back many parties. Generally it is best to bear toward its middle at the start. It may then be necessary to climb into and out of several large crevasses while trending right toward the south side of the glacier. The route changes season to season and within each season. Use your best judgment and move quickly. Once atop the icefall (10,600 feet), the base of the West Rib is due north. Traverse to the base of the broad access couloir, also known as the Chicken Couloir.

Route

The access couloir starts at 11,200 feet and rises 1,200 feet before meeting the ridge crest. The angle of the couloir reaches a maximum of 50-55 degrees. The couloir is a garbage chute for surrounding cliffs and rock-fall is common. It is prudent to climb the couloir under cold, stable conditions. Climb the couloir on its left side, using rock, snow, or ice protection when needed. If belaying, this will require seven to eight pitches. Near the top of the couloir, climb straight to the ridge crest. Once on the ridge crest, the first of two snow domes is encountered. These short crux ice bulges steepen to 50 degrees. Just after the first 400-foot snow dome at 12,900 feet is Apex Camp, the first okay camp site on the ridge. Climb the second 400-foot snow dome to where the ridge angle decreases considerably at 13,900 feet. A cornice forms along the left side of the ridge, forcing climbers to keep a good

A climber ascending the lower rib. Photo by Dylan Taylor

distance to the east. A good but exposed camp can be made here. A more protected campsite can be found at 14,800 feet in a bergschrund. Continue up snow and ice slopes on the east side of the crest, avoiding rock outcroppings. Eventually you will want to reconnect to the ridge crest and this can be done via many different variations. Near 15,700 feet is a good place to rejoin the crest and is also a good spot to descend to the 14,000-foot Camp on the West Buttress. Several small but protected campsites can be found between here and the base of the next crux couloir (16,400 feet) leading up to the 17,000-foot Camp. A great location is at 16,300 feet next to a rock thumb. For many parties, this makes the best high camp since the 17,000-foot Camp is extremely exposed to weather. Follow the ridge to 16,400 feet where there is a huge rock buttress split by a narrow couloir on the left. Ascend the 50-degree winding couloir for 600 feet using rock and snow protection. There is some dubious fixed gear here and there. At 17,000 feet the couloir ends on a flat area.

The route continues up another 800 feet through bouldery terrain to where the "rib" essentially ends at 17,800 feet and snow couloirs lead to the summit plateau. From here there are two options. The first option is easier and safer but less direct. From the last rocks on the West Rib, traverse up and across the Orient Express heading for the couloir on the left (west) side of the major rock outcropping above. This option stays at a lower angle but reaches the summit plateau at a lower elevation. A choice of two similar gullies can be taken to reach the crest around 19,300 and rock protection is available. The second option is to continue straight up the main couloir on the right (east) side of the rock band. There is a cornice that forms at the top of this couloir and the last 100 feet is steep, topping out at 19,500 feet. Both options top out on the "Football Field" of the West Buttress route. Be prepared for a change in winds and weather when topping out on the route. Also be sure to wand the descent if planning on returning back down the West Rib. Walk east to pick up the well-beaten path of the West Buttress and follow it up to Kahiltna Horn and then to the summit.

West Rib Cut-Off

A popular variation on the West Rib is to climb the West Buttress to 14,200 feet, then ascend snow slopes east out of the basin and intersect the West Rib between 15,700 and 16,200 feet. This is essentially a bail-out route for parties that had planned on doing the entire West Rib but were overwhelmed with the mountain for various reasons. Nowadays many parties come to Denali intent on only doing this variation, which lacks in aesthetics but is a good alternative to the crowds on the upper West Buttress. From the 14,000-foot Camp on the West Buttress, climb moderate snow slopes east out of camp aiming for 16,000 feet on the West Rib. This slope is avalanche prone and is prone to falling rocks from the myriad of rock bands overhead. Allow three to five hours to reach the crest of the West Rib.

Descent

If carrying over the mountain, descend the West Buttress route. Otherwise, return to 19,300 feet and begin down-climbing the ascent route. It may be tempting to head straight down the major couloir called the Orient Express. Due to its colorful history of accidents, this is not recommended. Nearly all parties descend the West Rib Cut-Off at 15,700 feet to the 14,000-foot Camp on the West Buttress and continue to descend this route.

Cassin Ridge

Difficulty: Alaska Grade 5, 5.8, AI 4

Elevation gain: On route: 8,000'. From Kahiltna Base Camp: 13,100'

Total time: 16-24 days

Approach time: From Kahiltna Base Camp: 10-18 hours. From the 14,000-foot Camp via the Northeast Fork: 9-16 hours; via the West Rib: 8-15 hours

Climbing time: Up: 3-7 days. Down: 1-2 days

Season: Mid-April to late-June, June is best

The Cassin is the quintessential technical climb of the Alaska Range. It is an elegant line that perfectly splits the enormous south face of the biggest mountain on the continent and is one of the most sought after climbs in the world. Many consider it a trade-route of the range, but judging by the actual number of ascents it has seen, it is still a modern testpiece and a lasting tribute to the visionary first ascensionists. The actual climbing is not that difficult by present technical standards. But the complete package of a long and dangerous approach, 8,000 feet of sustained climbing, high altitude, arctic cold and storms, and difficult retreat make this route a serious endeavor. The quality of the climbing is absolutely classic. Bradford Washburn wrote that the route had "unequivocally excellent climbing from start to finish." Both the rock and the ice on this exceptional route are superb.

FA: July 19,1961; Riccardo Cassin, Luigi Airoldi, Luigi Alippi, Giancarlo Canali, Romano Perego, Annibale Zucchi.

History

It was only time before this amazing line was sought out. Washburn, the master of finding potential new lines in the Alaska Range, divulged in 1956 that this ridge was the "last and probably the most difficult and dramatic of all potential new routes on Mount McKinley." So the call went out to alpinists around the world. In 1961 Ricardo Cassin of the Italian Alpine Club answered the call and in July of that year he and his team of six made international climbing history. Their climb was the 23rd ascent of the peak, but only the fifth route to be climbed. Except for Cassin and one other member of the team, it was their first trip outside of Europe. None of them was quite prepared for the extreme cold that the arctic weather brought. But they were prepared for the technical difficulties of the ridge, both with modern gear and talented

Mark Westman at 16,700 feet on the Cassin. Photo by Joe Puryear

abilities. The climb was done expeditionary style, fixing ropes and hauling loads. Because of Washburn's suggestion, the team started the climb from the East Fork of the Kahiltna, an approach rarely used these days. They started the climb in late June and over the course of three weeks they had shuttled their gear and established three camps on the route. Throughout their climb they were battered by gale force winds and heavy snowfall, but the persistent Cassin and his team continued upward progress. The six climbers left their final camp at around 17,000 feet on the morning of July 19. They climbed through bitter cold conditions for 17 hours until they finally reached the summit.

All of the team suffered from cold extremities. They were only using alpine gear designed for the Alps. One team member, Giancarlo Canali, suffered major frostbite and his swollen feet did not fit into his boots. Through much teamwork and tenacity, they escorted the injured climber down. At one point, Canali and his rope-mate slipped, but Cassin stopped them with his ice axe. Lower down, another teammate slipped and the belay did not hold, but Cassin was able to grab the rope

with his hand and stop them. Toward the bottom, Cassin was completely buried in an avalanche and he lost both his crampons, but continued down unharmed. The team eventually all made it to the safety of the glacier and was soon flown back to Talkeetna. For this epic ascent, the climbing community afterwards graciously bestowed the name Cassin to this "great central bulge" of Denali.

The second ascent of the Cassin was made in May of 1967 by a Japanese team. The Japanese made two important contributions to the route. One was the opening of the Japanese Couloir on the western flank of the lower buttress. This straightforward ice couloir bypassed a lot of more technical and meandering climbing. The Italians actually traversed into this couloir near its top, but avoided the ice and opted for the rock on its side. The entire couloir was overlooked by the Italians because at the time of their climb steep ice was deemed much harder than fifth class rock. The Japanese Couloir is now the standard route of ascent. The Japanese party also bypassed the third rock band above 16,700 feet, deviating from the ridge crest, but providing a much easier and faster line. This too has become part of the standard route. The Japanese used a different approach for the climb as well. They headed up the Northeast Fork of the Kahiltna, which is much faster but much more perilous. This is now the standard approach for the climb.

The Northeast Fork of the Kahiltna became known as the Valley of Death after a mysterious disappearance and a close call in 1980. A Canadian team of four people ventured up the Northeast Fork in July of that year. The team disappeared and an extensive and expensive search ensued. Their bodies were never found. Earlier that year on June 5, four climbers were camped underneath the Kahiltna Peaks when a massive avalanche broke off from above. The truck-sized debris came within six feet of their tent, but everyone escaped unharmed.

In the summer of 1976, a single bold and visionary climber soloed the Cassin. Little is known about Charlie Porter's climb, but his accomplishment was certainly ahead of its time. It is written in the 1977 American Alpine Journal, "With his usual reticence, Porter has given us no details." He apparently made an impressive 36-hour single push from the top of the Japanese Couloir to the summit. Another notable solo started on June 4, 1991. The legendary Mugs Stump left the 14,000-foot Camp in the afternoon and descended (partly on skis) the West Rib to the base of the route. He then climbed the route in a mere 15 hours and returned back to his camp in a record setting 27 and a half hours round trip.

In March of 1982, three competent Alaskan climbers not only made the first winter ascent of the Cassin, but the second winter ascent of Denali as well. The ascent was completed by Jonathan Waterman, Roger Mear, and Mike Young. Waterman stated they wanted to "push the limits by climbing alpine style on a technically difficult route in subzero conditions." On March 7, after eight days of climbing they stood on the top, unacclimatized and exhausted, but setting a standard for winter

alpinism that few will ever match.

Today there are still the remains of tattered fixed ropes here and there. Near 18,000 feet there are old bags of pitons and ice screws and piles of fixed ropes. An admirable cleanup project conducted by the park rangers in 1996 cleaned up 200 lbs. of fixed ropes and trash out of the Japanese Couloir and off Cassin Ledge. Luckily most climbers have currently adapted an alpine ethic for climbing this route. Each year dozens of prospective climbers register with the NPS to do the Cassin. Only about 10 percent actually step foot on the route, and even less complete it. Climbers still find it very intimidating and most dislike the prospect of traveling up something called the Valley of Death. However, many climbers consider an ascent of the Cassin a career defining accomplishment.

Strategy

The route is no longer commonly done expedition style. Most parties acclimatize on the West Buttress route, and then wait for a spell of good weather to attempt the Cassin alpine style. Plan for a minimum three-week trip in the range. This allows for four to five days to reach the 14,000-foot Camp on the West Buttress. Seven days can be spent acclimatizing on this route by making trips to either the 17,000-foot Camp or the summit. Depending on the party strength and conditions, three to seven days are used to climb the route and descend back to the 14,000-foot Camp. One day will be needed to descend back to the airstrip. This allows one to five storm days. A longer trip will allow more leeway for choosing a good weather window. Some parties have taken over four weeks total to climb the route. I've seen too many fit and qualified parties run out of time because they thought they were going to blitz the route. Don't underestimate Alaskan weather.

There is of course a fine line between taking too much food and fuel and too little. Going as light as possible will definitely increase your chances of success, especially since good weather spells commonly don't last more than four to five days. Route-finding is generally

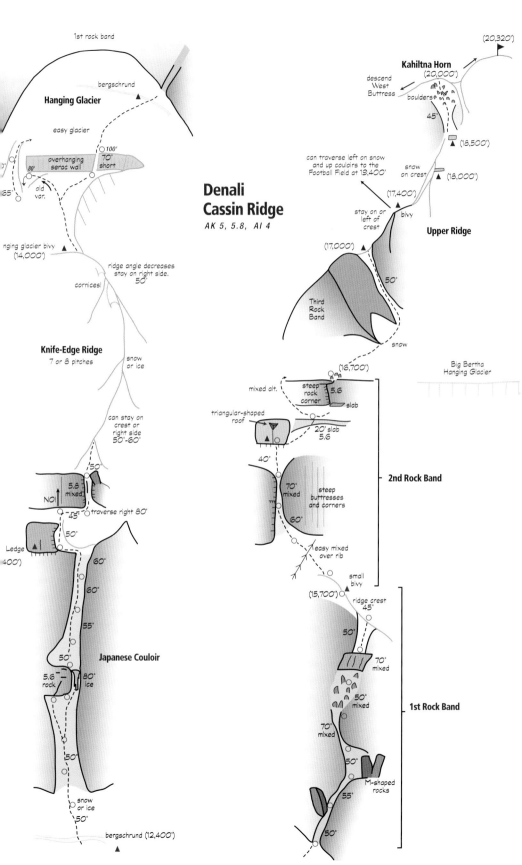

straightforward, allowing much of the route to be climbed in low-visibility conditions. But beware; the south face of Denali is no place to be in a big storm. Only a couple locations on the route lend themselves to digging in a protected bivy. Most bivies are small and exposed.

Specific Hazards

Regardless of the approach used, climbers must enter the Valley of Death. Catastrophic avalanches are common here and climbers must accept a certain level of risk to travel into this area. The Japanese Couloir is prone to natural rock and ice fall, especially in the late afternoon sun.

Gear

Take six to eight ice screws, five to six cams to 2", one set of stoppers, and two to four pickets. Rope selection has many alternatives. A team traveling very light and fast may only need one 165 or 200-foot rope, if all pitches are lead with a pack and retreat is doubtful. Two 200-foot double or twin ropes allow a good safety margin for leading and retreating and allow an extra line to haul a pack on if needed. The

average climber considering this route will be able to lead a great deal of the climb even with a heavier pack. Bring two ice tools per person.

Snowshoes can be very useful up the Northeast Fork for the approach. Use a lightweight pair that you can put on your pack and carry up the route. An additional two lbs. of weight on your pack may seem like a lot, but they are sure going to be useful when a storm dumps six feet of snow while you are camped at the bergschrund, and you need to walk back out. If conditions are good or a trail is broken, you may be able to walk in. While useful for acclimatizing on the West Buttress, skis are not recommended for the approach because they would be difficult to retrieve after the climb. Some parties purposely break a trail to the Safe Camp or to the base of the icefall with skis, return to the 7,800-foot Camp, and then walk back over the broken trail when it is cold and firm. One other option involves climbing up the West Buttress and the West Rib Cut-Off and descending the West Rib. The bottoms of the two routes are very close together, necessitating only crampons for traveling. This option should

only be considered for very advanced teams that wish to move fast.

Many climbers will bring extra comforts for the West Buttress route that won't go along for the Cassin. These can be a real moral booster if pinned down for many days, waiting for the weather. Consider bringing a larger base camp tent in addition to the small bivy tent. Some climbers even bring two sleeping bags, a lighter one for the route and a heavier one for the approach.

Most parties will leave a cache at the 14,000-foot Camp on the West Buttress. This generally includes a few days of food and fuel, the base camp tent, and the rest of the heavy amenities that are not necessary. It can also be a good idea to leave the climbing gear, climbing food, and fuel for the route in a cache at the Northeast Fork. This allows lighter loads to be carried up the West Buttress. Unfortunately, there has been reported theft of caches at the Northeast Fork in recent years, so use your best judgment.

Mark Westman atop the crux gully above Cassin Ledge. Photo by Joe Puryear

Camps

The following is a list of recommended locations to camp for this route. See the West Buttress Route for other camp locations.

Safe Camp (9,450 feet): Located on the Northeast Fork of the Kahiltna, this is a relatively crevasse-free area. The camp is threatened by only the most catastrophic avalanches. It may not be such a safe place during a storm. The camp sits on a rise in the center of the glacier, set back from the ominous north face of East Kahiltna Peak. Use good judgment when camping here.

Bergschrund (12,200 feet): Just under the bergschrund, there is a small serac that provides a small area to camp. Although it doesn't seem threatened by icefall, past pictures suggest that the entire base of the Cassin and even Kahiltna Notch can be decimated by avalanches off the South Face.

Cassin Ledge (13,000 feet): This is a very small ledge underneath a huge rock buttress at the top of the Japanese Couloir. Many

are disappointed upon seeing it for the first time, but with a little work, camping here can be a fun experience. Try gathering some surrounding snow to fill in the bouldery ledge. The ledge is barely wide enough for a small single-wall tent, although two may fit end to end. There are good rock anchors on the wall above.

Hanging Glacier (14,000 feet): Just after the end of the knife-edge ridge, this is the route's most comfortable camp. A large and safe location big enough to accommodate several tents and possibly dig a snow cave.

Hanging Glacier Bergschrund (14,700 feet): This small bivy site is reached just before the first rock band. With a little work it can provide a decent protected bivy, but it is not as comfortable as the Hanging Glacier camp just a few hundred feet lower.

Top of First Rock Band (15,700 feet): This is a small exposed location between the two rock bands that may require chopping out a platform. This makes a good intermediate camp to split up the two rock bands.

Climbing along the knife-edge ridge. Photo by Joe Puryear

Middle of Second Rock Band (c. 16,400 ft.):
A small ledge beneath a small triangular shaped roof after the crux provides a small bivy location. An excellent finger crack in the wall provides good anchors.

Top of Second Rock Band (16,700 feet):
At the top of the technical difficulties, this spot is low angle but very exposed. It may be possible to chop out a good platform next to the rocks, but it is recommended to continue to the upper ridge for a more protected location.

Upper Ridge (17,300 feet), (17,700 feet): At the top of the couloir that regains the ridge is a small exposed col. This makes an okay spot but a better spot is located just a bit further in a higher col (17,700 feet). This makes a good final camp before the summit bid. There are some higher spots that afford exposed bivies next to boulders at 18,100 feet and 18,700 feet.

Approach

Northeast Fork Approach
From Kahiltna Base Camp (7,200 feet), follow the West Buttress route 5.5 miles to the base of Ski Hill (7,800 feet). Here is the junction of the Northeast Fork (a.k.a. Valley of Death). Alternatively, if you are starting from the 14,000-foot Camp, descend back down the West Buttress route to the same spot. The Northeast Fork will require tenacity and good decision making to arrive at the base of the Cassin unscathed. It is extremely inadvisable to enter the valley until 24 to 48 hours after any snowfall—more if it was a big storm. The valley is flanked on both sides with hanging glaciers and seracs. In places, the seracs are higher up one side than the width of the valley. Avalanches can sweep the entire valley floor and up the other side. While you can mitigate the amount of time you are in supreme danger, you must accept the unavoidable risk of traveling into this awesome and rewarding place. Many parties travel though the valley at night to reduce avalanche danger. However, serac fall can happen at any time day or night.

Turn northeast and ascend into the valley. The first three miles are not exceedingly dangerous or crevassed. Take the best path through the center of the glacier. At 9,000 feet, there is a spot between two buttresses on either side of the valley that provides a relatively safe place to take a long break. The best place to rest or camp on the glacier, dubbed Safe Camp, is reached at 9,450 feet, in the middle of the glacier.

From here keep ascending east toward the big ice-fall and crevasses that split the glacier end to end. The valley starts to narrow and the danger is perceived to increase. The icefall can be quite difficult and has turned back many parties. Generally it is best to bear toward its middle at the start. It may then be necessary to climb into and out of several large crevasses while trending right toward the south side of the glacier. The route changes season to season and within each season. Use your best judgment and move quickly. Once atop the icefall (10,600 feet), the base of the West Rib is due north. A spot on the west side of the West Rib Couloir is a safe spot if you need break, but it is a bit out of the way and it's not that far to the base of the Cassin. Head up and toward the South Face of Denali. In this area there are multiple ice cliffs, between one and five thousand feet above you. Traverse left around several crevasses then head back right to the bergschrund near the base of the Japanese Couloir.

West Rib Appoach
From the 14,000-foot Camp, ascend the West Rib Cut-Off to about 16,000 feet on the West Rib. Descend the rib by down-climbing and rappelling. Refer to the West Rib route for more route details. From the base of the rib, walk quickly to the base of the Cassin. While this may seem a safer and maybe faster option, consider the inherent difficulties in descending 5,000 feet of steep snow and ice. Time wise, it is probably only a couple hours faster, and there is still acute danger when traversing to the base of the Cassin.

Joe Puryear approaching the first rock band. Photo by Mark Westman

Route

Japanese Couloir

At the base of the Japanese Couloir (12,300 feet), cross the small bergschrund. Climb four pitches of snow or ice at an angle of 50-degree. Above, the couloir splits, presenting two options. On the right is a short step of steep ice (up to 80 degrees) or on the left is moderate and protectable rock (5.6). Climb either one, then continue four more rope lengths, using ice and rock pro, up the steepening couloir (up to 60 degrees). Just below its top, traverse left for 30 feet. From here look left and behind you (west) and you will see the tiny Cassin Ledge beneath a steep wall (13,400 feet). From the right side of Cassin Ledge, climb a pitch of snow straight up to the big rock wall above. Don't be tempted up by the old fixed lines. Instead, make an exposed traverse right for half a rope length until an easier looking gully appears around a corner. Climb this rock crux (5.8) and belay off slings up and right.

Knife-Edge Ridge

The next section is the Knife-Edge Ridge. This can consist of brutal hard blue ice,

snow over terrible ice, or anything in between for about eight rope-lengths. The ridge starts off steep and sharp, then lies back with cornices. Protection can vary dramatically. Reports contrast from having sinker screws all the way to not being able to place any protection but for two poor pickets near the end. For the first several rope-lengths, it may be possible to climb directly on the ridge crest. Higher up, the ridge becomes corniced with the cornices overhanging to the west (left). Here it is best to traverse on the east (right) side of the crest. The ridge eventually dead ends into the hanging glacier and the biggest camp on the route (14,000 feet).

Hanging Glacier

Climb the easy glacier up to the infamous ice headwall. Currently this once formidable obstacle can be passed by a conspicuous break on its right side. Climb through this short step (up to 70-degrees) then up the low angle glacier. This new passage appeared in the spring of 2000, and may disappear as the glacier moves and changes. Prior to this there were two options to overcome this barrier. One was to ascend the 60 to 80-foot gently overhanging wall

3rd Rock Band

2nd Rock Band

Big E

M-Shaped R

1st Rock Band

Hanging Glacier

Knife-Edge Ridge

Cassin Ledge

Japanese Couloir

directly, using aid or free climbing. This is a difficult but straightforward endeavor. The other option was to climb up and left from the camp to the left most edge of the wall. From here it is possible to make an 80 foot V-thread rappel into an ice gully below. The gully is steep for the first bit, then eases off and climbs around the hanging glacier. Exit right to the lower angle glacier above. This variation is exposed to icefall. Once on the glacier above the ice headwall, make a rising traverse right looking for a gully that cuts into the rock band above. This right-slanting gully is several hundred feet below the apex of the hanging glacier and is marked by a prominent prow-shaped rock on its left side. At the top of this gully a set of M-shaped rocks can be seen with some imagination. Near the top of the glacier, cross the small bergschrund (14,700 feet).

First Rock Band

Climb the ice gully (up to 55 degrees) in two pitches using ice and rock pro. This leads to a small bowl left of the so-called M-shaped rock. Climb straight up a pitch to a rock wall at the base of a tight gully on the left. Climb this difficult mixed chute (70-degree mixed). Then climb up and right for two pitches through moderate ice gullies and boulders. A short difficult mixed section (70-degree mixed) is climbed in a pitch. One more pitch leads to a left-trending snow arête between the two rock bands. Climb this for a pitch up to a small bivy at the base of the second rock band (15,700 feet).

Second Rock Band

From the bivy, traverse up and left over a small rib for two pitches to avoid the intimidating climbing above. Look for a main weakness and gully to the left. One crux pitch (70-degrees mixed) will lead to easier mixed terrain above. The next pitch leads to a big rock with a noticeable small triangle-shaped roof. Here there is a small ledge and good belay and possible bivy. The next pitch traverses right, then up a short and stuborn snow-covered slab (5.6). Next traverse right and mantle onto another sloping slab, then up a beautiful left-leaning dihedral (5.6). Another option is to climb

out left then back right on easier mixed ground. This takes you to 16,700 feet and the end of the technical climbing.

Upper Ridge

The terrain here is a broad plateau that is not very steep. Climb out and right onto the broad slopes of the southeast face above Big Bertha, then back up and left in the first couloir. Watch the avalanche conditions on this slope. This bypasses the third rock band and leads back to the ridge crest (17,300 feet). Follow the bouldery ridge, bypassing obstacles on the left. Many variations exist here. Pick the path of least resistance and try to stay on good ice or snow. Between 18,400 feet and 18,700 feet, the ridge is broad and snowy. Above this, the ridge becomes less distinct. Follow snow or ice slopes up and slightly left into a depression with easy mixed terrain. This turns into a face that is climbed directly to the top of Kahiltna Horn (20,120 feet). Drop your pack and run up the ridge (east) to the summit.

Descent

Descend the West Buttress route. If descent is necessary from the route, rappel and down-climb the line of ascent. There are many fixed anchors, but if you are high on the route, expect to lose all of your rack and then some. The most difficult section to retreat is the knife-edge ridge. If the ice conditions are bad, rappels will be difficult and down-climbing scary. Before starting up this section, make an honest assessment as to your party strength. It is only 11 rappels to the ground from here.

Mount Foraker

Mount Foraker (17,400') is second highest mountain in the Alaska Range and the sixth highest in North America. Its massive bulk is made up of a complex arrangement of steep faces and long, sharp, meandering ridges, capped by a broad, rounded summit. The Koyukon tribe named the mountain Deenaalee Be'ot or Denali's wife. It was the Tanaina (or Dena'ina) tribe, also Athabascan, from the Cook Inlet area that named the mountain Sultana also meaning the woman or wife of Denali. Lieutenant Joseph S. Herron of the 8th U.S. Calvalry crossed the Alaska Range in 1899 via Simpson Pass, naming Mount Foraker on the way after Senator Foraker. Joseph B. Foraker was a corrupt senator and former governor of Ohio, who was removed from his position after a monetary scandal involving an oil company. Unlike Denali, the name Mount Foraker stuck and is used much more often than its common native name of Sultana.

The mountain was first ascended by its Northwest Ridge in July and August of 1934 by Charles S. Houston, Chychele Waterston, and T. Graham Brown. This was an enormous undertaking in a vast and remote wilderness. With the ease of access to the southern aspects, few people venture to the north side of the mountain anymore. The number of climbers attempting Foraker is substantially lower than Denali, as is the overall success rate. Only 20 to 40 climbers attempt Mount Foraker each season, with an average success rate around 20 percent. Without the network of climbers breaking trail, fixed lines, and nearby rescue services, this shorter mountain can be much more difficult overall.

Profiled here are two diverse and extremely aesthetic routes. These two routes make up the bulk of current attempts on the mountain, although as of 2005, the Infinite Spur had only seven successful summit teams.

Sultana Ridge

Difficulty: **Alaska Grade 3, 55-degree snow**

Elevation gain: **From base: 10,500'. Total climbing gain: over 12,500'**

Total time: **14-21 days**

Approach time: **2-4 hours**

Climbing time: **Up: 3-10 days. Down: 2-3 days**

Season: **April to June; Mid-May to early-June is best**

The Sultana Ridge of Mount Foraker is perhaps the most pure and scenic ridge climb in the Alaska Range. The seven-mile ridge undulates endlessly as it climbs over several smaller peaks along the way to Foraker's massive summit. After ascending the first peak, Mount Crosson, the ridge comprises the crest of the Alaska Range. The left side pours its ice into the Kahiltna Glacier, which runs south, eventually ending up in Cook Inlet. The right side heads to the great tundra of the north, eventually feeding the mighty Yukon River, which deposits into the Bering Sea. The Sultana ridge is a good alternative to the busy West Buttress of Denali. The climbing is similar in difficulty, but retreat is more difficult, camps more exposed, and there is no support network on the route. For this, you will be rewarded by a true feeling of remoteness and serenity. It is not uncommon to have the entire route to yourself.

The ridge is also the most common line of descent for the more technical routes on the peak. Many parties having more technical ambitions ascend this route not only for acclimatization purposes, but also to familiarize themselves with its intricacies.

FA: Upper Northeast Ridge: July 7, 1966; Hideo Nishigori, Yasuhiko Iso, Takeshi Ogawa, Kazuya Murayama, Yasuo Kubota, and Yuuzo Samura.

Sultana Variation: March 15, 1979; Brian Okonek, Dave Johnston, and Roger Cowles.

History

The Sultana Ridge route is a compilation of two variations that culminate in the ascent of the upper Northeast Ridge of Mount Foraker. The first route to be done traveled up a hideously crevassed icefall beneath the incredibly dangerous east face of Mount Foraker. Ice cliffs and seracs lie at multiple elevations up to 8,000 feet above this basin and tremendous avalanches come off at alarming frequency to devastate the route. The route climbs onto a small spur of the Northeast Ridge before joining it at 11,550 feet. Then a sweeping ridge of near perfect proportions leads to the summit. The route was attempted by three separate teams before a group of six Japanese came to the Kahiltna on June 4, 1966. After completing the third ascent of Mount Hunter, Yasuhiko Iso, Takeshi Ogawa, Kazuya Murayama, Yasuo Kubota, Yuuzo Samura, and leader Hideo Nishigori of the Gakushuin Alpine Club established base camp on June 28, below the icefall at 7,000 feet. Without mishap, they traversed through the icefall and onto the spur ridge making a camp at 9,600 feet. From July 1 to July 12 they reported it to snow every day. In bad weather they pushed onto 11,550 feet near where the spur intersects the Northeast Ridge. After waiting out a three-day storm, three team members Iso, Samura, and Nishigori made an eight hour dash to the summit. They made the descent in heavy snowfall and returned to their base camp "in terror of avalanches and falling seracs." To cap off their excellent season, they finished their trip by walking out to Talkeetna in a week.

Over the next several years, several Japanese teams came to climb this route. All were successful until two teams came in 1976. Three members of one team were lost to fatigue and exposure while three members of the second team were lost in a colossal avalanche at 7,500 feet. The excessive and unnecessary risks associated with this variation certainly keep most sane climbers away.

The more aesthetic and much safer Sultana Ridge Variation was completed by Brian Okonek, Dave Johnston, and Roger Cowles in March of 1979 as the first winter ascent of Mount Foraker. This has now become the standard ascent and descent route of the mountain. The route had been attempted at least eight times before and each section of the ridge eventually was climbed. But it was not until their final winter climb that the ridge was linked completely. The team flew in on March 2 and started up the next day. They spent six days in a snowstorm at 11,000 feet on Mount Crosson, then proceeded up and down the scenic ridge and finally reached a third snow cave at 12,300 feet. At 8 A.M. on March 15 they left for the summit. They topped out at 2 P.M. with the temperature at a measly -30 degrees Fahrenheit. They descended and three days later reached base camp.

Strategy

Being almost 3,000 feet lower than Denali, Mount Foraker generally requires much less acclimatization time. For parties that are not acclimatized and attempting the route expedition style, allow a minimum two weeks in the range. For parties that have previously acclimatized and attempting the route alpine style, plan on taking five to eight days round trip. With seven miles of ridge traversing and over 2,000 feet of climbing required on the "descent," most teams carry extra supplies in the chance that they get stuck high on the route.

If a party is acclimatized it is feasible to climb Mount Crosson the first day (or night during warm weather), traverse most of the flatter ridge the next, make a high camp at 14,000 feet on the third day, then summit and return to the base on days 4 and 5. A minimum of three extra days of food should be carried.

For parties wishing to acclimatize on route, a minimum two weeks of supplies should be carried up the route, necessitating double carries and several more camp locations.

Specific Hazards

The initial couloir accessing Mount Crosson is a typical south-facing avalanche prone gully. Natural rock fall is a concern here. Cornices are generally not a major concern on the route. The ridge crest, however, is

Mark Westman contemplating the ridge ahead. Photo by Joe Puryear

heavily crevassed, necessitating extra care and route-finding.

Gear

Take standard glacier travel gear. One ice axe and one second tool per person is recommended. Wands are highly recommended to mark the way on Mount Crosson and the broad upper ridge, as well as crevasses and cornices on the narrower sections. Take 60-100 wands. Carry skis or snowshoes only to the base of Mount Crosson.

Camps

The Sultana Ridge provides endless places to set up camp, but often the ridge is quite narrow. The following is a list of locations that climbers have most often used on successful ascents.

Base of Route (6,700 feet): This is a safe location on the main Kahiltna Glacier near the toe of Mount Crosson. Some parties camp in the approach icefall (7,100 feet), but this location is exposed to avalanches off the south face of Mount Crosson.

Crosson Camp 1 (8,500 feet): At the top of the couloir that accesses the Southeast Ridge of Mount Crosson, the broad slope affords a large safe camping location.

Crosson Camp 2 (10,000 feet): A small notch in the mid section of the steeper part of this ridge makes a good place to dig a protected camp.

Upper Southeast Ridge of Mount Crosson (11,100 to summit): Several locations next to serac walls or on the ridge crest allow good camping opportunities. The summit of Mount Crosson (12,800 feet) is a broad flat area that climber's have used as a campsite. There is also a Park Service repeater antenna that is placed here each year.

Col between Mount Crosson and Pt. 12,472 (11,000 feet): This broad col is a great location to set up camp.

Between Point 12,472 and base of upper Northeast Ridge: Numerous locations exist along the ridge crest. Be sure to probe the camp well for hidden crevasses.

Mark Westman traversing around Pt. 12,472. Photo by Joe Puryear

Col at base of Northeast Ridge (12,300 feet): For many teams, this will be their high camp. This broad col is an excellent spot to set up a solid camp with snow walls or even dig a snow-cave.

High camp (14,000 feet): On the final climb up the Northeast Ridge, the angle decreases slightly around 14,000 feet. This is the only good spot for camping on the upper ridge. The ridge is usually very icy, making it occasionally difficult to make a tent area.

Approach

From Kahiltna Base Camp, travel west down Heartbreak Hill following the track of the West Buttress. Once on the main body of the Kahiltna at the base of the hill (6,800 feet), head straight across the Kahiltna toward the icefall just left of toe of the Southeast Ridge of Mount Crosson. Climb the central crevasse-free slope up the ice fall to 7,200 feet, and then cut across to the south-side of the toe of the Southeast Ridge.

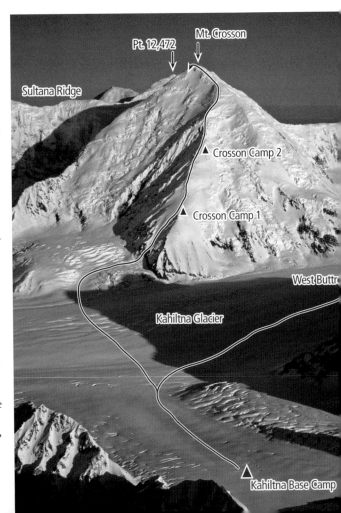

Sultana Ridge · Pt. 12,472 · Mt. Crosson · Crosson Camp 2 · Crosson Camp 1 · West Buttr · Kahiltna Glacier · Kahiltna Base Camp

Route

Ascend one of several couloirs up the south side of the Southwest Ridge (35 to 50 degrees). Once on the broad ridge, continue up, bypassing rock obstacles on the right side. There are a few steeper sections up to 55 degrees, and for the most part, the way is straightforward and direct. After summiting Mount Crosson, take a good look at the way ahead. Most of the ridge is laid out before you. Continue by descending nearly 1,100 feet off the back side of Mount Crosson to the col adjoining Pt. 12,472. Climb up the east ridge of Pt. 12,472. If avalanche conditions are safe, most climbers bypass the summit of this peak and traverse across its southeast face at around 12,200 feet. Descend the peak's south ridge and continue on toward Mount Foraker. The next three miles are a long series of ups and downs, cornices, crevasses and occasionally tedious climbing along the narrow crest of the Sultana Ridge. There are two specific knife-edge sections on the ridge. One comes just below 12,000 feet on the descent off Pt. 12,472. The next comes over half-way across the traverse, at 12,100 feet, after descending off the small point where a major spur ridge comes up from the east called The Way. Eventually the ridge meets the broader upper Northeast Ridge at a col at 12,300 feet. For many teams this is a good high-camp, leaving a 5,100-foot summit day. An advantage of camping here is the ability to dig in a good snow-cave, a difficult task on the slopes above.

Climb up the snow slopes out of the col. It is imperative to mark your way on the upper slopes. The slope is broad and undefined. A route-finding error during a white-out could have serious consequences. The slope becomes less steep around 14,000 feet where an even higher camp could be located. This is an extremely exposed location and should only be used in excellent weather. Continue up the low angle slopes until the Northeast Ridge merges with the summit plateau at 17,100 feet. Head west and slightly south to the large flat and non-distinct summit area.

Descent

Descend the exact line of ascent. Unfortunately, to descend requires re-ascending over 2,000 vertical feet of ridge to get back to the summit of Mount Crosson.

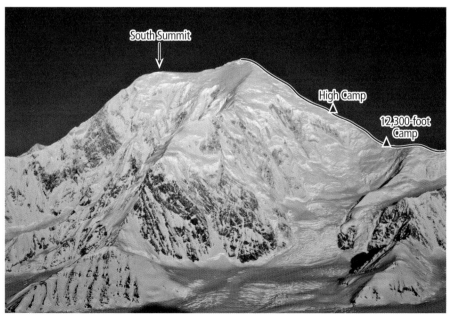

South Summit

High Camp

12,300-foot Camp

Photo by Joe Punyear

Mt. Foraker from the east showing the upper Sultana Ridge. Photo by Joe Punyear.

Infinite Spur

Difficulty: **Alaska Grade 6, 5.9, M5, AI 4**

Elevation gain: **On route: 9,400'. With approach: 11,500'**

Total time: **14-21 days**

Approach time: **10-16 hours from Kahiltna Base Camp**

Climbing time: **Up: 5-8 days. Down: 2 days**

Season: **April to early-July, June is best**

The Infinite Spur is Alaska's ultimate test-piece and one of the world's finest alpine challenges. This aesthetic arête soars nearly nine thousand feet directly up the south face of the second highest mountain in the range, providing a uniquely safe passage up a wall of total chaos. The extended length and extreme commitment required make this route a formidable and intimidating endeavor. However, the rewards of climbing such a perfect line on this incredibly complex mountain are immeasurable. This route has been a distinguishing highlight in the lives of each alpinist that has completed it.

FA: FA: June 25 to July 6, 1977, summit on July 3; Michael Kennedy and George Lowe.

History

The first recorded attempt of the central spur of the south face of Foraker was made by Alex Bertulis and party in 1968. Due to rock-fall, the team retreated after just a few hundred feet. They went on to do the first ascent of the Talkeetna Ridge just left of the Infinite Spur.

In June of 1977, Michael Kennedy, George Lowe, and Jeff Lowe came to Alaska to try some first ascents alpine style. They had two routes on their minds, an unclimbed ice rib on the central north face of Mount Hunter, and a huge unclimbed spur on the south face of Mount Foraker. While attempting the new route on Mount Hunter, Jeff Lowe fell and broke his ankle high on the route. Kennedy and George Lowe lowered him to safety and Jeff Lowe flew out. The two then went back up and completed the new route on Hunter in excellent alpine style.

Their next objective laid heavily on their minds. They thought that the team was not as strong without Jeff Lowe. A party of two, however, would perhaps be able to move faster. Becoming overwhelmed with intimidation, they gave up on the idea and decided on doing the easier Cassin Ridge on Denali instead. The idea constantly pestered them though and at the last second they decided to go for Foraker.

The duo reached the snow shoulder near the base of the route at 10 A.M. on June 26. It was here that the route came into full view before the climbers. Kennedy wrote that it "looked immense and beautiful, almost powerful in the crystal morning air." It also appeared not as intimidating as they had expected. With no reason to turn back, they started up the spur at 3 A.M. on June 27. They moved efficiently up pitches of pure rock and mixed terrain climbing the entire day through the hardest parts of the lower rock bands.

The next day, snow started falling as they made their way through the last mixed pitches before the ice rib. They chopped a small uncomfortable bivy a couple pitches up the rib. The snow continued into the next day but they kept upward progress. Visibility was poor but they eventually saw the black band coming into view. They had seen this obstacle in pictures of the route, and now they were directly under it. They had no idea how they would break through this menacing obstacle that Kennedy described as "grim, black, loose, and horribly steep."

As the ice rib ended, they looked desperately for a place to sleep. They had been climbing for 18 hours and were exhausted. There was nowhere to dig in and they had to move onward into the crux. Lowe yielded the leads to Kennedy who was feeling tired but strong. Kennedy wrote, "My mind was clear and surprisingly calm as I visualized the way ahead, keenly aware of the chalkboard-screech of crampons on rock, the rattling thud of an axe in too-thin ice, a sling on a frozen-in spike, the dull ring of a bad piton behind a loose block, calf muscles screaming for relief, choking spindrift in eyes, throat, down the neck.". After three of the most difficult and scary pitches imaginable, they passed the crux and chopped a bivy into the snow above.

The next day they traversed endlessly along the knife-edge ridge to where the spur ended below the final exit slopes above. A large campsite allowed them to un-rope for the first time on the route. After a needed day of acclimatizing in a storm, they summited July 3 at 4 P.M.

Immediately they began their descent down the Southwest Ridge. This was the standard ascent route at the time. They made good time at first, running down the lower angled upper section. But soon the ridge became badly corniced, requiring much care. All of a sudden, a cornice collapsed under Lowe and sent him falling into the abyss. Kennedy fell down the other side of the ridge, but was yanked back toward the crest as the rope went tight. Kennedy imagined himself "shooting over the edge and the two of (them) falling helplessly to the chaotic glacier 8,000 feet below." Fortunately he stopped just 20 feet from the edge, and Lowe, unhurt, was able to climb back up to the ridge. They carefully continued the descent and arrived

in base camp at 3 A.M. on July 6. Kennedy and Lowe's ground-breaking ascent was not repeated for 12 years. On June 14, 1989, Jim Nelson and Mark Bebie stood on the summit after 14 days on the route. A storm stranded them for four days high on the route. They worried as over four feet of snow stacked up on the upper mountain before gale force winds scoured it away, leaving their old footsteps raised six inches above the icy surface.

The route wasn't climbed again until 2000 when two teams made almost simultaneous ascents. Barry Blanchard and Carl Tobin summited on the morning of June 3, with Glen Deal and Gren Hinton topping out about an hour after. Hinton and Deal climbed a new variation to the start of the spur. At the spur's base they ascended the obvious left trending gully directly under a huge hanging glacier, avoiding most of the lower technical difficulties. They were hit by a serac avalanche but continued up unharmed, connecting back into the spur just below the ice rib. Due to the extreme avalanche danger, this variation is not to be recommended. Blanchard and Tobin. climbed a new variation through the black

band, traversing left near its bottom and climbing up steep snow and mixed ground on its back side.

In May of 2001, Rob Owens and Eamonn Walsh climbed a variation to the black band that at least part of will become the favored route. They climbed a straightforward three-pitch gully that splits up the center of the band, then continued straight up the rib for another four good pitches up to M5. Most parties will find the gully the favored route, but will traverse left at its top on moderate ice around the rib to easier ground.

In 2001, Steve House and Rolando Garibotti made an impressive effort to climb the route in a single push. They left Kahiltna Base Camp midday on June 8 and made their way to the base. Starting at 7:15 the next morning, they climbed the route to the summit in just 25 hours. They descended the Sultana Ridge in another 20 hours, and arrived back in base camp in less than three days after they started.

Strategy

Plan for at least a three-week trip in the range. This will allow time to acclimatize and maybe make a warmup ascent. Every ascent of the route has been made in good alpine style. Aside from one speed ascent of the route, the average time for completing

the climb round trip has been eight or nine days.

A good option for acclimatization is to climb up onto the Sultana Ridge. This will allow you to become familiar with what will become your descent route. Just don't lose your motivation after you see what this route involves. Another good option is to head up the West Buttress on Denali. Spend a couple days at the 14,000-foot Camp, and take a trip up to the 17,000-foot Camp. This is about the same height as the summit of Foraker, so if you feel good here you should be good to go for the route. Watch the weather and wait patiently for a high pressure system to give you a good jump on the route.

For the approach it is recommended to take skis or snowshoes to the base of the second pass. From here you should be able to climb the pass and walk to the base of the route. If you are wallowing in deep snow, you may want to reconsider your objective. After completing the climb and descent, it will be necessary to retrieve your equipment, so having an extra pair of skis or snowshoes at base camp is a good idea. If snow conditions are good on the Kahiltna, you could feasibly walk to the base of the route at night and not have to worry about using skis or snowshoes.

An overview of the south side of Mt. Foraker and the approach to the route. Photo by Mike Gauthier

Mark Westman climbing a short crux pitch in the second rock band. Photo by Joe Puryear

1st Pass

Kahiltna Glacier

Mt. Crosson

Lacuna Glacier

Southeast Ridge

2nd Pass

French Ridge

Snow Shoulder

The Infinite Spur

Talkeetna Ridge

Lacuna Glacier

Specific Hazards

The final approach to the base is severely threatened by seracs. The first snow pitches getting onto the spur proper are threatened by natural rock fall. The hanging glacier at 14,800 feet is active and should be approached with care.

Gear

Take six to eight ice screws (include one stubby), six to eight cams to 3", one set of stoppers, a selection of three to five pitons, and two pickets. Take two 165 to 200-foot ropes. This allows better retreat options and two ropes will be useful in protecting the knife-edge ridge section (one rope on each side). Hauling the leaders pack may be necessary on some of the crux pitches. Bring two ice tools per person.

Camps

Snow Shoulder (7,600 feet): This is the last ridge to cross before the base of the route. The shoulder provides a safe camp and excellent view of the route.

Top of Crux Couloir, First Rock Band (c. 9,400 feet): This good bivy is located at the top of the opening crux pitches where the route gains the ridge. A small platform can be dug and good rock anchors found above.

Snowy Hump, First Rock Band (c. 9,600 feet): Just two pitches higher, a larger area can be found on top of a hump in the ridge, but it lacks good anchors. It may be possible to dig a platform just over the hump at the base of the rock wall, but this is exposed to rock-fall.

Base of Rock Step (c. 10,800 feet): After the first rock band, the angle decreases and a platform could be chopped out of the slope below the next short rock step. This spot is exposed to localized avalanches if it snows.

Top of Second Rock Band (c. 11,500 feet): Just one pitch below the ice rib, a tiny snow hump can be chopped off to form a very small platform. There is an excellent rock anchor on the wall above. This spot is exposed to avalanche runoff from the ice rib above.

Ice Rib (c. 11,800 feet): If snow conditions on the arête allow, a couple locations on the lower part could provide a good protected bivy, but it may be difficult to get adequate anchors.

Top of Black Band, (c. 13,500 feet): Several parties have had to camp in this area out of desperation. Unfortunately, there is really no good spot. At the top of the central (recommended) variation, knock off a small snow blob to provide a three by four foot platform. Otherwise, chop out a ledge in the ice slope above and enjoy what one ascensionist called "the world's worst bivy."

Hanging Glacier (14,800 feet): This is the best bivy on the route and the only one where you might actually feel like taking the rope off. This is where the spur ends into a big serac. A large tent platform can be made here. If it snows a lot, watch for avalanches coming off the slopes above.

South Summit Area (15,900 to 16,800 feet): Several places along the low-angle ridge above the spur provide good protected camping and possibly a snowcave.

Approach

The approach is long and somewhat involved, adding even more to the mystique of the route. From Kahiltna Base Camp, go west toward the main body of the Kahiltna. Instead of following the tracks down Heartbreak Hill towards the West Buttress route, start heading southwest toward the toe of the long west ridge of Peak 8,060. Don't cross the Kahiltna airstrip.

Once on the main Kahiltna (6,700 feet), travel southwest heading for the toe of the Southeast Ridge of Foraker (6,500 feet), and the main low pass below the French Ridge (7,250 feet). Look up and right at the Southeast Ridge and confirm your decision not to consider descending this route. Head up and over the pass. Stay right and descend the back side of the pass, then climb back up this new glacier (a small fork of the Lacuna) through a small icefall. When the glacier flattens, traverse across (west), heading for the big couloir to a notch in the next ridge line. If you brought skis or snowshoes, leave them at the base of the couloir at 7,000 feet. This 600-foot couloir gets steep at the top (up to 55 degrees) and may contain exceptionally bad snow, but rock protection is available. Climb the couloir to its top (7,700 feet). Walk off the backside and traverse straight across to the

snow shoulder directly west. Climb up on the shoulder and enjoy the first view of the route. To this point will take 10 to 16 hours. This is an excellent spot to camp before getting on the route. Watch the icefalls on either side of the route to gauge the risks involved in the final approach. Climb higher on the shoulder until a short down-climbable couloir to the west presents itself to access the glacier below (7,900 feet). Descend this, then walk up the glacier (north) toward the route. The objective danger here is extreme. Hangers on both sides of the spur are perched at multiple elevations up to 8,000 feet above. Move very quickly. Once across the bergschrund (8,200 feet), the icefall danger decreases.

It is also possible to fly directly to the base of the Southwest Ridge of Mount Foraker (6,500 feet). This cuts off about six miles of the approach, but adds another three to the descent. It also puts you farther from many other popular climbing objectives.

Route

First Rock Band:

At the bottom of the spur there is a broad open snow slope above a short rock band. Aim for a thin gully in the middle to access this slope. Once on the 45-degree slope, traverse several hundred feet up and left to its left apex, heading for the main weakness that will access the crest. Climb two full pitches of M4 to M5, then a half pitch of steep snow to reach the spur proper (9,400 feet). This spot makes an excellent bivy. Climb straight up the spur crest for two pitches (5.6-5.8) then climb over a big snowy hump. Here the crest butts into a broad headwall. Climb up snow then rock following a right trending system for two full pitches (5.7). At this point the system continues up, but becomes very difficult. Instead, look for a blocky ledge traverse around the buttress to the left. Another gully system climbs up on the other side. This gully has some loose rock and can be difficult to protect in spots. Climb the gully pitch (5.8) to a ledge on the left. The next

difficult to protect in spots. Climb the gully pitch (5.8) to a ledge on the left. The next pitch climbs up and right fifty feet then back left through a weakness on less than perfect rock. Belay below a nice looking left leaning dihedral corner. Climb the steep and fun corner (5.6), and then up on mixed ground to a good single #3 Camalot belay. This is the top of the first rock band.

Second Rock Band:
Climb 45-degree snow for two pitches to the base of a short stubborn wall blocking the way (c. 10,800 feet). A bivy could be chopped here. Climb the 40 foot rock step (5.8), and then continue up three pitches of steepening snow and ice entering a right-trending gully that splits the rocks above. When the gully ends abruptly on a small arête, climb a mixed pitch (M4) up and left taking weaknesses in the blocky rock, and then take a small gully system to its top. This spot is a half pitch below the ice rib (c. 11,500 feet). To the right, a tiny snow hump can be chopped into for a bivy with a good rock wall and anchor above. Otherwise, traverse horizontally left for 40 feet then up and onto the rib.

Ice Rib:
Ascend the 40 to 55-degree arête staying on or right of the crest (c. 11,500 feet to 13,000 feet). This can consist of either chest deep snow shoveling or firm step-kicking (both without adequate pro), or 15 to 20 pitches of bullet-proof dinner-plating blue ice. If there is snow, a bivy may be possible at various places along the slope.

Black Band:
Ahead lies the route's crux, the notorious Black Band. While most of the rock to this point is excellent shattered granite, this formation is rotten black diorite. The band diagonals up and right across the slope. It is narrow at its lower left edge and gets progressively taller as it traverses across. Over the years, three variations have been climbed here, the last one described being the most recommended.

The original route follows the ice rib up and right along the base of the black band to the rib's apex. Three pitches of up to 85-degree ice and very bad 5.9

rock break through a weakness and onto the knife-edge ridge above. The second variation (not recommended) was done out of desperation to get off the waist deep snow on the ice rib as quickly as possible. Approach the band on its lower left side and exit left across and over somewhat solid rock. This leads to very steep snow slopes and mixed climbing on the other side of the band. Climb this to meet up with the last variation. The final and recommended way takes a narrow gully at mid-height in the band, in a direct line with the ice rib. Climb two pitches of AI4 or M4, depending on conditions. Climb one more steep snow pitch to the base of the huge wall above. A bad bivy can be chopped here (c. 13,500 feet). The wall above has been climbed directly (four pitches of M5), but an easier 50-degree horizontal traverse left for a pitch, bypasses this obstacle. Climb five pitches of 50-degree snow or ice to intersect the knife-edge ridge.

Knife-Edge Ridge:
This is one of the grandest features of the route and one of the wildest spots in the Alaska Range. The ridge is near vertical on one side and averages 60 degrees on the other. It offers no good protection other than a "Fairbanks" belay. Tiptoe along the two-foot-wide ridge for 10 pitches. Eventually the ridge butts into a 40-foot rock wall. Climb the pitch (5.6) with good pro. One rope-length leads to the first real good bivy on the route, underneath a large hanging glacier (14,800 feet). From here there are two options. Climb the 100-foot serac wall directly (up to 90 degrees) and pull onto the snow slopes above or traverse horizontally right from the bivy (50-degrees) then up for one pitch. This is a dangerous traverse under an active part of the hanger.

Exit slopes:
From either point, climb up 10 rope lengths of 50 to 55-degree snow or ice to where the slope eases off and joins the French Ridge to the east (15,900 feet). Continue up easy snow slopes to the south summit (16,812 feet) and then make the one-mile traverse north to the main summit.

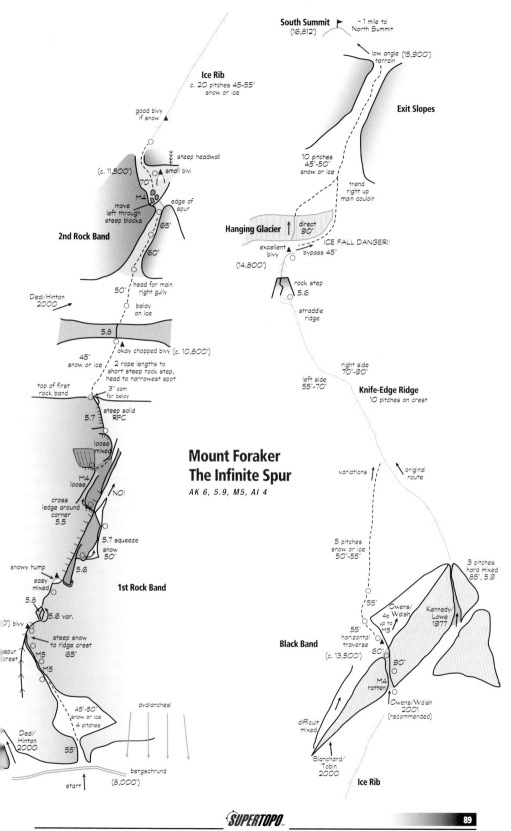

South Summit
(16,812')
~ 1 mile to
North Summit

low angle (15,900')
terrain

Exit Slopes

Ice Rib
c. 20 pitches 45-55°
snow or ice

10 pitches
45°-50°
snow or ice

good bivy
if snow

trend
right up
main couloir

steep headwall

(c. 11,500')   small bivi

Hanging Glacier   direct
                     90°

70°

M4   edge of
          spur

move
left through   65°
steep blocks

2nd Rock Band   60°

excellent
bivy   bypass 45°

(14,800')

ICE FALL DANGER!!

rock step
5.6

straddle
ridge

head for main
right gully

50'

Deal/Hinton
2000

belay
on ice

right side
70°-90°

left side
55°-70°

5.8

45°
snow or ice

okay chopped bivy (c. 10,800')

Knife-Edge Ridge
10 pitches on crest

2 rope lengths to
short steep rock step,
head to narrowest spot

top of first
rock band

3" cam
for belay

steep solid
RFC

5.7

loose
mixed

variations   original
                   route

Mount Foraker
The Infinite Spur
AK 6, 5.9, M5, AI 4

M4
loose

NOI

cross
ledge around
corner
5.5

5.7 squeeze
snow
50°

5 pitches
snow or ice
50°-55°

3 pitches
hard mixed
85°, 5.9

snowy hump

easy
mixed

5.6

1st Rock Band

55°

Owens/
4p Walsh
up to
M5

Kennedy/
Lowe
1977

5.8

') bivy   5.6 var.

55°
horizontal
traverse

60°

90°

spur
crest   steep snow
            to ridge crest
M5   65°

Black Band

(c. 13,500')

M4
rotten

M5

Owens/Walsh
2001
(recommended)

45°-50°
snow or ice
4 pitches

avalanches!

difficult
mixed

Deal/
Hinton
2000

55°

Blanchard/
Tobin
2000

bergschrund

start   (8,000')

Ice Rib

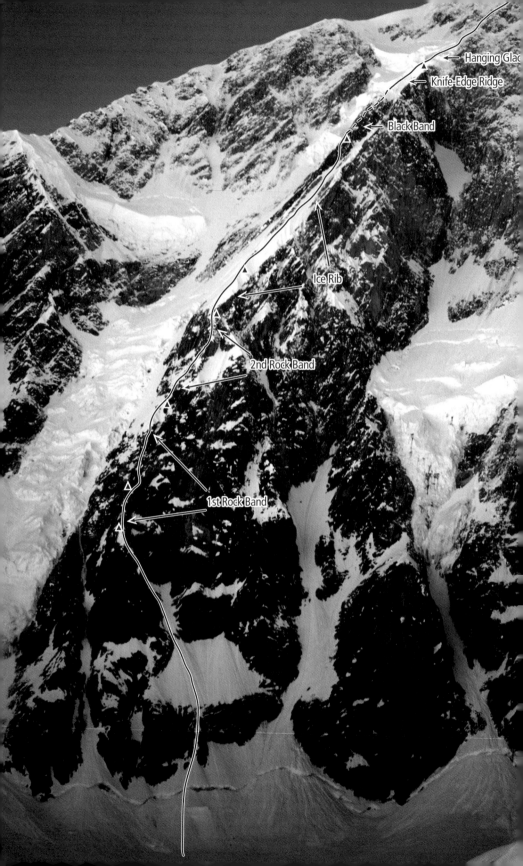

Hanging Glac

Knife-Edge Ridge

Black Band

Ice Rib

2nd Rock Band

1st Rock Band

Joe Puryear leading into the first rock band. Photo by Mark Westman

Descent:

The best descent option is to go down the Sultana Ridge. This is a big undertaking by itself and is only recommended when visibility is good. Traversing out the ridge requires gaining over 2,000 feet of elevation and descending nearly 13,000 feet. It is corniced and crevassed and there can be avalanche danger when descending Mount Crosson. Refer to the Sultana Ridge route for a complete description. The first and second ascensionists descended the Southeast Ridge. This route is dangerous and has claimed many lives over the years.

I do not recommend this.

Descending the Infinite Spur would be difficult and gear intensive down low. There is little to no fixed gear, but good anchors exist from the bottom of the ice rib down. Once above the ice rib, it is probably easier to continue up than retreat—a bit of a point of no return. Rappelling the rib may be difficult due to poor ice, and downclimbing it would be very scary at best. Retreating from high on the route would require an extreme amount of ingenuity.

Mount Hunter

One of the "Big Three" in the Alaska Range, Mount Hunter (14, 570') is considered the most difficult fourteener in North America and perhaps the world. For what Mount Hunter lacks in height compared to its taller neighbors, it makes up in bulk and complexity. Standing like a giant fortress, a three-mile-long summit plateau is rimmed with sheer cliffs up to nearly 7,000-feet high. Splitting down between these cliffs are long and narrow corniced ridges, giving it a scorpion-like appearance from above. Three distinct summits stand along its upper plateau; the northern one being the highest.

Mount Hunter was first referred to as Begguya, meaning the "High One's Child," by the Athabascan people. Robert Dunn, who was on Frederick Cook's first Alaskan expedition in 1903, labeled the now called Kahiltna Dome (12,525') Mount Hunter after his aunt Anna Flaconnet Hunter, who donated $1,000 to their trip. Due to a surveyor's mistake in 1906, the name Mount Hunter was applied to the much larger peak to the south on the government maps and this is the name still used today.

Two classic routes of very different character are profiled here. The North Buttress climbs Mount Hunter's sheer north wall, while the West Ridge ascends a 4.5-mile narrow icy ridge.

Mt. Hunter from the north. Photo by Mike Gauthier

West Ridge

Difficulty: **Alaska Grade 4, 5.8, AI 3, extensive cornicing**

Elevation gain: **8,000'**

Total time: **10-14 days**

Approach time: **2-4 hours**

Climbing time: **Up: 3-6 days. Down: 1-2 days**

Season: **April to mid-June, May is best**

Although not technically the easiest route to the summit, the West Ridge was chosen the first ascent route and is considered the standard route to the summit. But don't be deceived, this is not a "dog route." The route and the mountain are a serious undertaking, considered much harder than its two higher neighbors. The climb is classically Alaskan, presenting a variety of climbing types. Offering rock, mixed, ice, and dazzling corniced ridge climbing, the route is constantly thought provoking. And unlike many climbs in the range, there is no easy way down.

The climb gets attempted about a half-dozen times each season. The success rate varies dramatically with the year's snow conditions. The mountain has in the past gone several years in a row without a successful ascent.

In addition to the standard route, there has been much interest lately in a variation that is purported to be the easiest route up Mount Hunter—the Ramen Route. This route is covered at the end of this section.

FA: July 5, 1954; Fred Beckey, Heinrich Harrer, Henry Mehbohm.

History:

It was 41 years after the first ascent of Denali that climbers first set foot on Mount Hunter. Exploration on its intricate and complicated slopes was stifled by its remote location and difficult approach. Climbers would wait for the ski-plane to be developed before attempting this and other smaller peaks in the range. Once again, Bradford Washburn created a route proposal for climbing Mount Hunter, via its western ridge of the north summit. In exceptional detail he laid out a description

based on his own aerial photographs. In a 10-page essay in the 1953 AAJ he described every aspect of the route, including camp sites, route-finding options, and expected difficulties. Washburn, who became famous for route proposals such as this one, figured that if he described it, they would come.

In June of 1954, three climbers who ended up having one of the single greatest Alaska seasons ever, flew on to the Kahiltna Glacier with Washburn's proposal in hand. Fred Beckey and Henry Mehbohm had earlier completed the first ascent of the Northwest Buttress of Denali, a grandiose achievement in itself. Heinrich Harrer, of the North Face of the Eiger fame, had made the first ascent of Mount Drum in the Wrangells. After a haphazard meeting in Fairbanks, the three went on to complete the first ascent of Mount Deborah in the Eastern Alaska Range by a bold and difficult ice route. In a wave of motivation and visionary accomplishment the three were destined to climb Hunter.

They landed on the Kahiltna Glacier on June 29, 1954 and the next day they made a reconnaissance of the route and cached some supplies at a col at 8,750 feet, past the first rock gendarme. The next day they set off with only eight days of food and minimal gear, employing a style of climbing that was unheard of at the time that would eventually become known as "alpine style." They quickly dispatched the first third of the ridge and set up their first camp below the first major crux—a 500-foot rock step. Later that afternoon, the trio went up and explored the complex towers and left several hundred feet of fixed rope on their return. From then on they started climbing at night to take advantage of more frozen snow conditions. They continued up the rock step, then up the heavily corniced and fluted ridge. Such an extremely corniced ridge had never been attempted in Alaska, so they were pioneering a risky technique. At one point a large section of cornice broke off right next to the climbers and tumbled thousands of feet to the glacier below.

On July 4 at 4 P.M. the climbers left their high camp for the summit. A long and difficult ice slope between 10,700 feet and 11,500 feet proved to be the ice climbing crux. Then more cornices followed by a maze of crevasses led to the 13,200 foot summit plateau. Upon climbing the final summit pyramid, they stood on the top in the full glory of the early morning sun. Their ascent time of five days is still considered fast by modern standards. And their achievement is one of the greatest in Alaska mountaineering history. The descent was long and tiring as they retraced their tracks back to the Kahiltna. Then if only to legitimize their climb, they spent the next several days walking out the unexplored Kahiltna Glacier over 44 miles to the road.

Strategy:

Nearly every ascent of the West Ridge has been done alpine style. Because of its lower elevation, most parties find that they can acclimatize on route as they ascend. The route is incredibly long and is on a much bigger scale than any other 14,000-foot peak in North America. A full 8,000 feet of actual climbing over nearly five miles of ridge awaits. It is usual to leave Kahiltna Base Camp and ski to the route's base for

an advanced base camp. Motivated parties will be able to leave Base Camp and make considerable progress on the ridge the first day, possibly reaching the top of the rock-band. Be sure to gauge your progress on the ridge and remember to save enough energy and supplies for the long and tedious descent down the ridge.

Specific Hazards:

The initial basin leading onto the ridge climbs through a frequently avalanched icefall.

Gear:

Take three to four cams to two-inches, six stoppers, four or five ice screws, and two or three pickets. Take one or two 200-foot ropes. Bring two ice-tools per person.

Camps:

Base of Ridge (6,550 feet): Camp on a small rise several hundred feet away from the base of the route. There is a risk of avalanches at the very bottom of the ridge.

Before Pt. 9050 (8,900 feet): A broad area before the rock tower makes a good area to dig in or even dig a snow cave.

Col (8,700 feet): This narrow col is not the best place to camp, but was used on the first ascent. A better camp is located in the next col at 9,200 feet.

Col at Base of Rock Band (9,200 feet): An excellent campsite that allows several options for digging a good protected camp.

Top of Rock Band (10,000 feet): Three pitches above the chimney where the ridge becomes lower angle, there is a monolithic boulder with a snow scoop on its south side. This is a great protected campsite with rock anchors available.

Col (10,550 feet): Several locations exist along the ridge to camp, but much of the ridge is corniced and crevassed. The col below the ice face is a good spot and may be a suitable high camp for a fast party.

Top of Ramen Route (11,400 feet): After traversing a level section of scary cornices, this small exposed spot is the last good camp on the ridge before the summit plateau. This is probably the best high camp location for the average party.

Summit Plateau (13,000 feet): Camp just about anywhere on the broad summit plateau but, unless you are descending from another route, most climbers won't bring their camping gear up this high.

Approaches and Routes:

Described below are two variations of the route. The first described is that of the original ascent and the one nearly all parties use to ascend. This is the most pure line and climbs the entire four and a half mile ridge directly to the summit. The second variation is what is now commonly referred to as the Ramen Route. Although it has seen only a few ascents, this may be the fastest and easiest route to the summit of Mount Hunter. It should only be considered an early season route, however, as the main couloir becomes a rock filled bowling alley later in the season.

The Northwest Basin Variation is purposely excluded from this guide because of the unnecessary dangers involved on this non-aesthetic variant.

WEST RIDGE ROUTE:

Approach:

From Kahiltna Base Camp, go west toward the main body of the Kahiltna. Instead of following the tracks down Heartbreak Hill towards the West Buttress route, start heading southwest toward the toe of the long west ridge of Peak 8,060. Don't cross the Kahiltna airstrip. Once on the main body of the Kahiltna Glacier, head due south staying on its left side. Straight ahead will be visible the West Ridge. The original route starts just around the first rock buttress that meets the glacier. Head straight toward this buttress. The route starts up the west-facing pocket glacier between this buttress and the next (6,550 ft.) This is a good place to leave your skis or snowshoes, as well as set up an advanced camp.

Route:

Ascend the center of the pocket glacier. At 7,200 feet an icefall is encountered. There are active seracs above the route so objective danger is high. Move quickly, the maximum exposure time is only about 20 minutes. Negotiate several large crevasses that are often filled with large ice blocks that provide straightforward passage. At the top of the icefall (7,800 ft.), head up the broad basin due east towards the skyline ridge. Climb up to the ridge crest and then traverse up and around the shoulder to the south. Make a flat traverse across a basin aiming for Pt. 9,050. At 8,900 feet, there is an excellent camp site.

Pt. 9050 is shaped like a set of cat's ears. It is necessary to climb directly between the ears, then rappel off the steep back (east) side. Locate fixed rappel anchors on the south side of the left ear. Two 200-foot rappels or three 100-foot rappels reach steep snow below the rocks. Study the rappel route and the climbing here. If you descend Mount Hunter this way, it will be necessary to re-climb this wall (5.6-5.7). Some parties opt to leave a fixed line here for the return. Down-climb 45-degree snow to a notch. Continue along the right side of the ridge up and over Pt. 9,500. This section is heavily crevassed and corniced, so watch your step. As you descend to the next notch at 9,200 feet, carefully observe the rock band ahead to determine the route. In the notch is an excellent campsite.

Start the rock band by making a rising traverse on the right (south) side of the ridge across the 45-degree snow face. Depending on the year, a steep snow fluting may develop on the face. Cross this fluting in the easiest spot, then head up and right to a major couloir that regains the ridge crest. The gully gets steep and mixed near its top (60 degrees), but has good protection. Just before the crest, climb around a gendarme on the right to a narrow notch at the base of the Beckey Chimney. This 50-foot chimney is the technical crux of the climb. There are some old fixed lines in the back of the chimney, but it is often choked with rotten snow and ice. Stem and grovel up the chimney (5.8) to a good belay. From here, three rope lengths of easier mixed ground on or right of the crest lead to a huge rock gendarme and good bivy site (10,000 feet). This is the last major rock on the crest of the ridge.

Continue along the right side of the corniced ridge, carefully walking the fine line between the cornice fracture line on the left and the avalanche fracture line on the right. There will often be times along the ridge where there are rock outcroppings below on the right. These provide some sense of security, in the hope that the rope would snag on them if a fall were to occur. On the ascent to Pt. 10,610, several steep snow flutings might be encountered. Tackling these directly could consist of vertical sugar snow. Instead, traverse right around them to the spot where they look least steep for the least distance. The Northwest Basin variation connects with the ridge at about 10,200 ft. Continue along the ridge, up and over Pt. 10,820 ft., and down to the notch at 10,550 feet. Here is another excellent bivy spot.

The next section is the ice face. This can be dispatched in four pitches of generally good 45 to 55-degree ice. Atop the ice section is probably the worst section of

cornices on the ridge. Below to the right (south) drops the Ramen Couloir and on the left the cornices are severe. Although only a couple of rope lengths long, this section requires utmost care. Where the sharp ridge broadens into the final slope (11,300 feet) is the last good bivy on the ridge proper. Many parties use this as their high-camp. This is a small spot, so parties with a larger tent may want to consider using the previous camp below the ice face.

Continue up, staying near the crest of the ridge, avoiding obstacles and crevasses. At the top of the ridge before the summit plateau there may be a large crevasse splitting the glacier end to end. There is generally a conspicuous way across this. Once on the expansive summit plateau, use wands profusely. This is a huge area and there is only one way back down. Storms up here are fierce and cold and descent in bad conditions would be difficult at best down the broad section of ridge below. From the broad plateau, the first ascent party contoured around the summit pyramid at the 13,000-foot level to access a snow ramp on the south side. This is a safer but certainly longer way to get to the summit. If conditions are good, head directly east towards the face leading to the summit. A 55-degree snow face just left of an active serac leads to the final summit ridge. Watch for avalanche conditions on this slope. Once on the summit ridge, walk northeast to the summit.

Descent:

Downclimb off the summit the same way you ascended. Continue down the west ridge to the ice face. Make several V-thread rappels down the face. Continue traversing down (and up) the ridge. Upon reaching the rock-band, down-climb to the top of the Beckey Chimney. Make several rappels from fixed anchors, retracing your ascent route. Continue along the ridge to the rock tower. Climb up to the rocks and set a belay at the base. The tower can be climbed in one long pitch. Ascend straight up broken terrain and moderate corners (5.6-5.7), aiming for the notch between the two towers. Belay off the fixed rappel anchor on

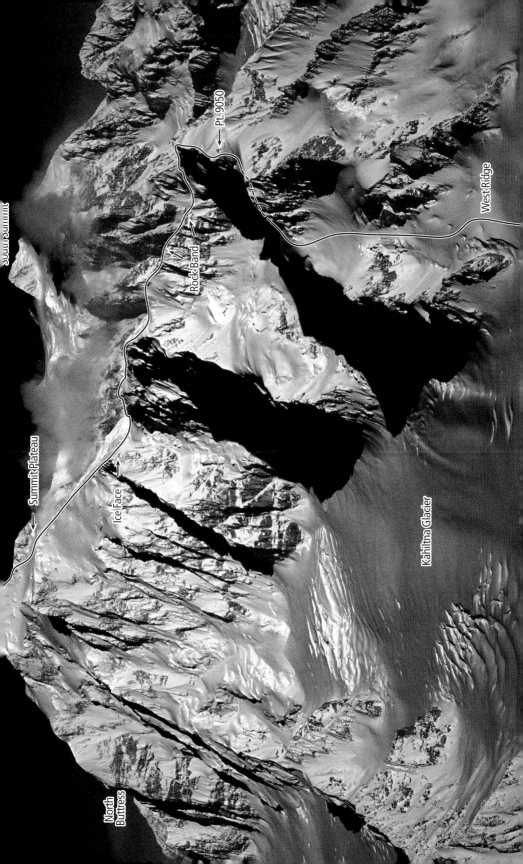

South Summit

Pt. 9050

West Ridge

Rock Band

Summit Plateau

Ice Face

Kahiltna Glacier

North Buttress

top. Continue down the ridge following the line of ascent to the Kahiltna Glacier.

THE RAMEN ROUTE:

The Ramen Route is a variation on Hunter's West Ridge first climbed by Dave Wills and Dan Donovan in April of 1999. This is a direct couloir on the south side of the ridge that bypasses all of the crux climbing on the ridge proper. The route is somewhat marred by the strange and difficult approach needed to reach the couloir's base. The route was skied in 2003 marking the first ski descent of Mount Hunter. Lorne Glick, John Whedon, Andrew McLean, and Armond DuBuque skied the route on May 15 after a 12 and half hour ascent to the summit.

Approach:

To get to the Ramen Route, continue

south down the Kahiltna Glacier. On the left, you will pass three distinct buttresses all descending from the West Ridge. Finally, a major side glacier between the West Ridge and the Central West Ridge (unclimbed) will come into view. One look at the appalling ice-fall in the glacier may cause you to instantly reconsider your objective. Although the second ascent of the route made passage through this, the first ascensionists opened up a safe and ingenious bypass to this daunting problem. They climbed a 1,500 foot couloir, then traversed mixed ground on the south side of the West Ridge, then descended 500 feet back down to the top of the ice-fall from above. Continue east up the glacier and look for the broad Ramen Couloir on the south face of the West Ridge that starts at 8,000 feet. A good camp can be set at 7,900 feet in the basin.

The ski team approached by tackling the ice-fall direct. They skied up the right side of the icefall, bypassing much of the worst terrain, but were forced back into the jumbled glacier near its top.

Route:

Climb the 40 to 60-degree couloir straight up to the ridge crest at 11,300 feet. Bypass rock obstacles on the right. Continue along the West Ridge route to the summit.

Ramen Couloir Descent: (2 200 foot ropes recommended)

An early season alternative to descending the entire West Ridge is to descend the Ramen Route. This 3,300-foot couloir drops south directly to the glacier, avoiding nearly all of the cruxes and badly corniced sections of the ridge. It can make a good alternative if a storm is fast approaching and you need to get off the upper mountain fast. However, this descent is not to be taken lightly and should only be attempted by advanced teams. This is huge avalanche prone couloir that deposits you into an unforgiving

The West Ridge from the southwest, showing the Ramen Route. Photo by Joe Puryear

cirque, far away from base camp. At the bottom of the glacier is a treacherous icefall that would be nearly impassable without having ascended it prior. There is, however, a secret way around the ice-fall.

From the bivy spot at 11,400 feet, traverse down the ridge a couple hundred feet and carefully look down the couloir below. On the left there is an active serac that (just barely) doesn't threaten the couloir. On the right is a narrow rock band. The couloir comes up the ridge crest at an angle of 55 to 60 degrees. If conditions are good, it may be possible to carefully down-climb this steep part for three rope lengths. Otherwise, set a V-thread in the underlying ice and rappel down to the rock band. Make one or two more rappels from rock outcroppings until the angle of the couloir decreases to 45 to 50 degrees. You may want to continue rappelling, or start down-climbing using available intermediate rock anchors as you go. Near the bottom the angle decreases even more (40 degrees). Watch out for the bergschrund then walk out onto the glacier below.

Looking down the glacier, you will notice the top of the icefall and on the right a large protrusion off of the West Ridge. This hump holds the key to the descent. Walk down the right side of the glacier.

At 7,900 feet start climbing up the easy snow face and at 8,600 feet traverse across the face to the major notch between this hump and the West Ridge. Two couloirs lead down the backside of the notch. The left (southern) couloir is the correct choice. Down-climb 120 feet toward a huge abyss. Locate a large rock horn on the right with fixed slings. Make a short rappel to the top of a giant cleft that looks like it has no bottom. Find more fixed slings or make a V-thread in the top of the frozen waterfall that flows down this cleft. Make a full 200-foot rappel into a cave on the climber's right side. Rappel 50 more feet off fixed gear to the base of the waterfall. From here, continue walking down the couloir to the edge of the glacier. The bottom part of the icefall is immediately to the left. Carefully cross the bergschrund and walk out (west) through crevassed terrain to the safety of the Kahiltna. Hopefully conditions on the Kahiltna are good because from here it is a 2.5 mile walk back to the base of the West Ridge route.

North Buttress

Difficulty: **Alaska Grade 6, 5.8, A2, M5, AI 6**

Elevation gain: **On route: 6,100'. From Kahiltna Base Camp: 7,400'**

Total time: **10-14 days**

Approach time: **1-2 hours**

Climbing time: **Up: 2-6 days. Down: via route: 8-16 hours; via West Ridge: 1-2 days**

Season: **Mid-April to early-June, May is best**

The North Buttress is the technical showpiece on Mount Hunter and like the Infinite Spur and the Cassin, it is considered a world class climbing objective. Although it has been called "The Nose" of the Alaska Range, climbers coming to find a similar type route up Mount Hunter will be quite surprised. The sheer 4,000-foot granite buttress replete with difficult ice, rock, mixed, and aid climbing has less than 20 ascents to the top of the buttress and far fewer to the true summit. For even the world's best climbers, an ascent is a career defining achievement.

The soaring tower stands prominent above Kahiltna Base Camp. Even an untrained eye may notice the thin ribbons of ice intertwining down sheer granite cliff bands and buttresses. These are the natural passageways that allow modern alpinists to ascend the intimidating buttress. Climbers attempting the route are on center stage for gawkers at the airstrip. The Park Service often has a high power telescope trained on the North Buttress so curious onlookers can track their progress. The remains of an old porta-ledge used on the first ascent of the Wall of Shadows can still be seen dangling above the Third Ice Band.

Each season there is a lineup of potential climbers wanting to ascend a route on the North Buttress. These so-called Moonies (from the Moonflower name) can be found lurking throughout Base Camp, posturing and waiting for the right weather and conditions. The buttress does not succumb easily and despite some good attempts, no one climbed to the buttress top in the years 2002 through 2005.

The Moonflower Buttress is a name that is widely used to refer the North Buttress route as well as the entire northern tower of Mount Hunter. In fact the Moonflower is the name that Mugs Stump attributed to his route after claiming the first ascent. Most of the route that is climbed today follows this line, but there are a few key differences between it and the standard North Buttress route described here. Stump and Aubrey began to the right of the commonly used start, the routes joining at the Prow. Above, Stump followed the line previously established by the White Punks on Dope team to the First Ice Band. This was the high point of other attempts. Stump continued up The Shaft and The Vision, and made a high point near the top of the final rock band below the upper ice face. Above the Third Ice Band, the North Buttress route follows the route of Bibler and Klewin who continued to the top of the pyramid and on to the summit.

FA: To near the buttress top: May 1981; Terrance Mugs Stump and Paul Aubrey; To the summit: June 3, 1983; Doug Klewin and Todd Bibler.

History:

The North Buttress route has a bit of a torrid history, which stems from an age-old dispute that climbers will debate for years: Is a route complete without the summit? There were 15 prior attempts on the North Buttress, mostly on the North Buttress Couloir, before 1980, when focus changed to a more central line. In 1980, a team calling themselves White Punks on Dope (WPOD) made a good effort on the line, reaching the first ice-band in 12 pitches. The team consisted of Doug Klewin, Pat and Dan McNerthney, and Rob Newsom. They came to realize that porta-ledges might be in order for such a steep route, so the next year they returned, with the necessary equipment and a new name: Back in Black. Starting up their same line, the team, now dressed in all black, made good progress until a broken porta-ledge forced their retreat. Their attempts have left a permanent mark on the route, with named features such as the Klewin Couloir,

the McNerthney Ice Dagger, and Tamara's Traverse (named after Rob Newsom's wife).

At about the same time, Mugs Stump, fresh off his and Jim Bridwell's bold new route on the East Face of the Mooses Tooth, teamed up with New Zealander Paul Aubrey for a more alpine-style attempt on the buttress. They took little in the way of food or gear and climbed with the vision and determination that made Stump famous. They started up a new variation to the right of the competing party's line, (now commonly referred to as the Mugs Start). Aubrey led two pitches then let Stump take over for the rest of the climb, Aubrey conceding to Stump's incredible skills. Stump and Aubrey joined the main line just below The Prow. Pitch after pitch of quality climbing fell beneath them as they approached the route's crux: a 400-foot vertical wall split with a narrow vein of ice dubbed "The Shaft." Stump, reluctant to free-climb the vertical and over-hanging ice, was able to aid cracks on the side in order to bypass the hardest sections. They continued up more challenging terrain and after the fourth night they were bivied on the Third Ice Band. Each night Mugs slept comfortably in a hammock, while Aubrey took hours chopping small ice ledges. On Day 5, they reached their high-point (still some six pitches from the actual buttress top, but at the end of every major crux) and rappelled off. Stump claimed the first ascent of the North Buttress of Mount Hunter and many people credit him with that, but it has been met with opposition in the climbing community. What are not disputed are the bold and visionary techniques used in making the ascent, bringing technical alpine climbing around the world to a new level.

Todd Bibler and Doug Klewin came back the next year to make the first complete ascent to the summit, setting an uncompromised standard that all climbers should strive for. Newsom and Pat McNerthney came back the year after and also completed the route to the summit, finally fulfilling their destiny.

In May of 2001, Marko Prezelj and Stephan Koch made the first free ascent of the route to the Cornice Bivy at the top of the buttress, freeing The Prow, the traverse into the McNerthney Ice Dagger, and The Vision. They completed their ascent in an incredible 25 hours and confirmed a free rating of M7, WI6.

Strategy:

There are several different schools of thought on how to approach this logistically complex route. Different techniques range

Pat McNerthney leading the Shaft on the second complete ascent of the North Buttress. Photo by Rob Newsom

The North Buttress of Mt. Hunter from the northwest. Photo by Joe Puryear

Mugs Start

from light and fast single push attempts to big-wall style, haul bag toting, multi-day affairs. Whatever style you choose, be aware that the North Buttress is a shitty place to be in a storm, whether you are prepared for it or not. There are no protected camp locations and the entire wall becomes a torrent of spindrift avalanches. Several different sleeping options can be considered, including porta-ledges, hammocks, bivy sacks, and small single-wall tents. Critical judgments must be made about the trade-offs between weight, comfort, and time spent preparing a bivy site. All of these different techniques have been employed on successful ascents of the route, so it is up to you to decide what will work for you.

A typical itinerary may look like this:

Because of the lack of really good bivys below the First Ice Band, many parties try to make it here the first day in a single push. This has historically taken parties anywhere from 12 to 24 hours, depending on party strength and route conditions. A partial rest day here is sometimes utilized. The next good bivy site is on the Third Ice Band, which can often be reached in another long day. From here you can make a lightweight summit attempt or you can move camp to the Cornice Bivy for an easier shot at the summit. After a summit bid or topping out on the buttress itself, most parties tend to descend the route the next day. This is an intense four to five-day schedule that leaves little room for technical or route-finding errors. Be sure to bring extra food or

Joe Puryear leading the Prow. Photo by Mark Westman

more importantly extra fuel for unexpected difficulties.

If you leave a cache in the basin below the route, be sure to mark it with an extra-long cache-marker. This area can receive excessive snow accumulation.

Specific Hazards:

The approach is severely threatened by the hanging seracs of Mount Hunter 1,000 to 5,000 feet above. Avalanches are a daily occurrence and more than one party has been hit in the center of the glacier. While most of the debris is generally pulverized into small pieces by the time it reaches the main path, it is not uncommon to see softball to grapefruit-sized chunks strewn across old ski tracks. The main avalanche zone is between 7,600 feet and 8,200 feet on the Southeast Fork of the Kahiltna.

Unstable snow-mushrooms on this route pose a serious and potentially deadly threat. In 1997 climber Steve Mascioli was tragically killed when a huge mushroom was dislodged above him. Similar to cornices, these gravity-defying features generally form underneath roofs or in other protected locations where the wind tends to eddy and swirl snowfall and spindrift. Because of their precarious locations and lack of any real structure or bonding to the rock, they are prone to falling, especially in warmer weather. There is one mushroom on this route that is of particular danger on top of Pitch 17. Do not touch or go near it and try to minimize your time underneath it.

The final 2,000 feet of northeast facing snow slopes to the summit are especially prone to avalanches. Assess conditions carefully before continuing to the summit.

Gear:

Take 10-12 ice screws (include one stubby), seven to eight cams to three inches, one set of stoppers, a selection of three to five pitons, draws, and long slings. Take one set of etriers each, and one set of ascenders. Take two 200-foot ropes. Hauling a pack may be necessary on some of the crux pitches. Bring two ice tools per person.

Camps:

Top of initial ice field (top of Pitch 4): Although not very high on the route, this is the only good camp site below the first ice band. At the top of the traverse across the lower ice apron, a small rib can be chopped out to make a nice sized bivy.

Top of Leaning Ramp (top of Pitch 7): At least one ascent party has camped here. Chop out a small ledge out of the ice below the Prow.

First Ice Band (top of Pitch 14): This is the most popular bivy spot on the lower part of the route. Ascend to the top of the ice band and chop a ledge out of the ice below the rocks. An alternative is to fashion a bivy under a boulder on the left side of the ice band about half way up.

Second Ice Band (top of Pitch 19): Climbing the Shaft and the Visions can be a tall order for a single day. If a bivy is required between, this is the place. With difficulty, chop a ledge out of the small amount of ice here.

Third Ice Band: The high camp for many parties, this is probably the best bivy on the entire face proper. A snow rib forms on the left side of the ice band that generally has a good amount of snow to dig a platform. Some parties may opt to climb up to the rocks above to set a rock anchor, and then run their rope down 50 to 100 feet to their bivy site.

Cornice Bivy: This is an excellent bivy site at the top of the real technical difficulties that puts you in good summit position.

Approach:

From Kahiltna Base Camp, go east up into the Southwest Fork of the Kahiltna Glacier. Climb up a hill between 7,400 and 7,600 feet (great for skiing). From here on, the way is threatened by the hanging seracs of Mount Hunter. Quickly head out toward the center of the glacier, passing crevasses on the right until under the North Buttress of Hunter (8,200 feet). As soon as you are a safe distance past the hanging glaciers, cut south directly to the route's base.

Route:

In 2001, the first two pitches of the original route catastrophically fell off. The rock below and right of the Klewin Couloir blew apart, taking with it the right hand side of the initial ice apron. Now the Klewin Couloir is virtually unattainable and the route starts farther left. Hopefully, there will not be further rockfall, or the entire start to the North Buttress route may disappear. There is always the Mugs Start should this happen. Follow the detailed topo to the buttress top.

From the Cornice Bivy, go south along the corniced ridge until it meets a rock buttress. Climb a steep ice slope on its left side (60 degrees). Above, the angle backs off and gentle but avalanche-prone slopes lead south to the summit.

Descent:

Option 1: Rappel the route. This is probably the most attractive option and one used most often. Rappelling a 4,000-foot face can be fraught with problems and it should not be taken lightly. However, if you do not plan on visiting the summit or are not familiar with the West Ridge, this is probably the best option. From the summit, descend the slopes back to the top of the buttress. A rappel may be necessary over the ice slope above the top of the buttress. From the Cornice Bivy, start rappelling the exact line of ascent, using V-thread anchors, rock anchors, and fixed anchors where available. When approaching Tamara's Traverse, rappel straight down toward the top of the McNerthy Ice Dagger so as not to have to repeat the traverse. This is a steep rappel and a fixed rock anchor can be found underneath a roof. From the bottom of the Twin Runnels, climb back up to the small ridge on the climber's left, then continue rappelling straight down over the Klewin Couloir. Rappel directly over the ice cliff and rock scar to the glacier. This descent takes from 8 to 16 hours.

Option 2: Descend the West Ridge or the Ramen Route. If rappelling a 4,000 foot wall is not your cup of tea, the West Ridge is a good scenic way down, but involves much difficult snow travel on corniced ridges. See the West Ridge route description for full details.

3rd Ice Band
The Vision
2nd Ice Band
The Shaft
1st Ice Band
Tamara's Traverse
The Prow
Twin Runnels
Start
Original Start
Mugs Start

The North Buttress of Mt. Hunter from the north. Photo by Joe Puryear

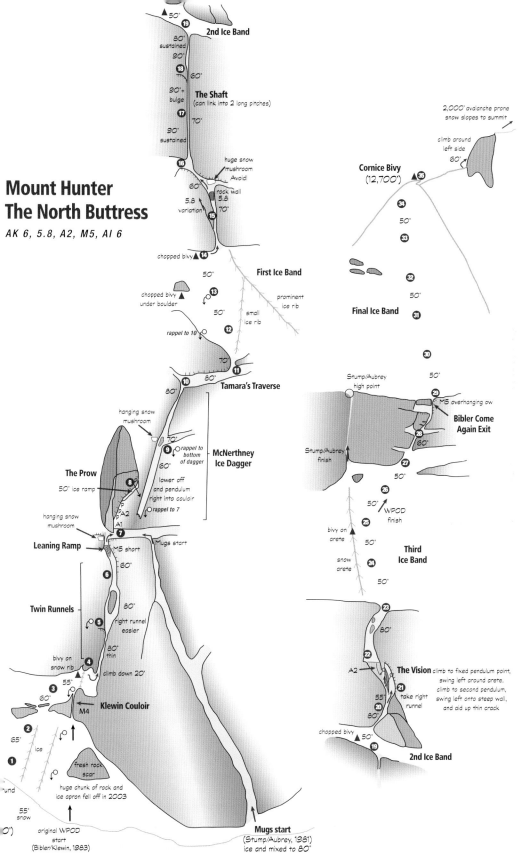

Mount Hunter
The North Buttress

AK 6, 5.8, A2, M5, AI 6

2nd Ice Band

▲50°

19

80° sustained

18

90°

60°

90°+ bulge

The Shaft
(can link into 2 long pitches)

17

70°

90° sustained

16

huge snow mushroom Avoid!

60°

rock wall 5.8

5.8 variation

15

70°

chopped bivy ▲14

First Ice Band

50°

prominent ice rib

chopped bivy ▲ under boulder

13

50°

small ice rib

rappel to 10

12

70°

11

80°

10

80°

Tamara's Traverse

hanging snow mushroom

70°

9

rappel to bottom of dagger

McNerthney Ice Dagger

60°

lower off and pendulum right into couloir

The Prow

50° ice ramp

8

P
P A2
A1

rappel to 7

hanging snow mushroom

7

Leaning Ramp

M5 short

Mugs start

60°

Twin Runnels

6

80°

5

right runnel easier

80° thin

bivy on snow rib

4

climb down 20'

3

55°

60°

M4

Klewin Couloir

2

65°

ice

1

fresh rock scar

huge chunk of rock and ice apron fell off in 2003

ʻund

55° snow

O')

original WPOD start
(Bibler/Klewin, 1983)

Mugs start
(Stump/Aubrey, 1981)
ice and mixed to 80°

2,000' avalanche prone snow slopes to summit

climb around left side

60°

Cornice Bivy
(12,700') ▲35

34

50°

33

32

50°

Final Ice Band

31

30

50°

Stump/Aubrey high point

29

M5 overhanging ow

Bibler Come Again Exit

28

60°

Stump/Aubrey finish

27

50°

26

50°

WPOD finish

25

bivy on arete ▲

50°

snow arete

24

50°

Third Ice Band

23

80°

22

A2

The Vision climb to fixed pendulum point, swing left around arete. climb to second pendulum, swing left onto steep wall, and aid up thin crack

21

55°

take right runnel

20

80°

chopped bivy ▲ 50°

19

2nd Ice Band

Mini-Moonflower, North Couloir

Difficulty: **IV, 85-degree ice**

Elevation gain: **On route: 2,000'. From Kahiltna Base Camp: 3,400'**

Total time: **1-2 weeks**

Approach time: **2-3 hours**

Climbing time: **Up: 8-14 hours. Down: 3-5 hours**

Season: **Late-March to early-June, May is best**

The Mini-Moonflower has had the unfortunate luck of being over shadowed and overlooked because of its immediate proximity to a world-famous alpine climbing monolith—the North Buttress of Mount Hunter. While not as grandiose as its neighbor to the west, this pointy satellite pillar of Mount Hunter boasts similar terrain, and by all means is a

stunning feature by itself. The top, however, is nothing more than a bump on the Northeast Ridge of Mount Hunter. The Japanese, who made the first ascent of the Northeast Ridge in 1971, did not traverse this point. They traversed into the Tokositna from the Ruth and climbed the Tokositna to its head, staying well left of the lower ridge crest on the ascent.

It is the northern aspect that has caught the attention of alpinists over the last several years. Here there are three steep and technical lines. In 2001 Ian Parnell and Kenton Cool opened up a central line on the steep north face called Kiss Me Where the Sun Don't Shine (VI, Scottish VII). The same year, Stephan Koch and Marco Prezjeli climbed Luna (V, M7, WI6+, A0) on the right side of the face. To the left of these two modern routes, a continuous and more moderate ice couloir splits up the face. The North Couloir has become popular in recent years, offering a worthy objective by itself or a warmup for harder test-pieces. It has also become an integral part of the Base Camp circuit of moderate routes, akin to the Southwest Ridge of Frances and the West Face of Kahiltna Queen. The couloir is characterized by 50 to 70-degree quality alpine ice, with a single difficult crux at mid-height. The final summit ridge gives a stellar head-on view of Mount Huntington, as well as an interesting perspective of the northeast slopes of Mount Hunter.

FA: May 1998; Kelly Cordes and Scott DeCapio.

History:

Kelly Cordes and Scott DeCapio made the first recorded ascent of the route in May of 1998. Although they did not find any previous signs of an ascent, Cordes maintains that such an obvious and accessible route may have

The Mini-Moonflower North Couloir from the base. Photo by Joe Puryear

previously been climbed but not recorded. It was a thin year for the range with less than normal ice buildup on the northern facing aspects. The crux pitch which is normally 85-degree solid ice, was a 95-degree bulge of unconsolidated ice and snow which they rated M6 R.

While belaying the final pitch to the top of the couloir, Cordes was hit hard by falling ice chunks. Relates Cordes, "I never saw it coming, and it knocked the hell out of me, almost flipping me over backward on the anchor and opening a horrific, several-inch-long gash above my left eye and up my forehead. Blood was everywhere, the gash wiggling open and shut whenever I blinked. Scott said it was wide enough to put TCUs in." In excellent style, Cordes continued leading to the summit, dripping blood the entire way.

Strategy:

Complete the ascent and descent in a day as there are no bivy sites on the route. If the weather is warmer, consider climbing the route at night so as to keep natural ice fall to a minimum. The couloir only gets sun in the early evening and can become quite active during this time.

Specific Hazards:

The approach is severely threatened by the hanging seracs of Mount Hunter 1,000 to 5,000 feet above. Avalanches are a daily occurrence and more than one party has been hit in the center of the glacier. While most of the debris is generally pulverized into small pieces by the time it reaches the main path, it is not uncommon to see softball to grapefruit sized chunks strewn across old ski tracks. The main avalanche zone is between 7,600 feet and 8,200 feet.

The couloir itself is capped by several large snow mushrooms that at some point during the season fall down the route.

Gear:

Take 8 to 10 ice screws, an optional picket for the summit ridge, draws, and slings. Take two 200-foot ropes. Bring two ice-tools per person.

Camps:

Since the climb is normally done in one day, Kahiltna Base Camp is the only recommended spot.

Looking down the couloir from high on the route. Photo by Joe Puryear

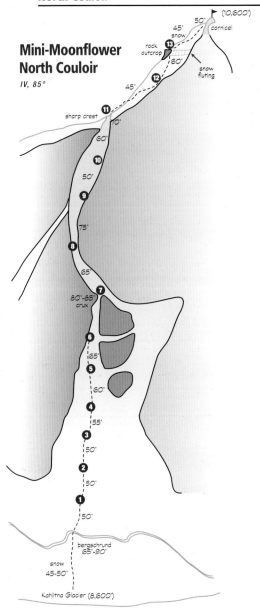

Mini-Moonflower
North Couloir

IV, 85°

on the right until under the North Buttress of Hunter (8,200 feet). This is a safe spot. Another ice-cliff between the North Buttress and the Mini-Moonflower should also be traversed quickly as you continue up glacier to 8,500 feet underneath the North Couloir of the Mini-Moonflower. From here the first nine pitches are plainly visible straight above.

Route:

Scout from below the best bergschrund crossing. Climb up steep snow to the bergschrund and climb over it onto 50-degree ice. Continue up five pitches of steepening ice to 65 degrees. The couloir narrows and climbs left into a slot. After the sixth pitch, belay on the left side in a protected stance below the steep ice crux. Climb straight up 80 to 85-degree ice, exiting right around a rock at the top. Belay on ice on top of the rock. Continue up the narrow 55 to 75-degree couloir for two pitches until it turns right and widens into a 50-degree ramp. After one and a half pitches the couloir narrows slightly between some rocks. The last 30 feet before the ridge crest steepens to 70 degrees. Climb over the sharp crest and onto the Tokositna side for an incredible topout to the couloir. Continue up the ridge and pass a steep snow fluting on the left, next to some flat rocks. This may be the last good place to make an anchor before climbing onto the final 250-foot summit snow slope. Climb to as near as the actual summit as you feel comfortable—it is a gigantic cornice.

Descent:

The upper snow pitches may need to be down-climbed because there is generally no ice available for rappelling. Once back to the rocks, a V-thread anchor or rock anchor can be made. Make the first rappel down the ridge crest, then the second rappel into the couloir. Continue rappelling down the couloir using V-thread anchors.

Approach:

From Kahiltna Base Camp, go east up into the Southwest Fork of the Kahiltna Glacier. Climb up a hill between 7,400 and 7,600 feet (great for skiing). From here on, the way is threatened by the hanging seracs of Mt. Hunter. Quickly head out toward the center of the glacier, passing crevasses

Kahiltna Queen, West Face

Difficulty: **IV, 60-degree ice and snow**

Elevation gain: **On route: 3,100'. From Kahiltna Base Camp: 5,200'**

Total time: **1-2 days**

Approach time: **3-4 hours**

Climbing time: **Up: 8-14 hours. Down: 3-6 hours**

Season: **March to early-June; April to mid-May is best**

Kahiltna Queen (12,380') often gets overlooked, standing amidst its more famous neighbors of Mount Hunter, Mount Huntington, and the South Buttress of Denali. But it is very significant, being the triple divide peak of three of the greatest glaciers in the range: the Kahiltna, the Ruth, and the Tokositna. It is only at this summit that all three of these glaciers meet simultaneously. It is similarly shaped to Mount Huntington and slightly taller, but its summit does not rise as far above its connecting ridges, giving it less overall prominence. Kahiltna Queen's East Ridge actually goes on to become Mount Huntington's Northwest Ridge. The peak was originally given the name Humble Peak in 1977 by its first ascensionist but because of its commanding position as viewed from Base Camp it is now more commonly referred to as Kahiltna Queen.

There are only five reported routes on the peak, with many opportunities for development. Dominating the head of the Southeast Fork of the Kahiltna Glacier is the peak's West Face. This is by far the most often seen and climbed aspect. A broad couloir splits up its right side, providing a natural passage through the steep and rocky upper slopes. This excellent climb is a great warmup for harder routes in the range or it may be a culmination of several of the Base Camp area climbs that can provide for a climbing trip by themselves.

FA: June 13 and 14, 1979; Brian Okonek and Arthur Mannix

History:

Kahiltna Queen was first climbed on May 11, 1977 by Alan Kearny, Chuck Sink,

and Mal Ulrich. They climbed the main couloir on the peak's South Face from the Tokositna Glacier in a 22-hour round trip effort.

In June of 1979, Brian Okonek, Arthur Mannix, and Mark Bloomfield flew onto the Kahiltna Glacier to have a look the peak. The three left camp on June 13 in unsettled weather and upon reaching the bergschrund, Bloomfield decided to bow out. Okonek and Mannix left him there (he later returned to camp on his own) and started climbing broad snow-slopes that lead into a steep couloir above. The pair passed rappel slings from an earlier attempt by an Anchorage team. The gully turned out to be 13 pitches of excellent climbing up to 60degrees. At one point they narrowly avoided natural rock fall as helmet sized rocks whizzed pass them. Four pitches below the summit ridge the duo stopped for a six-hour bivy. Afterwards, a few more pitches led to the sharp ridge crest, which they followed to the summit, making 19 pitches in all. They rappelled without incident to camp arriving 36 hours after they left.

Strategy:

The ascent and descent should be completed in a day as there are no decent bivy sites on the route. Some parties may wish to make an advanced camp near the base of the route. This will certainly make a more manageable day. Just be careful where you place your camp: there are many hanging glaciers in this valley and the west face of the mountain can be prone to avalanches as well. If the weather is warmer, consider climbing the route at night so as to keep natural ice fall to a minimum. The couloir gets sun in the afternoon and can become quite active during this time.

Specific Hazards:

The approach is severely threatened by the hanging seracs of Mount Hunter 1,000 to 5,000 feet above. Avalanches are a daily occurrence and more than one party has been hit in the center of the glacier. While most of the debris is generally pulverized

Daniel Zimmermann climbing up the lower slopes. Photo by Joe Puryear

into small pieces by the time it reaches the main path, it is not uncommon to see softball to grapefruit sized chunks strewn across old ski tracks. The main avalanche zone is between 7,600 feet and 8,200 feet.

The entire couloir up to the ridge crest is prone to rockfall and snow avalanches. Be sure to make the ascent under cold and stable conditions.

Gear:

Take two or three cams to two inches, six stoppers, four to six ice screws, two or three pickets, and two 200-foot ropes. Bring two ice tools per person.

Camps:

Advanced Base Camp (8,600 feet): Camp near the head of the valley being mindful of avalanche danger.

Approach:

Follow the Mini-Moonflower approach. When under the North Buttress of Mount Hunter, continue straight up the center of the glacier toward Kahiltna Queen.

Route:

The climb starts at 9,300 feet below a short rock outcropping at the base of the face. Many variations exist to access the broad

snow face above. Find the best bergschrund crossing and climb one of many couloirs through the rocks. Once on the broad 45 to 50-degree face, climb several pitches, trending towards the main couloir up and right. After several hundred feet, the rock on the left side of the couloir is reached, and good protection is available if necessary. Follow the couloir for 10 pitches (up to 60 degrees) using rock on the left side and ice in the couloir for belays and protection. The couloir comes to a bottleneck and then opens into a large bowl. Follow snow up the left side of the bowl into easy mixed terrain. Three pitches lead to the crest of the south ridge.

Follow the narrow ridge for four pitches to the last rock on the ridge. Cornices form on both sides of the ridge, so it is necessary to keep on the correct side. Climb a short steep pitch (60 degrees) through the last rocks. From here, follow the ridge east, traversing below the crest on the south side, for three rope-lengths to the summit. Be careful, the summit is a huge cornice!

Descent:

Down-climb and rappel back down the ridge until over the snow bowl. Four rappels from rock or ice anchors lead back into the main gully. Continue rappelling or start down-climbing with fixed rock anchors or V-thread anchors. After the last rappel from the rocks at the base of the couloir, it will be necessary to down-climb back to the lower rock outcroppings. Be careful late in the day, as the sun can turn this face into mush. Point release avalanches are common. One more rappel may be necessary through the rock outcropping over the bergschrund.

Mount Frances, Southwest Ridge

Difficulty: **IV, 5.8, 60-degree snow**

Elevation gain: **3,600'**

Total time: **1-2 weeks**

Approach time: **30 minutes**

Climbing time: **Up: 8-16 hours. Down: 3-4 hours**

Season: **April to early-June, May is best**

Mount Frances' rocky hulk sits immediately north of the Kahiltna Base Camp. Over a thousand climbers each year walk right around this peak without even giving it a thought. But this multifaceted satellite peak of Denali's South Buttress holds some quality routes. The peak's central location on the Kahiltna Glacier makes the views from its flanks and summit incredible. The summit is *the* best place to view all three of the Alaska Range giants from one location.

As with many of the moderate routes around Base Camp, the Southwest Ridge of Mount Frances has been long overlooked by climbers more focused on the bigger peaks. It's quite unfortunate because this

long and fun mixed climb is a superb alpine challenge, similar in character to the more wellknown Southwest Ridge of Peak 11,300. Mount Frances is nearly as long but overall not as sustained or committing. The individual rock cruxes on Mount Frances however are more challenging than those on 11,300. Given its proximity to Kahiltna Base Camp, this route is destined to become a very popular objective and range classic.

Note: What looks like the summit from Base Camp is actually a false summit 400 feet lower and a half mile distant from the northern true summit.

History

The first ascent of the peak was made by its gentle East Ridge in July of 1960 by John Newman et al. They dubbed the mountain "Bergchen", slang for "little mountain" in German. The team also made the first ascent of East Kahiltna Peak, Mount Crosson, and Peak 9,000 southeast of Mount Foraker.

The mountain was renamed Mount Frances after Frances D. Randall, Kahiltna Base Camp manager from 1975 to 1983. Randall was an avid climber, with ascents

of Denali, Mount Bona, Mount Churchill and a first ascent of Pinnacle Peak in the St. Elias Range. She played a key role in numerous rescues on Denali and was like a mother to all that flew onto the Kahiltna. She died in 1984 of cancer at age 59. According to longtime Denali Climbing Ranger Roger Robinson, "After Frances passed away, many of us (climbers and NPS folks) felt that this peak would be an appropriate monument to all her years assisting everyone at Base Camp. With the help of Bradford Washburn, her name was put on newer additions of his map." The name, however, is not officially recognized by the USGS Board of Names.

The first ascent of the Southwest Ridge is undocumented. Several ascents have been made in the last few years.

Strategy:

With good conditions, the route can be climbed in one long day round-trip from Base Camp. Most of the route can be simul-climbed while belaying the individual short rock and mixed cruxes. Although the descent is straightforward, it could be very difficult and dangerous in whiteout conditions. Be aware of changing weather if unfamiliar with the East Ridge descent.

Specific Hazards:

The East Ridge couloir descent is prone to avalanches, especially late in the day.

Gear:

Take four to six cams to two inches (one three to four-inch piece is optional), six to eight stoppers, slings and draws. Take one or two pickets, and one or two ice screws. One 165 or 200-foot rope is sufficient unless using twins or doubles. Take one or two ice-tools per person.

Camps:

Since the climb is normally done in one day, Kahiltna Base Camp is the only recommended spot. However there are numerous locations on the route and descent for planned or emergency bivies.

Approach

From Kahiltna Base Camp go northwest toward the toe of the ridge. Not far from camp, you encounter a series of north-south trending crevasses. Navigate these out onto the smooth glacier below the south face of Frances. You can access the ridge from several places between 6,850-7,000 feet on its south side. For the purest ascent, continue to the toe of the ridge (6,850 feet) and start up its left side.

Route:

Scramble several hundred feet up boulders, scree and snow, staying near the ridge crest until a steep step (Tower 1) blocks the way. Climb over the tower (5.7, more solid on the right) and into a small notch on its back side. Scramble on the crest a bit further until Tower 2 is reached. Climb this via a central depression (5.6). Continue along the knife-edge ridge for a pitch. The ridge broadens again and a low angle slab with several cracks blocks the way. Climb the tricky slab and traverse off its left-hand edge onto a snow ledge after 60 feet. Above a steep and intimidating gendarme blocks the way (Tower 3). This tower would probably go free at a moderate grade with rock shoes, but most parties traverse off the ridge around it. Traverse left to the toe of the tower. A steep snow fluting often forms here at the edge making a difficult exposed step down. Once on the 45-degree snow beside the left edge of the tower, climb up and left around the base of a rock spur coming off the top of the tower. Climb a steep mixed pitch straight up and left of this spur to regain the ridge crest.

Continue up past a long rock fin on its right then straight up to the top of the Gendarme and fixed rappel station. Rappel 80 feet into the Notch. Climb out of this small col to a rock buttress, which is passed on either the left or right for a pitch (some mixed). Another couple pitches of snow on the ridge crest leads to Tower 4. Climb a wide crack (four inches) then step left to smaller cracks that lead to a central depression (5.8). Exit over steep blocks onto a snow ramp. Continue up the ramp to a belay in a small col. Climb up broken rock

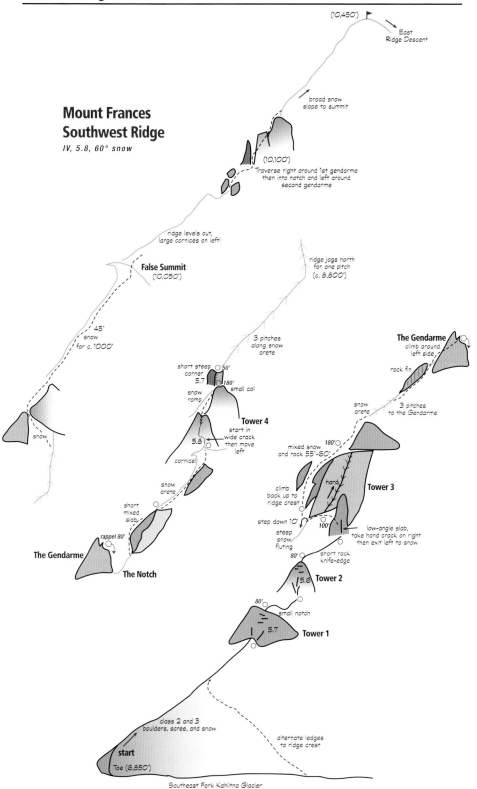

**Mount Frances
Southwest Ridge**

IV, 5.8, 60° snow

(10,450')

East
Ridge Descent

broad snow
slope to summit

(10,100')
Traverse right around 1st gendarme
then into notch and left around
second gendarme

ridge levels out,
large cornices on left

False Summit
(10,050')

ridge jogs north
for one pitch
(c. 8,800')

45°
snow
for c. 1000'

3 pitches
along snow
arete

The Gendarme
climb around
left side,

rock fin

short steep
corner 50'

5.7 180'

snow small col
ramp

snow
arete 3 pitches
to the Gendarme

snow

Tower 4
start in
wide crack
then move
left

5.8

cornice!

mixed snow
and rock 55°-60° 180'

hard

Tower 3

snow
arete

climb
back up to
ridge crest

short
mixed
slab

step down 10' 100'

low-angle slab,
take hand crack on right
then exit left to snow

steep
snow
fluting

The Gendarme rappel 80'

The Notch

80'

short rock
knife-edge

5.6 **Tower 2**

80'

small notch

5.7 **Tower 1**

class 2 and 3
boulders, scree, and snow

alternate ledges
to ridge crest

start
Toe (6,850')

Southeast Fork Kahiltna Glacier

to a short steep corner with a thin crack on the left. Mantle over the top and onto easier ground.

Climb up the ridge crest for three more rope-lengths until the ridge jogs north for a pitch. Bypass the rock-band above by climbing through a snow couloir on the left then back onto the northeast trending ridge. Climb up the 35 to 45-degree ridge for a thousand feet until reaching the false summit (10,050 feet). This is the summit seen from Base Camp with a large cornice on its left. From here the ridge flattens out. Pass huge cornices on the right side for several rope-lengths until you reach a rock tower is half way across the traverse. Climb a short mixed bit on the crest, then weave right around a gendarme, through a notch, then left around a second gendarme and back to the ridge crest. Follow snow slopes north to the summit.

Descent:

While retreat is always an option, descending the route would be a long and tedious endeavor involving many rappels. The best descent from the summit is down the gentler East Ridge. In clear weather, the ridge descent is quick with little difficulty. With poor visibility and without a marked trail, it could become an epic. From the summit, descend 1,600 feet due east toward the col between Mount Frances and Peak 12,200. In several places along the ridge, huge snow-flutings and ice cliffs bisect the broad crest. In poor conditions, it would be possible to walk right off these 100-foot cliffs. Generally, all of the obstacles are passed by skirting them on the right (south) side, which involves down-climbing a short bit then traversing back left (north) under the cliff.

The Southwest Ridge from the southwest. Photo by Joe Puryear

There are also several crevasses to negotiate. Cornicing is generally not a problem. About 100 feet above the col, a couloir snakes to the right (south) back to the Southeast Fork of the Kahiltna Glacier. Descend the 700-foot 40 to 45-degree couloir. Once in the basin below the southeast face of Frances, head southwest back toward Base Camp. Stay on the right side of the glacier using the avalanche snow cones coming off of Mount Frances to bypass large crevasses. Beware of a hanging glacier on that face that must be traversed under.

Other Climbs:

Kahiltna Dome, Northeast Ridge
This easy snow ridge leading up from Kahiltna Pass is an enjoyable day climb that provides excellent views of the West Buttress route and the north side of the range. It's best to start the route by climbing up to the notch between Mount Capps (Pt. 10,790) and Kahiltna Dome, then stay on the ridge crest to the summit. Descend the route.

Pt. Farine (Pt. 9,300), Southeast Ridge
This unique little peak was named in honor of Jacques "Farine" Batkin, who died near here on the first winter ascent of Denali. The climb and summit provide a different perspective on the Kahiltna area and is a worthy day trip to escape the daily grind of the Kahiltna Glacier. Climb up into the basin created by the South and Southeast Ridges, and then access the Southeast Ridge via a short snow couloir to a col on the right. Continue up the ridge to the summit. Descend the route.

East Kahiltna Peak, South Ridge
This is an excellent moderate snow route to the fourth highest summit in the Central Alaska Range. The summit lends unparalleled views of the South Face and South Buttress of Denali. The climb can be done in two to three days from Kahiltna Base Camp. The upper part of the route is visible from here. An advanced base camp can be made at the base and the climb done in a day from there. Head up the East Fork of the Kahiltna Glacier and start up the right side of the ridge's toe. Climb up to the sharp ridge crest and continue up. A natural break in the ridge often forms near 13,000 feet, which requires traversing off the ridge around it. From the summit it's possible to traverse to West Kahiltna Peak to the west. Descend the route.

Mount Crosson, Southeast Ridge
A very popular objective is this nice symmetrical ridge that is the start of the much longer Sultana Ridge route on Mount Foraker. Follow that route description. The climb can be done in a long day round trip, with a two-day schedule allowing for a more relaxed pace. This also makes for an excellent ski descent.

Mount Frances, East Ridge
Used as the descent route for the harder Southwest Ridge, this easy snow climb is by itself a classic ascent. The climb takes a half-day round trip from Kahiltna Base Camp and is frequently guided. From

The South Face of Peak 12,200. Many routes and variations exist on the central part of this face. Photo by Joe Puryear

SUPERTOPO

ALASKA CLIMBING

camp, go northeast into the glacial cirque below Frances' southeast face. Stay close to the face for the easiest way up the glacier, but be mindful of the hanging glacier above. Climb a left-trending couloir to a col at 8,750-feet, then follow the ridge up to the summit. A few short snow walls and ice barriers are best passed on the left. Descend the route.

Mount Frances, Base Climbs

For those climbers who are in the Kahiltna Base Camp area in late May on, the base of Mount Frances has numerous established rock routes from one to five pitches in length, up to 5.11 in difficulty. The Denali Climbing Rangers have been particularly proactive in developing the area and are the best resource for finding out what the best lines are. Most of the climbs are along the base of the east face of Frances.

Pt. 8,670, Various Routes

Known also as the Radio Control Tower, this very small peak stands dominant to the east of the Kahiltna Base Camp. Its West and South Faces have some moderate to difficult couloir routes, while its East side has an easy walk-up ridge commonly climbed by guided groups.

Peak 12,200, South Face

A good moderate line exists here for those climbers looking for a little adventure. This 4,000-foot face is directly across from the North Buttress of Hunter and it cannot be seen from Base Camp. To the right of a large hanger, there are a series of rock bands and gullies that are negotiated to reach a broad 50-degree snow field on the upper face. A couloir to the right bypasses these rock bands and may actually provide a decent ski line. Follow the snow slope directly to the top of Pt. 12,000, then follow the crest up to Peak 12,200. The descent down the Southwest slopes, which can be seen from Base Camp, is dangerous and tricky. Study the descent options well before heading up.

New Climbs:

As one can imagine, the upper Kahiltna Glacier is pretty climbed out of safe new lines. One area that has perked the interest of climbers in the last few years is the East Fork of the Kahiltna. There may still be a few good new lines in there for those willing to explore a little. Also the area around the Thunder Fork of the Kahiltna (underneath Thunder Mountain) may hold some new route potential.

Ruth Glacier

The Ruth is the veritable playground of the Alaska Range. With a high concentration of quality routes and easy approaches, the climbing possibilities seem endless. There are numerous objectives throughout the climbing season, from easy snow climbs to technical ice and mixed routes, short and long alpine rock climbs to alpine big walls.

The Ruth Glacier is huge, being nearly 35 miles long, and the Ruth Amphitheatre itself encompassing 25 square miles. In 1992 a research team from the University of Alaska used a seismic reflection system and small explosive charges to determine the depth of the ice in the Ruth Gorge (also known as the Great Gorge) near Mount Dickey. It was found to be 3,805 feet deep near the center of the glacier and moving at a rate of 3.1 feet per day. This "valley" is about 1.2 miles wide at the glacier surface and just over two miles wide at the top. Without the ice, the Ruth Gorge would be the deepest, narrowest gorge on the continent being nearly 9,000 feet deep from the top of Mount Dickey!

The Ruth Gorge got a bad rap over the years for having horrible and treacherous rock. While this is certainly true for many routes, there are a plethora of routes that have generally excellent rock and other routes with overall good rock, but with short stretches of bad rock. This can be said of most major alpine rock routes around the world. Come with an open mind to climb in one of the most enormous and accessible alpine venues to be found anywhere.

Getting There:

Because a walk-in approach is a long and complicated task, nearly all parties fly in with a licensed air service out of Talkeetna. The flight takes about 30 minutes one way.

There are four main landing spots:

The Mountain House: Used to access all climbing routes off the Ruth Glacier. Offers reliable landing and pickup.

The Root Canal: Primarily used to access Ham & Eggs and Shaken, Not Stirred. Not convenient for other climbing areas. Landing and pickup is very weather and condition dependent.

The Ruth Gorge: Used to access all climbing routes in the Ruth Gorge, including the Mooses Tooth, Mount Barrill, Mount Dickey, the Eye Tooth, the Stump, and Hut Tower. Landing and pickup is very condition dependent. Parties that land here may have to be picked up at the Mountain House.

The West Fork: Primarily used to access 11,300, but can also be used for Mount Dan Beard. Landing and pick-up is very condition and weather dependent.

Make sure to contact your chosen air service to verify your proposed landing and pickup locations. All of the air services will fly to the Mountain House, but not all will fly to the other locations.

Base Camps:

The following locations allow climbers to keep a main camp in one place and try multiple objectives.

The Mountain House (5,700 feet): Just south and west of the airstrip a camp can be set up just about anywhere. Be aware that the entire nunatak containing the Mountain House hut is private property and trespassing is prohibited. This is a busy airstrip and can be very noisy during the peak season. This location can be used for a base camp for any of the climbs in this section, but if you're planning on staying a while it may be better to move camp closer to your objectives.

The Ruth Amphitheatre (5,530 feet): Camping in the middle of the Ruth

Amphitheatre is an excellent choice for a general base camp for the area. Dan Beard, Barrill, and the Mooses Tooth can all be readily accessed for here. This location receives maximum sunlight and is away from the busy Mountain House landing strip. It also receives less wind than the narrow Ruth Gorge.

The Ruth Gorge (4,400 feet to 4,900 feet): This is a good place to set up a base camp to attempt many different routes in the Gorge. The Mooses Tooth, Mount Dickey, Mount Barrill, the Stump, and the Eye Tooth are all close by and Hut Tower is just a couple hours ski. Camp in the center of the glacier. The best spots are the area between Barrill and Dickey and the area between Dickey and Bradley. These places allow for the most sunlight in the evening.

Stump Camp (4,700 feet): This great camping spot is located under the Stump formation on the Wisdom Tooth, not far from the Ruth Gorge camp. It has the advantage of being protected from the constant wind that blows down the Gorge, as well as the possibility of cooking and/or camping on rock. Later in the season this entire area is a huge talus field on top of the glacier. The site does not get any morning sun, but it receives late evening sun. Running water is available by early to mid-June. Please help keep this camp clean by using a Clean Mountain Can or depositing human wastes in crevasses far downstream of the campsites. Another advantage of this camping area is its close proximity to the Wisdom Tooth cragging area and multi-pitch climbs on the Stump.

Emergency:

A CB radio is fairly useless on the Ruth Glacier. There is no one that constantly monitors any channels and most aircraft are not CB-enabled. The best bet is an aircraft radio (for emergencies only) or better yet a satellite phone. A cell phone works from certain summits such as the Eye Tooth and the Mooses Tooth, but reception can be inconsistent. A good reasonable method is to stomp a large (10-foot by 30-foot or larger) SOS into the snow. Enough planes frequent the area that it is bound to be seen. Self-rescue to the Mountain House airstrip is always the best option if possible.

The western rampart of the Ruth Gorge and the Ruth Glacier. Denali in the distance. Photo by Joe Puryear

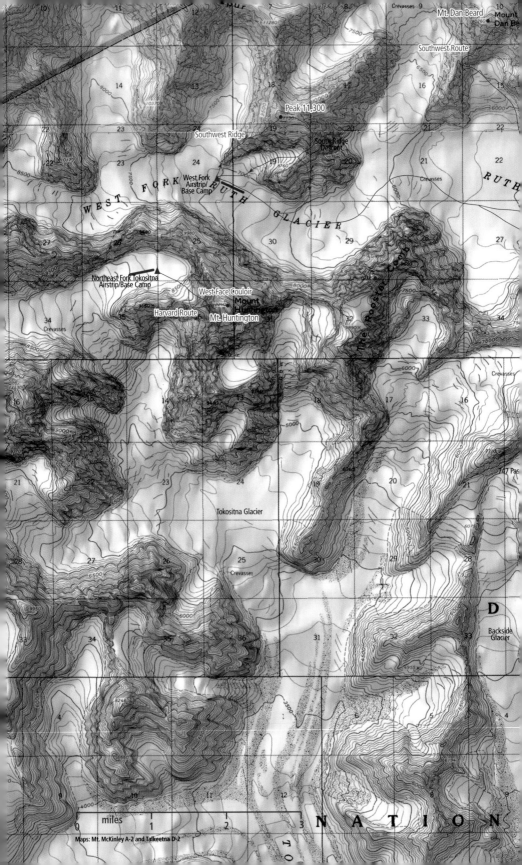

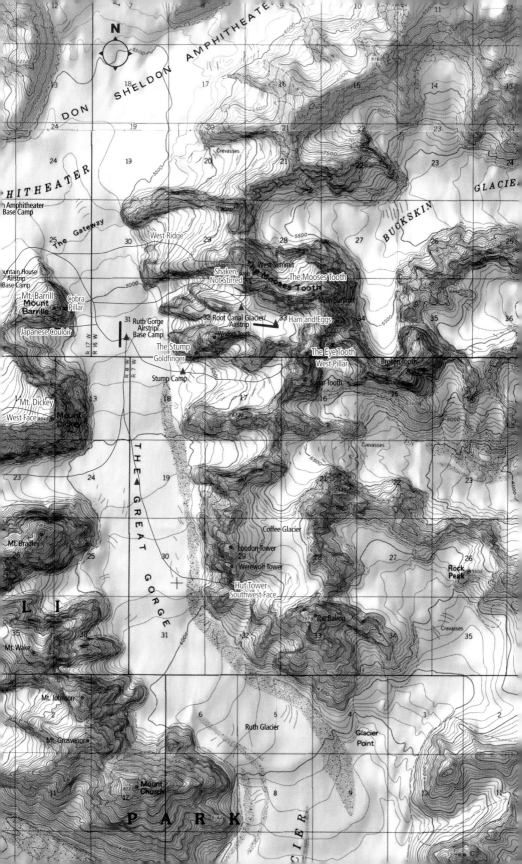

Mount Barrill

Mount Barrill (7,650') is the northern cornerstone of the great western Ruth Gorge peaks. Although significantly smaller than its monstrous southern neighbors, it still sports an El Capitan-sized east wall. It also has generally better rock than its southern counterparts. Mount Barrill was named after Edward Barrill, who guided the fraudulent Dr. Cook on his claim of the first ascent of Mount McKinley. It was first climbed up its glaciated northwest slope by a group of Mazamas in 1910. This mellow snow climb is still climbed today, but it can hardly be recommended as an ascent route because of its extreme avalanche danger. Beginning alpine climbers and hard-core rock climbers alike journey to the east side of Mount Barrill for some of the finest climbing in the Gorge. Here, two climbs of distinctively different character are recommended.

A June sunrise on Mt. Barrill. Photo by Joe Puryear

Japanese Couloir

Difficulty: **III, 55-70 degree snow or ice**

Elevation gain: **2,750'**

Total time: **1-2 weeks**

Approach time: **From the Mountain House: 1-3 hours. From the Ruth Gorge: 30 minutes**

Climbing time: **Up: 5-10 hours. Down: via route: 2-5 hours; via the Northwest Face: 2-3 hours**

Season: **March to mid-July; April and May are best**

The western wall of the Ruth Gorge seems almost impenetrable except by the deep notches between the peaks allowing access to the lower angle back sides. Mount Barrill, however, holds a secret little couloir that soars straight up its eastern façade, allowing relatively simple access up this forbidding face. This southeast couloir, first climbed by the Japanese, is "in" for a long part of the season. This makes it an attractive climb, either as a proud objective for a beginning climber, or as a quick romp for a seasoned alpinist. It is also a good descent route for the more technical rock climbs on the east face, so potentials for those climbs may want to climb it to familiarize themselves with their future descent.

FA: July 25 and 26, 1975; Teruaki Segawa, Kansei Suga, Masayuki Suemasa, and Eiji Tsai.

History:

The southeast couloir of Mount Barrill was first ascended by members of the Hone to Kawa (Bone and Skin) climbing club. After nearly being killed by an avalanche on the east ridge of Mount Huntington, they abandoned their attempt and then made the second ascent of Peak 11,300 across the valley. Their next objective was Mount Barrill. After resting in the Mountain House during a rainstorm, they set off and circled around into the Great Gorge to the base of Barrill. The mountain was covered in fresh snow and obscured by clouds, but they were able to just see the bottom of the couloir. They made their way easily up the couloir and at midnight, they slept on a rock terrace near mid-height. The next day

they climbed a crux 70-degree chimney that led to a notch near the south ridge. Earlier in the season this chimney is usually filled in with snow and is climbed on much lower angled slopes. From there they traversed to the south ridge, then up the mellow ridge to the summit.

Strategy:

The route is commonly done in day either from the Mountain House or the Ruth Gorge. If leaving from the Mountain House, consider either walking around Barrill on foot or on snowshoes. This way you do not have to leave any gear at the base and you can descend off the backside to camp. If you were to ski around to the base, you could descend back down the couloir and then ski back around to the Mountain House. Similarly, if you start from the Ruth Gorge, the best option may be to rappel the route. Otherwise, if you descend the backside, you are forced to walk back around Barrill to camp.

Specific Hazards:

The couloir can be particularly dangerous after a storm or during a warm spell. Several large snow mushrooms overhang it and the couloir is essentially a garbage chute for the surrounding cliffs. Later in the season there can be much natural rock fall.

Gear:

Take two to three cams to one inch, six to eight stoppers, three ice screws, and two pickets. If climbing over the mountain, one rope will be sufficient. If planning on descending the couloir, take two 200-foot ropes. Bring two ice tools per person.

Camps:

The best base camp locations are the Mountain House, the Ruth Amphitheatre, the Ruth Gorge, or Stump Camp. Check the Ruth Glacier introduction for base camp details.

Approach:

From the Mountain House airstrip (5,600 feet), descend down the hill to the north.

David Gottlieb nearing the top of the couloir. Photo by Joe Puryear

As you approach the bottom of the hill and the Ruth Amphitheatre (5,400 feet), start turning east around the toe of Pt. 6,000, a sub-peak of Mount Barrill. This section is fairly crevassed, but there is always a good way through. Turn south into the Ruth Gorge and head toward the center of the glacier. It is best not to try to skirt the base of Barrill—it is heavily crevassed. At 4,900 feet the couloir will be plainly visible. Go east toward it, navigating a small crevasse field near its base.

The Northwest slope of Mt. Barrill, commonly used for the descent. Photo by Joe Puryear

Route:

Climb up the large avalanche cone and cross a small bergschrund. Continue up the 45-degree couloir. The couloir bends left, then back right as it steepens to 50 degrees. The couloir narrows significantly for the last 300 feet. Early in the season this is a 55-degree snow gully. As the season progresses, there may be a section of water ice, or a short mixed step here. Continue up to the col above.

This col is a bit of an enigma, as you

realize that the couloir does not actually intersect the West Ridge of Barrill. The col is actually on a separate spur, but the West Ridge is only a couple hundred feet away. To gain the West Ridge, downclimb 50 feet of steep snow off the back (west) side of the col. Make a 50-foot left traverse under a rock wall (rock protection available). Then climb 200 feet up a 50-degree gully to intersect the crest of the West Ridge at 7,200 feet. Follow the ridge up low-angle snow slopes and over two false summits to the top of Barrill. Watch out for the huge cornice on the north and east side of the summit.

Descent:

There are two descent options:

Rappel the route:
This is the recommended descent. Walk back down the West Ridge and then down-climb and repeat the traverse back to the col. From the col, either down-climb the couloir or make a series of rappels down its upper portion, then down-climb or walk down the lower-angled bottom section. The first fixed rappel anchor is located on the north side of the col. Several more fixed stations can be found on the climber's right-hand side of the couloir.

Descend the Northwest Face:
This offers a quick descent to the Mountain House, but is not necessarily recommended due to serac and avalanche danger. Study the slope carefully from the Mountain House and the amphitheatre before considering it for a descent route. The best way down can change year to year. In general, descend the West Ridge to the around 6,800 feet. Cut back north on a large bench above and below large seracs on the northwest face. Follow the bench toward the center of the face until a central gully is reached that drops to the bottom of the face. Quickly descend the avalanche prone gully to the base of the face. From here, either traverse southwest back to the Mountain House or circle back around Barrill to your camp in the Gorge.

Mt. Dan Beard

Ruth Amphitheatre

Ruth Gorge

Cobra Pillar

Difficulty: **VI, 5.11, C1+, 50-degree snow**

Elevation gain: **2,750'**

Total time: **1-2 weeks**

Approach time: **From the Mountain House: 1-3 hours. From the Ruth Gorge: 30 minutes**

Climbing time: **Up: 2-3 days. Down: via Japanese Coulior: 2-5 hours; via the Northwest Face: 2-3 hours**

Season: **June and July**

This highly sought after route takes a direct line up the central pillar of Mount Barrill's East Face. It somewhat resembles a cobra from certain aspects. While most really big routes in the Gorge are generally a horror show only attempted by the world's best climbers, this route is manageable by more mortal seasoned alpine rock climbers. Much of the rock on the Cobra Pillar is clean, solid, and enjoyable, but there is the occasional section of what makes the Gorge famous—the Cracker Jack gravel that you can literally chop steps in with your ice-tool. The combination of easy access and straightforward descent makes the Cobra Pillar a great all-around alpine route.

FA: Jim Donini & Jack Tackle; June 5-10, 1991.

History

Jim Donini and Jack Tackle attempted the route in June of 1989, making four trys, all thwarted by storms. In 1990 Donini and another partner made it up 17 pitches that ended up left of the original line. They were stopped by a seamless section of rock that would require extensive drilling to continue. Donini and Tackle came back in June of 1991. They were determined to attempt a mostly free line and keep the drilling to a minimum. On the first day they fixed four ropes up the first six pitches. The next day they made it back up to the headwall to their original high point. After attempting to drill and hook up it, they gave up. It wasn't the type of climbing they had come to do.

Without being discouraged, they searched the rock for some kind of weakness that would allow passage. In the middle of the headwall, they spotted a possible traverse from their left crack system to a more central system 50 feet to the right. Donini moved out horizontally on thin holds into blank terrain. Half-way across with no pro between them, and looking at a horrendous pendulum fall into a corner, he decided one bolt was in order. He placed it, then continued over to an amazing splitter crack system that went up for three full pitches. Halfway up this crack, the crux of the route came as a four-inch off-width for 50 feet. With only a three-inch piece for pro, Donini made difficult and bold moves well above his protection. It was the turning point of the climb.

As the duo neared the top of the pillar, they thought they were home free. All of a sudden the beautiful crack systems they were climbing ended on a small pillar below a completely blank wall with no crack in sight. Too difficult to climb on-sight, Donini hooked and bolted up 60 feet in a bitter cold wind. Each bolt took 30 minutes to drill in the compact granite. This turned out to be the last difficult pitch, though, and the climbing eased to several pitches of moderate snow. The last great obstacle was the overhanging summit cornice, which they climbed direct, by aiding off their ice-tools in slushy snow.

They made the summit on the sixth day, then descended the Northwest slopes back to the Mountain House. In keeping with their snake theme, Donini and Tackle went on that season to climb a new route on Mount Foraker, naming it Viper Ridge.

As of 2005, the Cobra Pillar had seen only five complete ascents to the summit. On June 13, 2004 Chris McNamara and Joe Puryear made the first one-day ascent, firing the route in 15 hours and 10 minutes. On June 29, 2005 Ryan Nelson and Jared Ogden accomplished a completely free ascent with variations at a grade of 5.11.

Strategy:

Although the first ascent took six days of work to climb the route, thanks largely to their efforts, the climb can now be done in about two days. Unless it is unseasonably

Mount Barrill
The Cobra Pillar

VI, 5.11, C1+, 50° snow

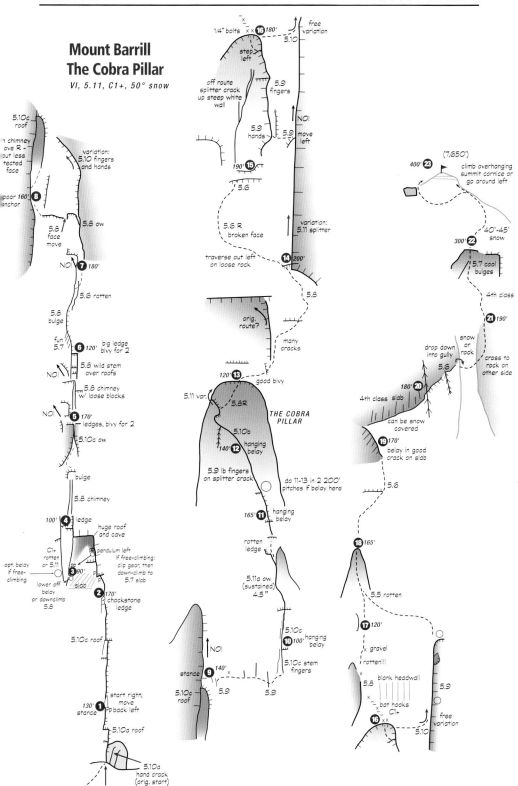

5.10c roof

in chimney
above R -
but less
rotected
face

poor 160' **8**
anchor

variation:
5.10 fingers
and hands

5.8 ow

5.8
face
move

NO! **7** 180'

5.6 rotten

5.8
bulge

fun
5.7

6 120' big ledge
bivy for 2

NO!

5.8 wild stem
over roofs

5.8 chimney
w/ loose blocks

NO!

5 170' ledges, bivy for 2

5.10c ow

bulge

5.8 chimney

4 100' ledge

huge roof
and cave

C1+
rotten
or 5.11

opt. belay
if free-
climbing

3 90' pendulum left
If free-climbing:
clip gear, then
down-climb to
5.7 slab

lower off
belay
or downclimb
5.8

slab

2 170' chockstone
ledge

5.10c roof

1 130' start right,
stance move
back left

5.10a roof

5.10a
hand crack
(orig. start)

start

---

x
1/4" bolts x x **16** 180'
step
left

free
variation

5.10

off route
splitter crack
up steep white
wall

5.9
fingers

5.9
hands

5.9
5.9 move
left

NO!

190' **15**

5.6

5.6 R
broken face

variation:
5.11 splitter

traverse out left
on loose rock

14 200'

5.8

orig.
route?

many
cracks

120' **13** good bivy

5.11 var.
5.8R

THE COBRA
PILLAR

5.10b

140' **12** hanging
belay

5.9 lb fingers
on splitter crack

do 11-13 in 2 200'
pitches if belay here

165' **11** hanging
belay

rotten
ledge

5.11a ow
(sustained)
4.5"

5.10c hanging
100' **10** belay

5.10c stem
fingers

stance **9** 140'
x

NO!

5.10c
roof

5.9 5.9

(7,650')

400' **23**

climb overhanging
summit cornice or
go around left

40'-45'
snow

300' **22**

5.7 cool
bulges

4th class

21 190'

snow
or
rock

cross to
rock on
other side

drop down
into gully

5.6

180' **20**

4th class slab

can be snow
covered

19 170' belay in good
crack on slab

5.6

18 165'

5.5 rotten

17 120'

x gravel
rotten!!!

blank headwall

5.8

bat hooks
C1+

16 xx

5.9

free
variation

5.10

cold, it is often not necessary to carry bivy gear while rock climbing in the Ruth because parties can comfortably climb throughout the night and sleep or rest during the day in the sun. This means much less gear needs to be carried up the climb, allowing climbers to forsake hauling bags all-together. Don't, however, be caught on a big route unprepared. Take the necessary equipment and clothing to sit out a major storm anywhere you go in Alaska.

Short-fixing and jumaring is an excellent strategy for speedy ascents. It is made easier by the large number of fixed anchors on route.

Specific Hazards:

Above the pillar proper, the upper pitches can be prone to rock or snow fall, especially when crossing into the summit gullies. The Northwest Face descent is prone to both slab and serac avalanches. The Japanese Couloir descent also has avalanche danger.

Gear:

Take two sets of cams to three inches and one or two four-inch pieces. Take one set of stoppers, two bat-hooks, ascenders, and etriers. If you don't plan on hauling or retreating, one 200-foot rope is sufficient. Otherwise take a combination of two 200-foot ropes. Bring at least one short ice-hammer per person for the snow pitches and the descent. Crampons are optional, but may be useful later in the season or for descending the Japanese Couloir.

Camps:

The best base camp locations are the Mountain House, the Ruth Gorge, or Stump Camp. Check the Ruth Glacier introduction for base camp details.

Route Bivies: At the top of Pitch 6 there is a great bivy, but unfortunately this does not get you very high up the route. The best spot is on top of Pitch 13, where there is usually snow for water. If you can make it here in one day you should be able to summit and descend the next day.

Approach:

From the Mountain House airstrip (5,600 feet), descend down the hill to the north. As you approach the bottom of the hill and the Ruth Amphitheatre (5,400 feet),

Pt. 6000

Japanese Couloir   Cobra Pillar

start turning east around the toe of
Pt. 6,000, a sub-peak of Mount Barrill.
This section is fairly crevassed, but
there is always a good way through.
Turn south into the Great Gorge and
head toward the center of the glacier.
It is best not to try to skirt the base of
Barrill—it is heavily crevassed. At 4,900
feet, across from the Japanese Couloir,
head west toward the base of Barrill
navigating crevasses. Once directly
under the Japanese Couloir, skirt
back north along the base of Barrill
until under the route. Some years it
is possible to navigate the crevasses
directly to the base of the Cobra Pillar,
but the above approach is a sure bet.

Route:

The original start begins with a
contrived hand crack on the right side
of the pillars base and then traverses
left to the main dihedral that forms the
left side of the pillar. A more logical
way is to ascend snow up a short ways
and start the climb directly in this
main dihedral. Follow the detailed
topo to the top.

Descent:

Northwest Face

This has been the standard descent for
this route, due to its ease and speed, but
it can hardly be recommended due to its
incredible avalanche danger. Unfortunately,
the best time to climb the rock routes in
the Gorge coincide with the worst time to
climb (or descend) snow routes. Study the
slope carefully from the Mountain House
and the Amphitheatre before considering
it for a descent route. The best way down
can change year to year. In general, descend
the West Ridge to the around 6,800 feet.
Cut back north on a large bench above and
below large seracs on the northwest face.
Follow the bench toward the center of the
face until a central gully is reached that
drops to the bottom of the face. Quickly
descend the serac-threatened gully to the
base of the face. From here, either traverse
southwest back to the Mountain House or

Chris McNamara leading the amazing splitter headwall crack.
Photo by Joe Puryear

circle back around Barrill to your camp in
the Gorge.

Japanese Couloir

This can be a good option if you brought
two ropes and crampons. It is certainly the
fastest way back to the Ruth Gorge. Later in
the season it is best to descend the couloir
at night to minimize rock fall. Check the
Japanese Couloir route description for full
details.

Descend the Route

Above Pitch 17, the route is difficult to
descend. Several parties have bailed off at
many different heights up to this point and
fixed anchors are numerous.

Mount Dickey, West Face

Difficulty: **II, 35-40 degree snow**

Elevation gain: **From the Ruth Gorge: 5,000'. From 747 Pass: 3,175'**

Total time: **1-2 weeks**

Approach time: **From the Mountain House: 2-4 hours**

Climbing time: **Up: From the Ruth Gorge: 5-12 hours. Down: 3-6 hours**

Season: **March to July**

Mount Dickey (9,545') holds one of the most impressive facades in all of the Alaska Range. Rising 5,000 feet straight out of the flat glacier, its east and south faces dominate the Ruth Gorge. Massive buttresses, fractureless planes, and insanely steep couloirs are intricately mixed to form a seemingly impenetrable bastion. It almost seems like cheating that you can easily walk up the western backside to the top of such a behemoth.

The West Face provides an excellent novice route that is equally enjoyed as a warmup for experienced climbers. The views are extensive, since Mount Dickey is one of the more prominent peaks in the area. In the 1956 American Alpine Journal, Bradford Washburn wrote of his climb of Dickey, "It would be hard to find a spot more easy of access where glorious glacier walks, easy lower climbs, and magnificent major ascents can all be accomplished out of the same air-supplied base camp, set amid North America's finest scenery and hardly a day's travel from New York!"

Mount Dickey was named after William A. Dickey (1862-1943). Dickey was a prospector who in 1896 named Mount McKinley after presidential nominee William McKinley of Ohio.

FA: April 9, 1955; Bradford Washburn and David Fisher.

History:

In the spring of 1955, four members of the Boston Museum of Science and one young climber from Britain flew onto the Ruth Amphitheatre to carry out survey work. Led by Bradford Washburn, the team accomplished several days of work from different points around the Gorge. This was also the expedition on which Washburn found the infamous "Fake Peak" in which Frederick Cook 50 years earlier had taken his bogus picture labeled "The Flag on the Summit of Mount McKinley." The team made several trips to Pittock Pass (7,250 feet), a western pass that separates Mount Dickey with its neighboring Pease Peak. On April 9, Washburn and David Fisher climbed Mount Dickey via this pass, hauling all of their survey gear to the summit. This peak was to be the main survey point of the surrounding area. They encountered no technical problems except for a short ice wall near 8,200 feet, which they found an interesting route through. With perfect weather they completed all their necessary observations, spending five hours on the summit. In his article Washburn wrote, "The view from the top of Mount Dickey is utterly magnificent...and has the added advantage of being readily accessible to civilization."

Strategy:

The route is generally done in a long day from the Ruth Gorge. If wanting to take a more leisurely two-day agenda, a good camp can be found at 747 pass.

Specific Hazards:

Watch for avalanche danger approaching 747 pass.

Gear:

Take standard glacier travel gear.

Camps:

The best base camp locations are the Mountain House, the Ruth Gorge, or Stump Camp. Check the Ruth Glacier introduction for base camp details.

747 Pass (6,370 feet): This is a good spot for an intermediate camp or snow cave.

Approach:

The original ascent crossed Pittock Pass from the Mountain House. This approach is not advisable due to the extreme avalanche danger in this area. The standard approach

Mt. Dickey from the west showing the two route variations. Photo by Mike Gauthier.

now is to drop down into the Ruth Gorge and circle around the south side of Dickey to reach 747 pass, the major col between Mt. Dickey and Mt. Bradley.

From the Mountain House airstrip (5,600 feet), descend down the hill to the north. As you approach the bottom of the hill and the Ruth Amphitheatre (5,400 feet), start turning east around the toe of Pt. 6000, a sub-peak of Mount Barrill. This section is fairly crevassed, but there is always a good way through. Turn south into the Ruth Gorge and head toward the center of the glacier. Pass underneath the east faces of Mount Barrill and Mount Dickey. Turn the corner around Mount Dickey and go west up the side glacier between Mount Dickey and Mount Bradley. At the head of the glacier, pass the icefall on its right side by a snow ramp. Gain the pass at 6,370 ft., also know as 747 pass.

Route:

There are two main route: one stays on or near the ridge crest on the right and the other stays on the main face and glacier on the left. The ridge crest generally has better snow conditions but has some steeper sections. The face is an easy consistent angle to the summit, but has more crevasses.

Ridge:

From 747 pass, climb directly up the 35-degree snow face, staying toward its right edge. Gain the ridge crest and climb to a short head wall at 8,500 feet. Climb up the 35 to 40-degree snow to a sharper ridge crest. Follow the crest to the top of a snow gendarme at 9,250 feet. Descend slightly, then ascend the wide slope east to the summit.

Face:

From 747 pass, climb up the broad slope staying either near the ridge crest or just to its left. At the point that the ridge rises steeply (8,500 feet) veer left above a large crevasse and into the broad basin in the center of the West Face. Ascend low angle slopes east to the summit, negotiating large crevasses.

Descent:

Retrace your steps back down to the base. If you are descending from another route and are unfamiliar with the descent, it's recommended to stay on the ridge because there are fewer crevasse and route-finding problems.

The Mooses Tooth

The western flank of the Ruth Gorge holds most of the great stalwarts—huge granite monoliths rising abruptly out of the glacier. Unfortunately they were designated with individual's names like Johnson, Wake, and Dickey. The east side, although generally less impressive, faired much better with peaks such as the Balrog, Werewolf Tower, and the Eye Tooth. And at the apex of these peaks is the greatest showpiece of all of the eastern part of the Central Alaska Range – the Mooses Tooth (10,300'). The mountain was originally named Mount Hubbard after Thomas H. Hubbard, president of the Perry Arctic Club. This name, given by Belmore Browne and Hershel Parker, was fortunately revoked by the USGS when they renamed the mountain to a translation of the indigenous Athabascan name. The exceptional name unfortunately forgot an apostrophe in the official spelling.

The rugged bulk of the Mooses Tooth sits directly across from the sheer east face of Mount Dickey, creating the grand Gateway to the Ruth Gorge. But unlike Mount Dickey, this complex massif has no forgiving route to the summit. Its north face is strewn with hanging glaciers; its colossal east face contains some of the most severe alpine routes in Alaska; its southern flank is a massive rock rampart split by thin ice couloirs; and the lower angled western slopes culminate in the narrow spine that creates the literal crown of the "tooth."

The following routes comprise the three easiest ways up the Mooses Tooth. Seeing that each one is a grade V puts this highly coveted summit into perspective.

The Tooth Peaks. The Mooses Tooth (left) and The Bear Tooth (right) are the highest two summits.
Photo by Joe Puryear

Ham and Eggs

Difficulty: **V, 5.9, AI 4**

Elevation gain: From the Root Canal airstrip: 2,900'. From the Ruth Gorge: 5,400'

Total time: 1-2 weeks

Approach time: From the Mountain House: 5-8 hours. From the Ruth Gorge: 4-7 hours. From the Root Canal airstrip: 5 minutes

Climbing time: Up: 8-16 hours. Down: 4-8 hours

Season: April and May; mid-April to early-May is best

Ham and Eggs is one of the ultra-classic routes of the Alaska Range, providing a direct line to this popular summit. The climbing is fun and moderate, and it gives the feel of a big Alaskan alpine route. The climb is characterized by many short crux ice and rock sections connected by easier snow climbing. The corniced ridge to the summit is mellow by Alaskan standards, but can still be attention-getting at times. The views from the summit are truly awe-inspiring: a commanding view of the Ruth Gorge, Denali, Hunter, Huntington, northern peaks, and the gnarly "Tooth" peaks adjoining the Mooses Tooth.

Oddly enough, the route took over 20 years to see a second ascent in the late 1990's, but it became a trade route almost overnight when Paul Roderick of Talkeetna Air Taxi started depositing climbers directly at its base. Now with its five-minute approach, this is a relatively safe and non-committing climb to test your Alaskan alpine skills.

FA: July 16-18, 1975; Jonathan Krakauer, Thomas Davies, and Nate Zinsser

History:

Three American climbers, Jonathan Krakauer, Thomas Davies, and Nate Zinsser, who were originally destined for the Kichatna Spires, somewhat stumbled across this line in the summer of 1975. Unable to fly into the stormy Kichatnas, they made a quick decision to fly into the Ruth, without even having a map of the area. After giving short consideration to the East Buttress of Mount Johnson, and a failed attempt on

Mount Barrill, the team made a miserable first ascent of Mount Cosmic Debris. From the summit of this measly heap of rubble they gazed across at the great Mooses Tooth and spied a perfect couloir splitting up the south face to a col just below the summit.

On July 11 they eagerly moved camp up onto the glacier below the couloir. They decided to go for a single push alpine style ascent, a bold undertaking for the time. However, this was to be the end of a perfect stretch of good weather. They started up in the evening of July 12. After a false start and three pitches of rock they continued up steep mushy snow. A difficult crux was reached on Pitches 8 and 9 requiring a bolt to be placed on a steep slab. By the time they reached Pitch 11, it was pouring down rain. Davies continued on, aiding up 90-degree ice with water pouring on him. Krakauer led the next difficult pitch as the rain got worse. As Zinsser started jumaring the rope, Davies accidentally started jumaring the same rope lower down, pinning Zinsser in a torrent of cold water. After a few expletives, they quickly remedied the problem, then started descending immediately. They crawled back to their wet tent, cold and exhausted.

The storm continued unabated for four days. Finally on July 16 they were able to dry out their gear and start again. They left at 8 p.m. and quickly made it to their high point. Once again it started to snow. They encountered the hardest climbing of the route on Pitches 11 through 15 where a narrow ice hose presented many short difficult steps of rotten 90-degree ice.

After another six pitches of 55-degree ice, they crested the ridge in a total white-out. They had been climbing for 20 hours and were exhausted. It was perhaps here that the route acquired its name. Krakauer wrote in his 1976 AAJ account of the climb, "If we had some ham, we could have some ham and eggs, if we had some eggs." Soon after, the clouds parted and three hours later they were on the summit. They started down tired and with snow falling heavily again. After a stuck rope and dozing off at a few anchors, they made it back safely to the tent, 33 hours after they started.

The route wasn't repeated until May 11, 1999. Peter Haeussler and Harry Hunt climbed the route in 25 and a half hours round trip. There were as many as 10 subsequent ascents later that year all confirming its classic status.

Strategy:

It is possible to fly directly to the base of the route onto what is known as the Root Canal Glacier. This is the best option if you are only planning to climb Ham and Eggs and Shaken, Not Stirred. Unless you can afford to be shuttled around the range, parties wishing to climb elsewhere in the Ruth may want to fly into the Mountain House airstrip or into the Ruth Gorge. A base camp can be made here and then climb a to an advanced base camp under the route. The climb has been done in a day from the Ruth Gorge, but most people will find this a difficult feat.

Many parties find the route climbable in one long day round-trip from the Root Canal. If moving slower, the broad col makes an excellent bivy. Climbing to here, then summiting and descending the next day can make for a great trip. For ambitious climbers, the route could be climbed in 24 hours round-trip from Talkeetna, assuming good weather. A fast party could feasibly fly into the Root Canal in the late afternoon, start the route early the next morning, and be back down on the glacier for a late afternoon pickup. Some parties have climbed both Ham and Eggs and Shaken, Not Stirred in a long weekend. Make sure you have a good forecast or you might find yourself late for work on Monday.

Specific Hazards:

Because Ham and Eggs is essentially a garbage chute for the surrounding cliffs and upper snow slopes, good judgment must be exercised when choosing the right temperatures and snow conditions for an ascent and descent.

Gear:

Take six to eight ice screws, four to six cams to three inches, and one set of stoppers. Take two 200-foot ropes. Bring two ice tools per person.

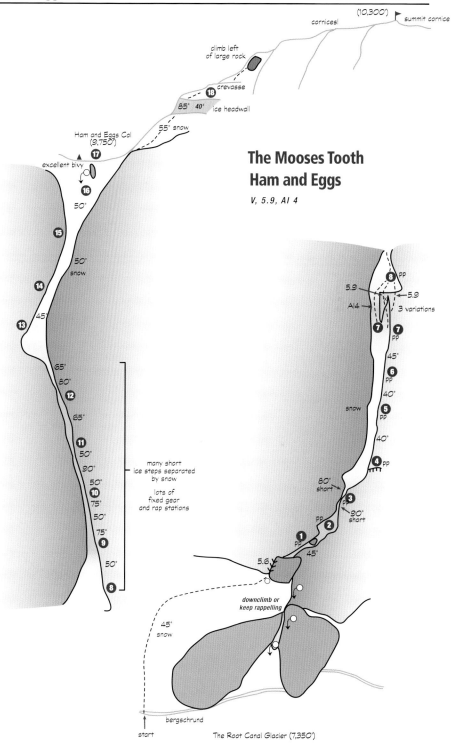

**The Mooses Tooth
Ham and Eggs**

V, 5.9, AI 4

(10,300')

cornices!   summit cornice

climb left
of large rock

crevasse

18

85° 40'   ice headwall

55° snow

Ham and Eggs Col
(9,750')

17

excellent bivy

16

50°

15

50°
snow

14

45

13

65°

80°

12

65°

11

50°

90°

10

75°

50°

75°

9

50°

8

many short
ice steps separated
by snow

lots of
fixed gear
and rap stations

8 PP

5.9   5.9

AI4   3 variations

7   **7**
             PP

45°

6 PP

40°

5 PP

snow

40°

4 PP

80°
short

3 PP

90°
short

PP
2

1 PP

5.6   45°

downclimb or
keep rappelling

45°
snow

bergschrund

start   The Root Canal Glacier (7,350')

Camps:

If not using the Root Canal Base Camp, the best base camp locations are the Mountain House, the Ruth Gorge, or the Ruth Amphitheatre. Check the Ruth Glacier introduction for base camp details.

Root Canal Base Camp (7,350 feet): If flying into the Root Canal, unload the plane and carry your gear about a hundred feet away and set up camp. Some climbers are concerned about the looming ice-cliff above on the Bear Tooth. Make sure you are camped a comfortable distance away (west), or camp at the safer Ridge Camp.

Ridge Camp (7,300 feet): For climbers coming up from the Ruth Gorge, this is a good place to set up base camp so as to not have to carry your load as far. Camp on the low ridge that separates the approach glacier with the Root Canal Glacier. This makes an excellent spot if you are planning on climbing Shaken, Not Stirred as well.

Col Camp (9,750 feet): The only reasonable campsite on the route is at the col atop the couloir. This is a broad area lending itself to several camping possibilities.

Approach:

From the Mountain House airstrip (5,600 feet), descend down the hill to the north. As you approach the bottom of the hill and the Ruth Amphitheatre (5,400 feet), start turning east toward the Mooses Tooth. Go southeast across the Ruth Gorge toward the northern-most glacier icefall that heads up to the basin beneath the south face of the Mooses Tooth. The icefall can be tricky to navigate and quite dangerous, especially after a storm. The best way through changes frequently but recent parties have found a gully on the right side of the glacier to bypass the icefall and access the slopes above. As you near the top of the glacier, the main couloir that splits the rock walls above is Shaken, Not Stirred. Continue up and right to a snow ridge and Ridge Camp (7,350 feet). Climb over and down the ridge about 200 feet to the east into the basin below. This is the Root Canal Glacier.

Route:

From the Root Canal airstrip, Ham and Eggs climbs directly up the main couloir to the north. Cross the bergschrund below and left of the steep rock buttress that defines the base of the couloir. Climb up snow left of the rocks, then traverse right up to the highest point where the snow butts into the short rock cliff left of the couloir's base. Climb 40 feet of low fifth class rock on the left-most section of this wall. Belay here or continue by down-climbing a short bit, then up a right-trending snow ramp. Pull a short boulder move, then traverse up and right to a fixed belay. Continue up and right to enter the couloir proper. Two short steps of steep ice lead to many rope lengths of easier climbing, using fixed rock anchors for belays. Above, the couloir splits. Choose wisely from the following options. The left way is pure ice (up to 80 degrees), but it may be thin or rotten. The right way has two variations. The better way is to climb a short ways up on 45-degree snow, then climb out right on flakes and cracks, 5.9, to the top of the barrier. Or, climb up to where the snow steepens considerably and make a move left on horns to a small stance on a crest. Clip the old 1/4" bolt at chest level, then make scrappy mixed moves over the slabs above, (5.9). This was the way of the first ascensionist, but is not recommended. Continue up moderate snow to where the couloir narrows again. Climb this section in four pitches of moderate-angled snow or ice with steep but short ice cruxes. None of the steps is over 50 feet. Belay and protect with fixed rock anchors and ice screws. Above this, four rope lengths of moderate snow reach the col. From the broad col, climb right (east) up a pitch of steepening snow to a short ice bulge. Climb this and belay on the lower angle slopes above. The ridge continues over flutings, cornices, and several false summits. A gigantic boulder is passed on the left by climbing a steep snow wall. The summit itself is a large cornice, so be careful.

Descent:

Down-climb carefully from the summit.

Make V-thread rappels over the ice bulge. Locate fixed rock anchors on either side of the gully and continue down. The rappel anchors are not always at perfect 200-foot stations. There are several short rappels here and there. Don't pass up a good anchor unless you are certain you can reach another one below. Be sure to test or back-up rock anchors. In general, the rock on the Mooses Tooth is poor. Near the bottom, instead of making the traverse back left (west) to the first rock pitch, you can make one rappel straight down the rock wall below. Down-climb the snow out to the left (west) from here. If the snow is mushy from the sun, you can continue to rappel off fixed anchors down the large slabs below, straight to the glacier.

Root Canal Airstrip

Shaken, Not Stirred

Difficulty: **V, AI 5**

Elevation gain: **From the Root Canal airstrip: 3,100'. From the Ruth Gorge: 5,400'**

Total time: **1-2 weeks**

Approach time: **From the Mountain House: 5-8 hours. From the Ruth Gorge: 4-7 hours. From the Root Canal airstrip: 20 minutes**

Climbing Time: **Up: to the West Summit: 8-15 hours; to the Main Summit: 2 days. Down: 4-8 hours**

Season: **April and May; mid-April to early-May is best**

This narrow ice ribbon splitting the immense granite walls of the south face of the Mooses Tooth is an alpinist's dream.

Mark Westman following up the lower-angled mid-section of the route. Photo by Joe Puryear

Although it doesn't provide an easy way to the actual summit, the outstanding nature of the climbing makes it exceptional. And with its easy access and short approach, this is about as good as it gets for Alaskan alpine climbing.

The climb is similar in ambience and slightly more difficult than its sister climb, Ham and Eggs. It has lots of easier climbing after an initial crux, which helps you gain elevation quickly. This leads to the narrows—an amazing 500-foot runnel of excellent quality alpine ice that is barely two shoulder widths, sometimes narrower. The highlight of the climb is a wildly steep and thin but short and well-protected crux high on the route. A trip to the West Summit is a good way to cap off the ascent.

FA: Late May, 1997; Jim Donini and Greg Crouch.

History

It remains a mystery how this excellent line remained unclimbed and perhaps unattempted for so many years. It wasn't until 1997 that Jim Donini stumbled across this gem while taking a picture of Mount Dickey from the Ruth Gorge with the Mooses Tooth in the background. There appeared to be a perfect ice line dropping directly down the South Face from Englishman's Col along the West Ridge of the Mooses Tooth. Donini and Crouch slyly left their camp in the Ruth Gorge at 1:30 A.M. Four hours later they arrived at the base of the couloir.

Having scoped the route from below, they expected to gain height rapidly on a long lower angle section in the middle of the route. However, right away they were forced with pitches of vertical rotten ice with marginal gear. Eventually they made it into the easier section and cruised up to what they thought would be the crux. Not knowing whether there was going to be any ice, they were pleasantly surprised to find a narrow slot of ice just a few feet wide. After 500 feet of incredible climbing, they expected to be done with the hard part. They rounded a corner and there in front of them was a huge chock-stone that had wedged itself into the gully. Over

SUPERTOPO

the top flowed a spattering of ice. Without hesitation they scraped their way up the crux and up to the top of the couloir. They decided to complete their ascent with a visit to the West Summit and descent via the West Ridge.

Strategy:

It is possible to fly directly to the base of the route onto what is known as the Root Canal Glacier. This is the best option if you are only planning to climb Shaken, Not Stirred and Ham And Eggs. Unless you can afford to be shuttled around the range, parties wishing to climb elsewhere in the Ruth may want to fly into the Mountain House airstrip or into the Ruth Gorge. A base camp can be made here and then climb to an advanced base camp under the route. The climb has been done in a day from the Ruth Gorge, but most people will find this a difficult feat.

Many parties find the route climbable in one long day round-trip from the Root Canal. If you plan on moving slower, you could bivy at the col, but be careful, the col has a cornice on its north side. If traversing to the Main Summit, a better bivy would be at the top of Ham and Eggs. A trip to the West summit is a good way to finish the ascent, but many parties simply descend from the col.

Specific Hazards:

Similar to Ham and Eggs, Shaken is essentially a garbage chute for the surrounding cliffs and upper snow slopes,

good judgment must be exercised when choosing the right temperatures and snow conditions for an ascent and descent. Be especially wary of descending in the late afternoon. The slopes off the West Summit can send sizeable wet snow avalanches down the lower part of the gully. Also be suspect of the rock anchors, especially near the bottom. The rock here is quite poor. In 2003, two climbers had a rock horn rap anchor fail, which sent them tumbling 1000 feet to the bottom. They miraculously escaped without serious injuries.

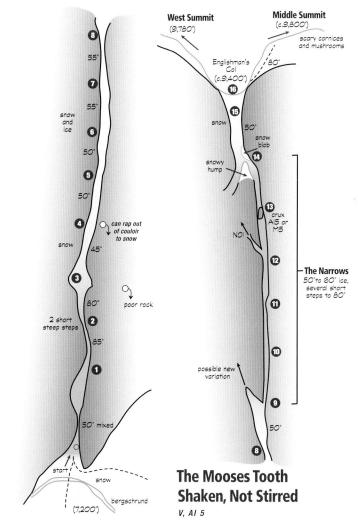

The Mooses Tooth
Shaken, Not Stirred
V, AI 5

Gear:

Take eight to ten ice screws, four to six cams to two-inches, and one set of stoppers. Take two 200-foot ropes. Bring two ice tools per person.

Camps:

If not using the Root Canal Base Camp, the best base camp locations are the Mountain House, the Ruth Gorge, or the Ruth Amphitheatre. Check the Ruth Glacier introduction for base camp details.

Root Canal Base Camp (7,350 feet): If flying into the Root Canal, unload the plane and carry your gear about a hundred feet away and set up camp. Some climbers are concerned about the looming ice-cliff above on the Bear Tooth. Make sure you are camped a comfortable distance away (west), or camp at the safer Ridge Camp.

Ridge Camp (7,300 feet): This is an ideal base camp or advanced base for the route. Camp on the low ridge that separates the approach glacier with the Root Canal Glacier. The camp provides an excellent straight-on view of the route.

Englishman's Col (c. 9,400 feet): If planning on camping on the route, this is probably the best spot. The narrow col has a cornice on the back side, but could be dug into for a small bivy.

Approach:

From the Mountain House airstrip (5,600 feet), descend down the hill to the north. As you approach the bottom of the hill and the Ruth Amphitheatre (5,400 feet), start turning east toward the Mooses Tooth. Go southeast across the Ruth Gorge toward the northern most glacier icefall that heads up to the basin beneath the south face of the Mooses Tooth. The icefall can be tricky to navigate and quite dangerous especially after a storm. The best way through changes frequently but recent parties have found a gully on the right side of the glacier to bypass the icefall and access the slopes above. As you near the top of the glacier, the main couloir that splits the rock walls above is Shaken, Not Stirred. Climb directly up to the bergschrund. If planning to make camp, continue up and right to the snow ridge (7,350 feet) that separates this glacier from the Root Canal Glacier.

Pete Tapley leading the crux of Shaken, Not Stirred in favorable conditions. Photo by Dan Gambino

If starting from the Root Canal airstrip, walk west and cross the low ridge (7,300 feet) to the head of the approach glacier. From the top of this ridge, traverse straight across above the bergschrund and down a little on snow to reach the base of the route.

Route:

Climb into the main narrow slot of the couloir. The first pitch may have some rock or thin ice, but is low angle. Pitch 2 is a steep step that may have rotten ice, snow, or mixed later in the season. One more short step leads to several pitches of fun and rambling snow and ice with good rock pro. The couloir then pinches down into the narrows. Here you will find excellent climbing with short cruxes. There is little rock pro to be found here and the belays are unprotected from falling ice. Expect to be beaten up a little. Climb this for 500 feet. The couloir turns left and widens a little before the crux, which consists of a huge chock-stone with a thin curtain of ice pouring over it (90+ degrees, short). A good screw and a one-inch cam can be placed before committing to the final moves. Don't be tempted by the easy snow runnel that leads up and left before the crux. A bit more moderate ice climbing and then you'll need to step left to a wide gully on the other side of a snowy hump. This traverse may consist of walking across a big improbable blob of snow stuck to the wall. This could be a scary proposition late in the day when the sun is on it. After making the 30-foot traverse, two more easy snow pitches lead to Englishman's Col (c.9,400 feet). If visiting the West Summit, head left out of the col. Climb a pitch of steep snow over a slab and then climb the broad ridge up. If traversing to the Main Summit, climb a pitch of 80-degree ice out of the col to the right. Traverse scary cornices and mushrooms for nearly a half mile while crossing the

The Shaken, Not Stirred couloir from the south. Photo by Joe Puryear

two central summits. Don't try to descend down between these two summits! Descend easier slopes into the col at the top of the Ham and Eggs couloir (9,750 feet). Climb the corniced and fluted ridge to the true summit.

Descent:

If coming down from the Main Summit, rappel the Ham and Eggs route using fixed rock anchors and a couple V-threads. To descend the Shaken gully, rappel the route using many V-threads and occasionally fixed rock anchors. If climbing to the West Summit, it is also possible to descend the West Ridge route back to the Ruth Gorge.

West Ridge

Difficulty: **To the West Summit: IV, 60-degree ice. To the Main Summit: V, 80-degree ice, extensive cornicing**

Elevation gain: **To the West Summit: 4,700'. To the Main Summit: 5,200'**

Total time: **1-2 weeks**

Approach time: **From the Mountain House: 2-3 hours**

Climbing time: **Up: to the West Summit: 1-2 days; to the Main Summit: 2-4 days. Down: 6-16 hours**

Season: **Late-March to mid-June, May is best**

Creating the long and sharp spine of the Mooses Tooth massif, the West Ridge is one of the most significant climbs out of the Ruth Glacier. This complex and somewhat precarious ridge was a ground-breaking first ascent to one of the hardest-to-attain summits in all of Alaska. The climb became even more well-known by being included in Steck and Roper's *Fifty Classic Climbs*, but it has fallen out of favor in recent years, due to the wild popularity of the south side routes. It is still a great climb up one of the most famous peaks in North America.

Few people that climb the West Ridge actually climb to the Main (east) Summit. Most parties are content with just the lower West Summit. The nature and seriousness of the climb certainly changes once you venture past this point. Make no mistake; the West Ridge is not the easiest route to the true summit. That would be Ham and Eggs. A moderate snow and ice climb to the West Summit becomes a difficult and dangerous ridge traverse, replete with steep ice climbing, dangerous cornices, and a high commitment factor.

FA:June 1-2, 1964; Klaus Bierl, Arnorld Hasenkopf, Alfons Reichegger, and Walter Welsch.

History

The West Ridge was first attempted in July of 1962 by the British team of Frank Smythe and Barrie Biven. They made a bold alpine-style effort, making the first ascent of the West Summit before being turned around in the vicinity of the col between the West and Central Summits. This col was named Englishman's Col in their honor.

On May 22, 1964, four German alpinists arrived on the Ruth Glacier beneath the Mooses Tooth. They had hoped to make the first ascent of Mount Huntington and climb Denali, but changed their goal to the Mooses Tooth after finding that Lionel Terray's French team was attempting Huntington. Klaus Bierl, Arnold Hasenkopf, Alfons Reichenegger, and Walter Welsch set their sights on a route up the south face from the high col between the Mooses Tooth and the Bear Tooth. Finding very steep and extremely rotten rock, they retreated to the basin below the south face. They made a vain attempt at what would eventually become the Ham and Eggs Couloir, and then withdrew everything back to the Ruth Glacier, setting their eyes on the West Ridge. At this same time, three American climbers Fred Beckey, Eric Bjørnstad, and Bob Baker arrived intent on the same objective. After an amiable discussion, they agreed to make a cooperative effort, but allowing the German team first crack at the summit.

The two teams started up the route climbing the initial icefall, then onto what the German team called the Moose's Back, the broad west ridge that leads to the sharper summit ridge. They established a high camp at 7,870 feet. On June 1 they left for a single-push summit bid at 6 A.M. The Germans led out in two teams with Bierl and Hasenkopf in the lead, the Americans followed behind later. They made their way with little technical difficulties to the West Summit. The climbing, however, was strenuous and demanding as they traversed across icy slopes to avoid the cornices. They rappelled into the col between the West and Central Summits and then started up the crux section. The climbing was steep and tenuous and one difficult pitch in particular they named the Himmelsleiter or "ladder to heaven." They crossed several snow and ice flutings, traversed around scary mushrooms and cornices, and intricately worked their way through exposed and challenging terrain. At one point, Hasenkopf fell on the steep ice and was caught by the rope just before he went over the steep southern edge of the ridge. Seventeen non-stop hours after leaving camp they arrived at the final col below the Main Summit.

After a short break, they made their way up the final corniced summit ridge. They arrived elated but exhausted on the untouched summit at 4 A.M. on June 2, 22 hours after they left camp. This was a glorious moment for the young Germans. They looked back to see two of the Americans retreating back along the ridge. They had only made it as far as Englishman's Col. The Germans retraced their steps along the ridge without incident, arriving back at their camp 41 hours after leaving.

Strategy:

The climb to the West Summit can be round-tripped in a long day from the Ruth Gorge. For a more comfortable schedule, make a high camp on the Moose's Back, then go for the summit the next day. If planning on climbing to the Main Summit, it may be best to carry your entire camp with you and descend via the Ham And Eggs Couloir. This straightforward descent, keeps you from having to re-traverse the difficult summit ridge.

Specific Hazards:

The initial ice-fall accessing the route is extremely hazardous, leaving some to question their decision to climb the route. The icefall becomes worse as the season progresses. Make an informed risk assessment and travel through the icefall quickly.

Gear:

Take two or three small cams, six to eight stoppers, and three or four pitons, including one Knifeblade. Take five or six ice screws and two or three pickets. Take two 200-foot ropes. Bring two ice tools per person.

Camps:

The best base camp locations are the Mountain House, the Ruth Amphitheatre, or the Ruth Gorge. Check the Ruth Glacier introduction for base camp details.

Mark Westman climbing along the final part of the ridge to the summit. The Middle and West Summits are in the distance.

Moose's Back Camp (7,000 to 8,000 feet):
Dig in a camp anywhere on the broad
ridge crest before the traverse into the
couloir. This was the high camp for the first
ascensionists.

Englishman's Col (c. 9,400 feet): The
narrow col has a cornice on the back side,
but could be dug into for a small bivy.

Ham and Eggs Col (9,750): This is a broad
area lending itself to several camping
possibilities.

Approach:

From the Mountain House airstrip (5,600
feet), descend down the hill to the north.
As you approach the bottom of the hill
and the Ruth Amphitheatre (5,400 feet),
start turning east toward the Mooses
Tooth. Straight across the Gateway to the
Ruth Gorge are the two icefalls used in
accessing the route. As you approach the
icefalls, gauge which one will provide the
safest passage. Generally the one on the left
(north) is better.

Route:

Ascend the 800-foot icefall and into the
basin above. Continue east up the center
of the glacier on the north side of the West
Ridge proper to around 6,900 feet. This is
generally the best place to start traversing
south to the ridge crest. One can also work
through crevasses right above the icefall
straight over to the ridge. Climb up onto
the broad ridge, then start ascending toward
its apex. At 8,700 feet, a huge rock tower
blocks the ridge crest and it is here that the
route takes a horizontal traverse off of the
ridge and into the couloir on its south side.
This traverse is usually made on snow over
granite slabs and can be thin at times. One
hard-to-protect pitch over 40 to 45-degree
slabs leads to the couloir. A fixed piton can
be found at the end of the traverse.

Once in the left-leaning gully on the
right side of the ridge, climb it straight up
to the narrow spine of the Mooses Tooth
at 9,300 feet. Another option is to traverse
into the next couloir to the right (south),
which is broader and may be slightly easier.
The couloirs are about five pitches of up to

Climbing the couloir below the West Summit. Photo by Mark Westman

The West Ridge of the Mooses Tooth from the west. Photo by Joe Puryear

55-degree snow and ice. Traverse along the 50-degree ridge crest for a pitch to a rock with a fixed piton. Continue up the steep corniced ridge to a false summit of the West Summit. A short section up to 60-degrees is encountered here. Traverse from the false summit to the West Summit along the very narrow and heavily corniced ridge.

From the West Summit, descend the broad low-angle slope to the east until it becomes sharp again. Either rappel or down-climb toward the major notch called Englishman's Col (c. 9,400 feet). This is the col that the route Shaken, Not Stirred comes into from the south. This would be a possible bail-out point in case of an emergency. Climb a pitch of 80-degree ice out of the col. Traverse scary cornices and mushrooms for nearly a half mile while crossing the two central summits. Don't try to descend down between these two summits! One or two rappels may be necessary off of rock horns coming off the first Central Summit. If returning this way, it may be beneficial to fix a rope. Descend easier slopes into the col at the top of the

Ham and Eggs couloir (9,750 feet). Climb the corniced and fluted ridge to the summit.

Descent:

From the Main Summit two options exist. It is possible to descend the Ham and Eggs Couloir after descending from the summit. This is a logical option to keep from having to retrace the entire ridge crest. The descent is very straightforward and once on the Root Canal Glacier one can simply walk back down to the Ruth. See the Ham and Eggs route description for more details.

Otherwise, it is necessary to down-climb, rappel, and re-climb the crest of the ridge back to the West Summit. From the West Summit, down-climb or make several V-thread rappels back to the bottom of the couloir. Re-lead the traverse back to the main ridge and retrace your ascent route back to the Ruth Glacier.

The Eye Tooth, West Pillar
Dream in the Spirit of Mugs

Difficulty: **V, 5.10c**

Elevation gain: **On route: 2,900'. From the Ruth Gorge: 4,300'**

Total time: **1-2 weeks**

Approach time: **From the Mountain House: 2-5 hours. From the Ruth Gorge: 1-2 hours**

Climbing time: **Up: 10-20 hours. Down: 5-10 hours**

Season: **June and July**

The Eye Tooth (9,000') is a southern sub-peak of the greater Mooses Tooth massif. Its tiny pointed summit caps one of the largest and steepest west facing walls on the east side of the Ruth Gorge. The West Pillar of the Eye Tooth is one of the finest alpine rock climbs in Alaska. This El Capitan-sized free climb scales an incredibly aesthetic buttress in the heart of the Ruth Gorge's Tooth peaks. While the route has an occasional loose block, the rock is overall very sound, well featured, and highly textured. On the climb, one gets the feeling of being "really out there" as a sea of granite sweeps up above and below you.

FA: July 7 and 8, 1994; Andi Orgler, Tommi Bonapace, and Raimund Haas

History

Master of the Ruth Gorge Andi Orgler laid eyes on this route for several years before getting a chance at it. In 1987 he had made a secret agreement with Mugs Stump, regarding both the Eye Tooth and the Sugar Tooth. Orgler accounts in his 1995 AAJ article, "The peaks ... were to be left for him, but tragically Mugs was lost two years ago and so the peaks were now 'free.'" So in June of 1994 he came to the Ruth Gorge with fellow Austrians Tommi Bonapace and Raimund Haas. The trio first went for the Sugar Tooth, the most southern Tooth Peak. A slabby and often wet affair, they made the first ascent of its West Face over three days in poor weather.

The team made a preliminary attempt on the Eye Tooth on July 1 but they were snowed off after eight pitches. On July 7 at about 6:00 P.M. they started up the route in marginal weather with their typical minimal gear. They were able to climb the first 12 pitches by midnight – an incredibly fast time for a first ascent. Bonapace decided to continue and lead the crux pitch above the bivy before turning in for a cold

Joe Puryear leading immaculate rock high on the route. Photo by Chris McNamara

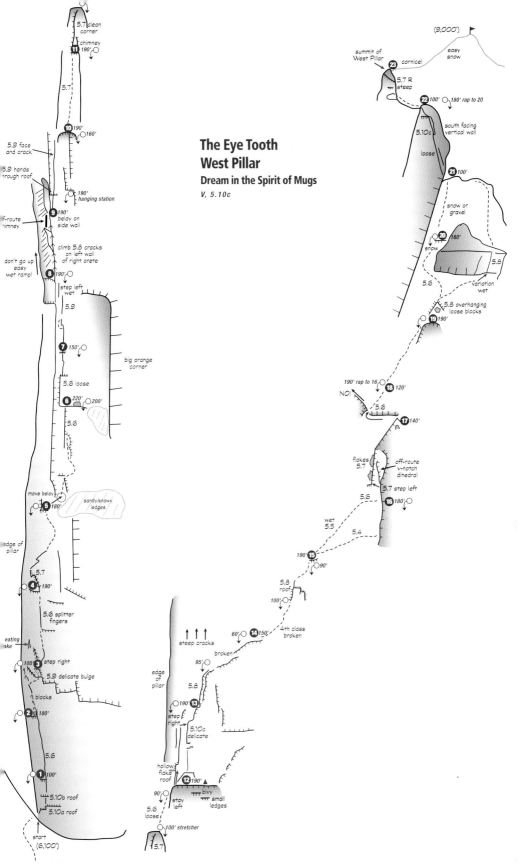

The Eye Tooth
West Pillar
Dream in the Spirit of Mugs
V, 5.10c

(9,000')

5.7 clean corner

chimney

11 190'

5.7

summit of West Pillar

cornice!

23

easy snow

5.7 R steep

22 100'   180' rap to 20

5.10c

10 190'   160'

5.9 face and crack

5.9 hands through roof

190' hanging station

off-route chimney

9 190' belay on side wall

climb 5.8 cracks on left wall of right arete

don't go up easy wet ramp!

8 190'

step left wet

5.9

7 150'

5.6 loose

6 220'   200'

5.6

move belay

5 180'

sandy/snowy ledges

edge of pillar

5.7

4 190'

5.6 splitter fingers

eating ake

3 100'   step right

5.9 delicate bulge

blocks

2 180'

5.6

1 100'

5.10b roof

5.10a roof

start (6,100')

south facing vertical wall

loose

21 100'

snow or gravel

20 160'   snow

5.6

5.8

variation wet

5.8 overhanging loose blocks

19 190'

190' rap to 16

18 120'

NO!

5.6

17 140'

flakes 5.7

off-route v-notch dihedral

5.7 step left

5.6

16 180'

wet 5.5

5.4

15 190'   90'

5.8 roof

100'

14 150'   60'

4th class broken

steep cracks

broken

95'

edge of pillar

5.8

13 190'

step right

5.10c delicate

hollow flake roof

12 190'   bivy

90'

stay left   small ledges

5.6 loose

100' stretcher

5.7

and snowy night. The weather continued to get worse so they raced for the top early the next morning reaching a point on the south ridge crest nine more pitches up, before deciding to rappel. The storm increased in fierceness and they were forced to continue rappelling continuously because they could not afford to bivy again so lightly equipped. After 24 rappels, they reached the base at 7:00 A.M. on July 9. Orgler states, "We were delighted to get to Base Camp minus one rope and some kilos lighter." Orgler remembered his friend Mugs Stump: "The line was a dream of his and also the style would have pleased him." As a dedication to Stump, they named their new route "Dream in the Spirit of Mugs."

Strategy:

A single push strategy will serve you well on this climb. With hard pitches right off the glacier, carrying bivy gear up the route can be a difficult task. If in need of a rest on the route, plan on climbing during the coldest part of the 24-hour day and resting in the warm mid-day sun with no bivy gear. Hauling the route is out of the question due to its lower angled sections. There are many fixed anchors and all of the belays are at a comfortable stance or ledge.

Specific Hazards:

The bottom six pitches of the route are severely threatened by rock and snow-fall from the large gully to the left of the route. Avalanches are common late in the day as the sun swings around and heats up the snow in the deep cleft. The debris can spill over and sweep the lower route. It is imperative not to be on the lower section of the route in the afternoon hours!

Gear:

Take a double set of cams to three inches, one set of stoppers, draws and slings. Two 200-foot ropes are obligatory.

Camps:

The best base camp locations are the Ruth Gorge or Stump Camp. Check the Ruth Glacier introduction for base camp details.

Bivy Site (top of Pitch 12):

One of the only decent places to bivy on the route. The ledge holds three seated people in different locations. Do not be lured into

bivy sites below Pitch 8 due to danger of rockfall.

Approach:

From the Ruth Gorge, head east up the side glacier beneath the Wisdom Tooth. It is easiest to cross the lateral moraines of the Ruth near the base of the Stump (4,700 feet). Ascend the center of the glacier and pass a small icefall at 5,700 feet. Continue to the route's base.

Route:

The route starts on the far left hand side of the huge granite apron that defines the bottom of the pillar. Due to glacial retreat, a new first pitch has most certainly been added since its first ascent, and nature didn't make it easy. A difficult series of roofs up the first crack system left of the major slabs forms one of the route's crux pitches. From there, follow the detailed topo.

Descent:

Rappel the route following the topo. Make note of the several short rappels down the upper pitches.

The Stump, Goldfinger

Difficulty: **IV, 5.11a**

Elevation gain: **1,800'**

Total time: **1-2 weeks**

Approach time: **From the Mountain House: 2-3 hours. From the Ruth Gorge: 20 minutes**

Climbing time: **Up: 5-10 hours. Down: 2-3 hours**

Season: **June and July**

This "small" 1,800 foot formation is often overlooked for the bigger peaks in the Ruth. The perfectly triangular face tends to blend in with the great walls of the Mooses Tooth and the Eye Tooth. It was named in honor of Mugs Stump after his tragic death in 1992. The Stump is technically part of the Wisdom Tooth formation, although all of its routes logically end on The Stump's lower summit point. The Wisdom Tooth has its own great south wall to the right of The Stump. The granite on these walls has a distinctively red color in places and is some of the best rock in the Ruth Gorge.

The south face is defined by two major dihedral systems that appear to converge perfectly at the summit. The left one holds one of the finest moderate rock climbs in the Gorge. This sustained moderate route on excellent rock sports good protection, easy access, and a straightforward descent.

FA: June 25, 2004; Chris McNamara and Joseph Puryear

History:

The lower part of the route was first climbed by Steve Quinlan and Mugs Stump while visiting the Gorge in late May to early June of 1991. Their main objective was a difficult new line on the South Face of Mount Dickey but the weather was not cooperating. During a clear day between storms they decided to go have a look at the rock by the Wisdom Tooth. They left early one morning from their campsite under Dickey and skied over to the base of the steep gold and red wall across the valley. On that same day, in a flurry of climbing, they ascended both of the major dihedrals cutting up the wall. On the left-hand of the two dihedrals they exited out left after their eigth pitch, topping out on a shoulder of rotten rock. From here they rappelled off,

Chris McNamara onsighting the crux pitch of Goldfinger on the first ascent. Photo by Joe Puryear

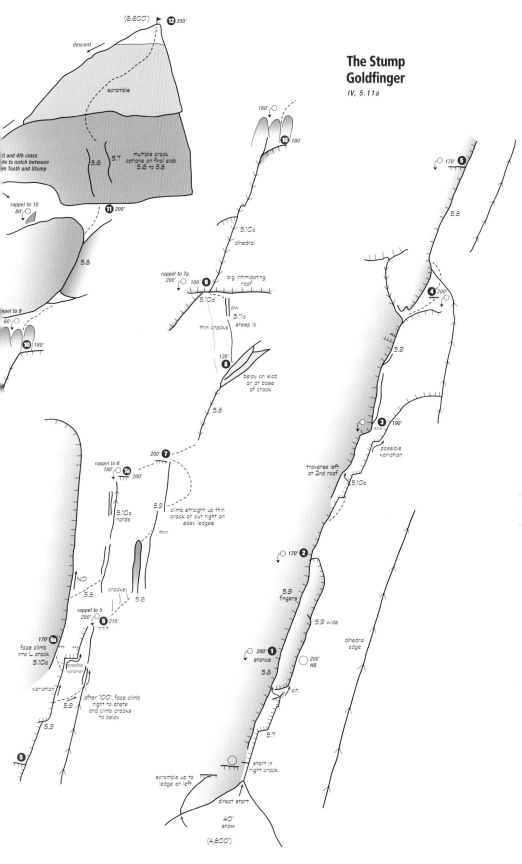

The Stump
Goldfinger
IV, 5.11a

not attaining the summit.

In June of 2004, Chris McNamara and I arrived on the Ruth Glacier. After a speed ascent of the Cobra Pillar and climbing the Eye Tooth and Hut Tower, we looked around for a moderate climb to give our poor fingertips a rest. We spied the beautiful stone on the south face of the walls below the Mooses Tooth. Having only a rough diagram of the formation referred to as The Stump, we liked the looks of the left-hand of two major dihedral systems splitting up the face. On June 22 we started climbing. Excellent stemming on super-solid and well featured rock characterized pitch after pitch. As we got higher, the route exited

off the south face and onto the west face, which contains some of the worst rock in the Gorge. Our climb was finished in a sea of sheer gravel and we were forced to half down-climb, half rappel off of bad anchors to return to the dihedral. We rappelled back to camp disappointed at how such spectacular climbing could end so poorly.

On June 25 we decided to give it another go and "straighten that route up" to the top. We quickly regained the top of Pitch 5. From there we deviated out to the arête defining the right edge of the dihedral and followed crack systems that pointed directly to the summit. However, when we topped out on the Pitch 8 our hopes faded as our intended route up a right dihedral was unreachable. We scanned the cliff above. The only other weakness was a steep and thin seam capped by an intimidating roof. After pondering our options for a few moments, Chris stepped up to the plate and said, "Well, I'll just go have a look at it." It turned out easier than it appeared as he walked the 5.11 roof up to a stance above. From there, the route was straightforward to the summit. In wanting to create a repeatable route we installed bomber rappel stations with clean pulls the entire way down. We named the route "Goldfinger" to speak to the golden nature of the rock and the beautiful climbing encountered.

Strategy:

Since the route can be rappelled from any point and all snow gear can be left at the base, climbers can focus on the actual rock climbing and

The Stump, Goldfinger. Photo by Joe Puryear

Mooses Tooth West Summit

Wisdom Tooth

Mooses Tooth Main Summit

Eye

The Stump

Wisdom Tooth Base Climbs

Overview of the Tooth Peaks and the Stump from the southwest. Photo by Joe Puryear

worry less about being on a major alpine route in the Ruth Gorge. The climb can be accomplished by most parties in a day. All but one of the belays has a comfortable stance or ledge, making it well suited to teams of two or three.

Gear:

Take two sets of cams to three inches. A four-inch piece is optional. Take one set of stoppers, draws and slings. Two 200-foot ropes are obligatory.

Camps:

The best base camp locations are the Ruth Gorge or Stump Camp. The approach from Stump Camp is about five minutes. Check the Ruth Glacier introduction for base camp details.

Approach:

From the Ruth Gorge, head directly to the base of The Stump, navigating a lateral moraine and a series of interesting crevasses. Leave your skis or snow travel gear at the base of the snow cone and

hike up the snow to the base of the main dihedral. Access a good rock ledge left of the dihedral by either climbing up the dihedral direct, then traversing across, or by scrambling up easy ground to the left of the ledge. This is a good place to organize gear and leave your boots.

Route:

Traverse back to the dihedral and climb directly up the main right crack. Follow the topo from here.

Descent:

From the summit, down-climb slabs and broken rock to the north to reach the notch between The Stump and the Wisdom Tooth. Traverse back south to the top of Pitch 11. Early in the season this traverse may be snow-covered, in which case it may be easier to set up a rappel back down to Pitch 11. Make 11 long rappels down the route to the base.

SUPERTOPO

ALASKA CLIMBING

Hut Tower, Southwest Face

Difficulty: **IV, 5.10c**

Elevation gain: **1,900'**

Total time: **1-2 weeks**

Approach time: **From the Mountain House: 3-5 hours. From the upper Ruth Gorge: 2-3 hours**

Climbing time: **Up: 4-8 hours. Down: 2-3 hours**

Season: **June and July**

This small pointy peak is the last summit of the great London and Werewolf Tower massif on the lower east side of the Ruth Gorge. The tower is completely hidden behind Werewolf Tower from the upper Gorge, lending to its relative obscurity. But this fin-shaped spire is a secret gem, consisting of some of the best rock in the Gorge. The Southwest Face of Hut Tower makes for a good warmup for harder rock routes in the Gorge, or it may be a great prize for intermediate climbers looking to get up any one of the legendary Ruth Gorge rock routes. First ascensionist Andi Orgler describes this route as "relaxing climbing in the afternoon sun."

FA: July 10, 1987; Andi Orgler and Sepp Jöchler.

History

The first ascent of Hut Tower or "Huttenturm" was made by Andi Orgler and Sepp Jöchler while on another trip to the Ruth Gorge in 1988. The two Austrians had just made the first ascent of Mount Bradley by its humongous 5,000-foot tall East Buttress. This superhuman ascent only took 14 hours to reach the summit. After Bradley they went on to make attempts on Mount Dickey and London Tower, but due to poor weather they were only able to summit Hut Tower. They started the climb in the late afternoon on the 10th of July, with only six pitons, thre cams, and five stoppers. Three hours and 45 minutes later they were on the summit. Orgler called it "a very nice and easy-going climb." The weather abruptly changed on the descent and they were back at their tent that evening in strong rain.

Near the end of their trip they made an impressive attempt on Mount Barrill, climbing a line to the right of but on the same feature as the Cobra Pillar. The next year they came back and finished the line, making the first ascent of the mountain's sheer East Face. They also finished their route on Mount Dickey, climbing the Wine

Chris McNamara leading solid granite low on the route. Photo by Joe Puryear

Bottle Route – a 51-pitch "Superthing" that is possibly the single greatest alpine rock climbing achievement ever done in Alaska.

Strategy:

Later season is generally better. A snowfield above the route can make for a wet Pitch 8. As the route sheds snow it becomes drier and easier. The route can be done in a long day from a camp in the upper Gorge. Leave your skis or snowshoes at the base, but bring your boots and possibly crampons or ice axe up the initially rock scrambling. The gear must be carried up to at least the top of Pitch 4. Here they can be tied off and left for the descent, which is by a slightly different route. As long as it is not too early in the season and the upper ledges are snow free, rock shoes should be fine for reaching the summit.

Hut Tower, Southwest Face. Photo by Joe Puryear

Gear:

Take one or two set of cams to three inches, one set of stoppers, draws, and slings. Two 200-foot ropes are obligatory. An ice axe and crampons may be needed for the slopes leading up to the climb if conditions are firm.

Camps:

The best base camp locations are the Ruth Gorge or Stump Camp. Check the Ruth Glacier introduction for base camp details.

Approach:

From the Ruth Gorge, travel south down the center of the glacier. Do not cut over to the base of the tower until you are directly across from it. Head east toward the tower, picking a way through a lateral moraine maze. Once at the base of the tower, find a flat rock, to leave your extra gear and skis, then start hiking up the slope to the start.

Route:

The route starts up the lower of two couloirs that trend up and right into the rock spur coming down the right side of the formation. The amount of snow in the couloir and on the rocky benches above can vary dramatically over the course of the season. At the top of the couloir, follow easy rock or mixed terrain up the lower angled spur ridge until it butts into the main upper face. From here the route starts up a steep right-facing corner with a roof near its bottom on the left edge of the south face. Follow the topo from here.

From the top of the last difficult pitch, several ramps and blocky terrain lead to the summit. Several 4th class and low 5th class variations are possible.

Descent:

Descend the upper section by the same route of ascent. Start rappelling from the first fixed anchor atop the last pitch. Make several long rappels to the top of Pitch 4, where your boots and gear are stashed. Instead of continuing down the ascent line, rappel straight down the west face five more times onto the glacier.

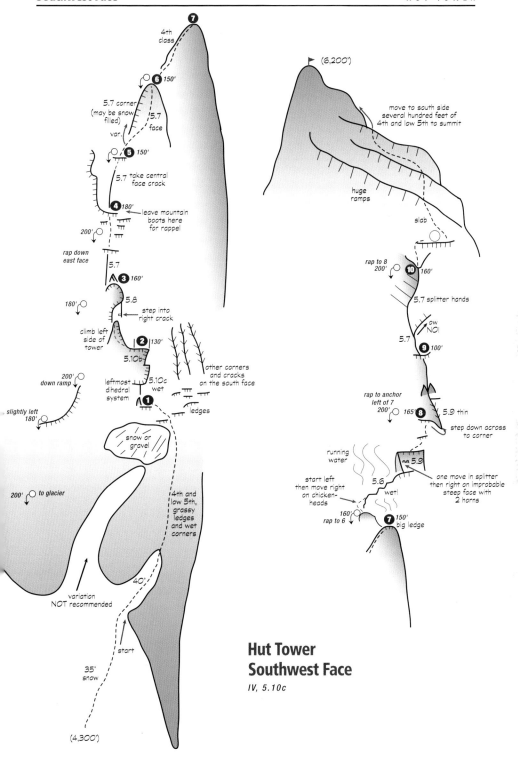

**Hut Tower
Southwest Face**

IV, 5.10c

Labels on topo:

- 7 — 4th class
- 6 — 150'
- 5.7 corner (may be snow filled) — 5.7 face var.
- 5 — 150'
- 5.7 take central face crack
- 4 — 180' — leave mountain boots here for rappel
- 200' — rap down east face — 5.7
- 3 — 160'
- 180' — 5.8
- step into right crack
- climb left side of tower
- 2 — 130'
- 5.10b
- 200' down ramp
- leftmost dihedral system — 5.10c wet
- other corners and cracks on the south face
- slightly left 180'
- 1 — ledges
- snow or gravel
- 200' to glacier
- 4th and low 5th, grassy ledges and wet corners
- variation NOT recommended
- start
- 40'
- 35' snow
- (4,300')

Right side:

- (6,200')
- move to south side several hundred feet of 4th and low 5th to summit
- huge ramps
- slab
- rap to 8 200'
- 10 — 160'
- 5.7 splitter hands
- ow NO! — 5.7
- 9 — 100'
- rap to anchor left of 7 200'
- 8 — 165' — 5.9 thin
- step down across to corner
- running water
- start left then move right on chickenheads
- 5.6
- wet
- 5.9
- one move in splitter then right on improbable steep face with 2 horns
- 160' rap to 6
- 7 — 150' big ledge

Mount Dan Beard, Southwest Route

Difficulty: **V, 60-degree snow and ice**

Elevation gain: **On route: 3,650'. From the Mountain House: 4,550'**

Total time: **1-2 weeks**

Approach time: **From the Mountain House: 3-4 hours. From the Ruth Amphitheatre Camp: 2.5-3.5 hours. From the West Fork Camp: 2-3 hours**

Climbing time: **Up: 7-14 hours. Down: 6-12 hours**

Season: **March to early-June, May is best**

Mount Dan Beard is a wildly mysterious mountain on the north side of the great Ruth Amphitheatre. Its complex bulk is a detached island that is oddly encircled completely by the Ruth Glacier. H. C. Parker and Belmore Brown named the mountain in 1910 after an American painter and illustrator and founder of the Boy Scouts of America, Daniel Carter Beard (1850-1940).

Even though it has an easy walk-up route on its back side, it is the south façade that really captures the imagination of climbers. It appears inviting yet appalling in the same glance. Because of this, or perhaps because it is so readily viewed from the popular Mountain House airstrip, this is where most attention is focused. The route opened by Peter Boardman and Roger O'Donovan in May of 1974 is a true mountaineering classic. While not technically difficult, the route requires good judgment and solid alpine skills. Only fast and very competent parties will be able to climb and descend the route in a very long day. The descent especially must not be underestimated as it can take nearly as long as the ascent.

FA: May 17 to 19, 1974; Roger O'Donovan and Peter Boardman.

History

The first ascent of Mount Dan Beard was made by the West Face on July 14, 1962 by Frank Smythe and Barrie Biven. They intended to climb the North Ridge, but found that way blocked by seracs and cornices. They made the trip round trip in 24 hours.

In May of 1974, Peter Boardman and Roger O'Donovan started their trip in the Ruth Amphitheatre by climbing Mount Dickey by the West Face on May 9. Their next objective was Mount Dan Beard, which at the time only had one ascent, and by a technically easy route. On May 17, they skied up into the small valley below the initial couloir, and climbed the couloir throughout the night. They continued up the complicated face the next day, heading for the large central depression on the face.

Mt. Dan Beard from the south. Photo by Joe Puryear

David Gottlieb descending off the south face in a storm. Photo by Joe Puryear

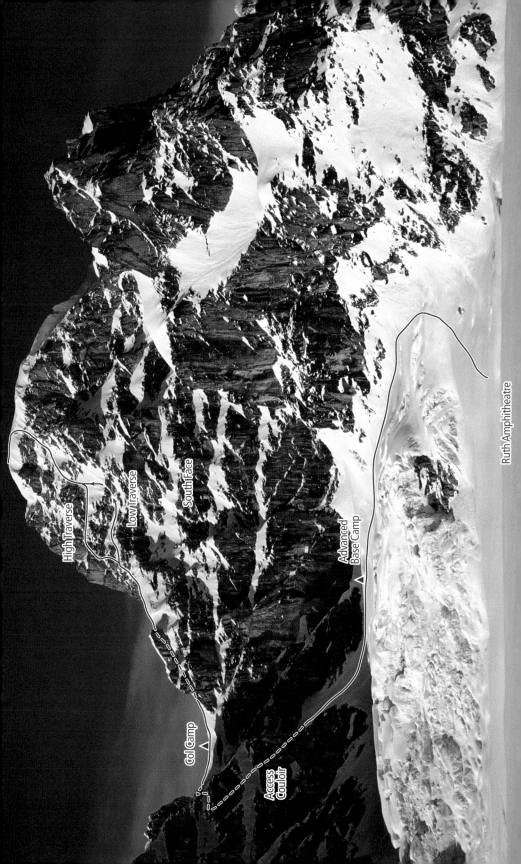

High Traverse

Low Traverse

South Face

Col Camp

Access
Couloir

Advanced
Base Camp

Ruth Amphitheatre

After two pitches of ice they were on the final summit slope just as a storm hit. They had been on the move for 23 hours and instead of descending, they opted to build an igloo on the summit to rest and wait out the short storm. The next day the weather cleared and they began their 14-hour descent in dangerous snow conditions.

Strategy:

Only under the best conditions can the climb be accomplished in a day round trip from the Mountain House. Most parties will need an intermediate camp, whether it be on the route or at the base. Climbing to the col is relatively straightforward, and the spacious area makes a great camp and good headstart on the upper sections.

Specific Hazards:

The gully that accesses the Southwest Ridge is avalanche-prone and should be climbed in cold conditions. The slopes on the South Face can also be avalanche-prone after a storm or in warm weather.

Gear:

Take four to six cams to two inches, one set of stoppers, one Knifeblade, one Lost Arrow, draws, and slings. Take two or three pickets and two ice screws. Take two 200-foot ropes. Bring two ice tools per person.

Camps:

The best base camp locations are the Mountain House or the Ruth Amphitheatre. Check the Ruth Glacier introduction for base camp details. The climb can also be accessed from the West Fork Camp.

West Fork Camp (7,000 feet): Camp near the base of the Southwest Ridge of Peak 11,300 or near where the pilot lands you. Make sure you are not camped under an avalanche run-out zone off of Mount Huntington.

Advanced Base Camp (6,500 feet): At the base of the route, a camp can be placed at the top of the small pocket glacier between the southwest and southeast ridges of Dan Beard. This is the recommended start point

for parties going for a one-day ascent. It is not recommended to camp here after a big storm due to avalanche danger from the surrounding cliffs.

Col Camp (7,950 feet): For parties making a two-day ascent, this is the best high camp option. Dig into the broad col, being mindful of crevasses that run through it.

Approach:

From the Mountain House airstrip descend the gentle hill to the north and out into the Ruth Amphitheatre (5,300 feet). Head northwest toward the small pocket glacier below the south face and between the arm-like southwest and southeast ridges of Dan Beard. Ascend the pocket glacier, avoiding a small icefall on its far right side. Move back toward the center of the glacier to avoid serac danger from the right, then up to the basin below the south face and the wide couloir which begins the route. This is a good spot for an advanced base camp.

Route:

Access Couloir:

Start up the couloir, crossing a small bergschrund. Continue up the couloir to where it pinches down on the left. Climb straight up to the wall above to a fixed belay. Traverse right over a fluting on an exposed ledge system. Protection is available in the wall above. Cross another fluting, then turn the corner and climb a couloir up to the broad col. Descend slightly into the col. Watch out for crevasses.

Southwest Ridge:

Climb north out of the col up a 400-foot, 45-degree snow face on the left side of a huge rock outcropping. Diagonal leftward up the slope to avoid the ominous cornice overhead and climb onto the southwest ridge proper. Continue up the ridge several hundred feet until a small knife-edged col is reached. Tip-toe across the col and climb up the mixed rock and snow ridge above. Two rope-lengths, passing a fixed anchor, lead to a large horn with a sling. From here there are two options, the first of which is the recommended way.

Option 1, Low Traverse:

The best option is to make a horizontal right traverse for three pitches to reach a gully accessing the main south face couloir. Depending on the amount of snow, there may be some mixed climbing on the traverse, otherwise expect 40 to 50-degree snow. At the end of the traverse there is an option of three gullies. The first heads up and left at a 50-degree angle and intersects the high traverse. The central is narrow and heads up and right at a 50-degree angle directly into the south face couloir. The third requires more traversing to the right, then heads into the same couloir. If conditions are good, the second couloir is the best option. Once into the broader south face couloir, climb straight up toward where the couloir narrows slightly.

Option 2, Upper Ridge and High Traverse:

Instead of making the low traverse, continue straight up the ridge, weaving through rock difficulties varying from 5.6 to 5.8, depending on the route chosen. After four pitches, a belay horn with a sling marks the beginning of the high traverse. Above here, the ridge is blocked by huge gendarmes. Traverse horizontally right on a steep snow ledge system at an angle of 45 to 55 degrees for three pitches, until it connects with the main south face couloir. Sparse protection is available in the rocks.

South Face Couloir:

Climb a narrow section in the couloir. In early season this is usually all snow. Later in the season, there may be a short mixed section. After a pitch, traverse up and right into the broad bowl above. Upon reaching the rocks above, make a right traverse over a snow fluting. After another pitch, the couloir narrows as it approaches a series of large boulders at its apex. Climb the couloir to its top and then exit right underneath the overhanging boulders to a belay at a large slung horn. Climb a small gully straight up for 40 feet and onto the summit ridge.

Summit Ridge:

Follow the low angle ridge over two small false summits to the broad summit area.

Descent:

It's best to descend the way you climbed. You can rap the south face couloir back to one of the traverses, or in good conditions down-climb it. One of the traverses must be re-climbed back to the main ridge. Then it is best to rappel back to the knife-edge col. From here, walk back down the ridge to the main col. Down-climb, rappel, or use a combination of both to cross the exposed ledge system above the main couloir. Once in the main couloir, walk or down-climb to the base.

Peak 11,300,
Southwest Ridge

Difficulty: **V, 5.8, 60-degree ice, extensive cornicing**

Elevation gain: **From West Fork airstrip: 4,400'. From the Mountain House: 5,700'**

Total time: **1-2 weeks**

Approach time: **From the West Fork airstrip: 20 minutes. From the Mountain House: 4-8 hours**

Climbing time: **Up: 1-3 days. Down: 6-12 hours**

Season: **April to June, May is best**

Just because a peak doesn't have a proper name, doesn't mean it is not worthy. With neighboring peaks called the Mooses Tooth, Mount Silverthrone, and the Rooster Comb, this striking peak has been largely overlooked by climbers. For years it was only contemplated by hard men in the know. But attention shifted when Steve House picked the Southwest Ridge of 11,300 as his favorite in the modern day tick list – Fifty Favorite Climbs. It instantly became a classic and "11,300" is now attempted several times each season. By all means the Southwest Ridge is a superb ridge climb, offering Cassin-like climbing at a lower elevation and less commitment. The rock is excellent and the climbing never too difficult, yet continually challenging. And the peak's location at the confluence of the West and Northwest Forks of the Ruth Glacier provides an unreal backdrop for a true technical mountaineering ascent. Rob Newsom, no stranger to hard climbs in Alaska, considers the top to be "One of the greatest summit views in the range."

FA: July 21, 1968; Niklaus Lötscher and Heinz Allemann.

History

Two Swiss climbers, Heinz Allemann and Niklaus Lötscher, made the first ascent of the Southwest Ridge while spending two weeks in the range in 1968. Theirs was the first ascent of the peak as well. Their ascent was in late July and much of the snow had melted off the ridge, making the rock climbing difficult. Because of the warm July temperatures they were forced to climb the summit ice field at night. They summited just after midnight on July 21, then descended the South Ridge back to the West Fork of the Ruth.

The Southwest Ridge of Peak 11,300 from the southeast. Photo by Joe Puryear

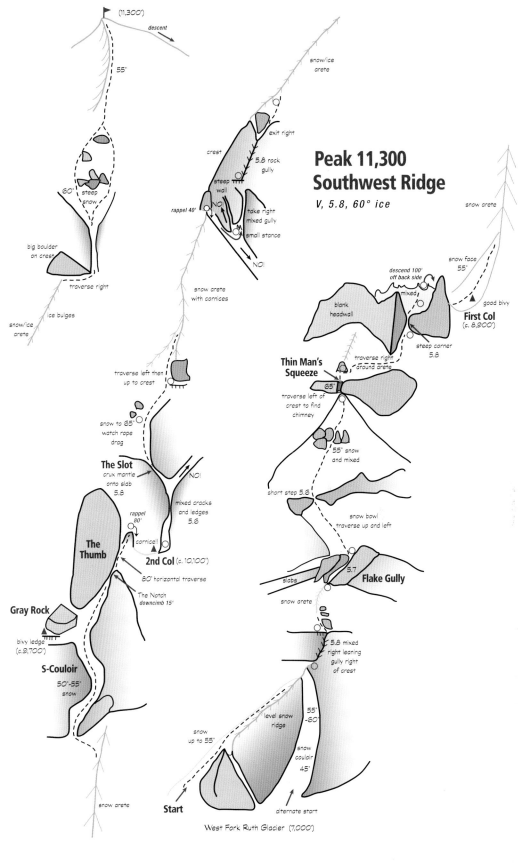

(11,300')

descent

55'

snow/ice
arete

60' steep
snow

big boulder
on crest

traverse right

ice bulges

snow/ice
arete

crest

exit right

5.8 rock
gully

steep
wall

rappel 40'

NO!

take right
mixed gully

small stance

NO!

snow arete
with cornices

Peak 11,300
Southwest Ridge

V, 5.8, 60° ice

snow arete

snow face
55'

descend 100'
off back side

mixed

blank
headwall

good bivy

First Col
(c. 8,900')

steep corner
5.8

traverse right
around arete

**Thin Man's
Squeeze**

65'

traverse left of
crest to find
chimney

55' snow
and mixed

short step 5.6

snow bowl
traverse up and left

traverse left then
up to crest

snow to 65'
watch rope
drag

The Slot
crux mantle
onto slab
5.8

NO!

mixed cracks
and ledges
5.6

rappel
80'

cornice!

2nd Col (c. 10,100')

**The
Thumb**

80' horizontal traverse

The Notch
downclimb 15'

5.7

Flake Gully

slabs

snow arete

Gray Rock

bivy ledge
(c.9,700')

S-Couloir

50°-55'
snow

5.8 mixed
right leaning
gully right
of crest

level snow
ridge

55'
-60'

snow
up to 55'

snow
couloir
45'

snow arete

Start

alternate start

West Fork Ruth Glacier (7,000')

David Gottlieb ascending the lower convuluted ridge. Photo by Joe Puryear

The duo went on to climb Peak 10,370 just east of 11,300. They had planned to make the complete traverse to the Southeast Spur of Denali, but were thwarted by the by bad snow conditions. They finished their trip with the first ascent of Peak 8,010 and Peak 9,090, both north of the Mooses Tooth, climbing the later on August 1, the Swiss national holiday, reaching the summit in fog and snow.

Says Lötscher, in his 1969 AAJ account, "Aside from my falling 35 feet into a crevasse, all went well on the whole expedition."

Strategy:

Fast and competent parties can do the route and descent in a single push, but this leaves little margin for error. Going light will definitely do you well as there is a lot of rock climbing that will be led with a pack on. If bivying on the route, a reasonable schedule would be to make it to the Second Col the first day, then to the summit the next. A bivy then could be made on the summit or somewhere on the descent if necessary.

Specific Hazards:

The standard descent route down the Southeast Ridge and down the small glacier below the south face is exceptionally dangerous. A massive hanging glacier lies perched above and commonly sweeps the entire glacier from side to side and down to the base of the Southwest Ridge. It is not uncommon to see huge ice blocks almost reaching the West Fork of the Ruth. Descending this glacier takes about 30 minutes but it is a total roll of the dice as to whether you will survive. Check the descent section for alternate descent options.

Gear:

Take four to six cams to two inches, six to eight stoppers, draws, and slings. Take three to four ice screws and one to two pickets. Take two 200-foot ropes. Bring two ice tools per person.

Camps:

West Fork Camp (7,000 feet): Camp near the base of the Southwest Ridge or near where the pilot lands you. Make sure you are not camped under an avalanche run-out zone off of Mount Huntington.

First Col (c. 8,900 feet): This spacious col is about a third of the way up the route and is by far the largest campsite encountered.

Grey Rock Bivy (c. 9,700 feet): This is an awesome bivy located underneath the prominent grey rock in the S-Couloir.

Second Col (c. 10,100 feet): This small col forms a huge cornice on its west side. A small platform can be dug on the north side of the col and rock protection can be found above.

Upper Ridge (10,300 to 10,800 feet): Several small and less distinct bivy sites exist on the upper ridge. They tend to be very exposed.

Summit (11,300 feet): An incredible spot that is a risky venture but super rewarding.

Descent (10,200 feet): Just below the upper snow field traverse and before the rock rappels is a nice flat area of the Southeast Ridge. Several more good and protected locations exist in and amongs the rappel line.

Approach:

There are two options for flying into 11,300.

Mountain House

Flying in here allows a greater versatility to climb other peaks in the Ruth and is less expensive. If it snows a lot, you are much likelier to be flown out from this busy airstrip as well. From the airstrip, go down (north) toward the Ruth Amphitheatre. Don't cut left toward the West Fork too soon or you will hit big crevasses. After about 1.5 miles at 5,350 feet, turn west and head toward the right hand base of the Rooster Comb. You can also head west, up and over the Mountain House hill from the airstrip where there is a smooth ramp that leads northwest into the amphitheatre. An icefall at the base of the Rooster Comb heading into the West Fork is usually navigated left of center as you turn the corner into the West Fork, but then it is advisable to stay on the right side of the glacier to avoid the massive seracs that hang off the Rooster

Comb and Mount Huntington. Continue up the West Fork to 7,000 feet near the base of the route.

West Fork Ruth Glacier:

If glacier conditions are good, a pilot may be able to land you directly at the route's base at 7,000 feet. Make sure you discuss pickup options with your pilot as he or she may require you to walk out to the Mountain House should conditions get bad. From 7,000 feet, it is a 20-minute walk to one of the start options of the route.

From the West Fork airstrip the route is plainly visible to the northwest. Go up the glacier to the toe of the ridge.

Joe Puryear cruising up moderate terrain low on the route.
Photo by David Gottlieb

Route:

The nature of the route allows many variations to be climbed. In general it is best to stay as close to the ridge crest as possible and follow the best looking weaknesses through the difficulties.

There are two ways to start the ridge, the latter being more challenging but more direct.

Option 1: Traverse around the left side of the ridge and climb up the initial snow slope, staying left of the rocks above, to the ridge crest. Traverse along the level and corniced ridge crest until the ridge steepens and the first major obstacle is encountered.

Option 2: Start the route on the right side of the ridge by climbing a moderate couloir that angles up and right to the same spot. Depending on the amount of snow in the couloir, a short mixed step may be encountered near its top.

Ascend right of the ridge crest and toward a right leaning depression in the rock. Climb mixed ground and mantle over a snow mushroom up to a huge boulder with an outstanding bivy site underneath. Pass the boulder on the left and continue up the snow for another pitch. The next rock step, the Flake Gully, is a right leaning ramp that narrows at the top. At the apex, make a face move left onto easier ground (5.8). The next three pitches have several variations. One is to traverse up and left on snow to a narrow weakness in the rocks above. Climb straight up mixed ground for several pitches until a large rock gendarme blocks the way.

The next pitch is the renowned Thin Man's Squeeze. This is a very short but tight water-ice chimney that forms a neat natural passage through this barrier. It is not obvious at first; climb around the left side of the block and you will find the unique hole. If you have a large pack or are a large person, you may want to haul your pack through the hole. Climb through then up the ridge above. Pass a fixed pin then belay at a boulder above with good cracks.

Traverse far to right to avoid the imposing headwall above. Climb up the first weakness and make a sequence of difficult moves up a corner system (5.8). Continue up one more pitch of mixed ground, going straight up at first, then right, and pull over and descend into the first col. This spacious col makes a superb bivy, but is only about a third of the way up the route.

The next several pitches involve only snow climbing. Climb down into the col and up the steep slope on the other side to a long snow arête. As the arête approaches the next rock section, a very prominent S-shaped couloir can be seen snaking through the rocks left of the arête. Half way up the couloir is the gigantic Grey Rock. Underneath this rock is a spectacular bivy site. Climb the S-Couloir, exiting right at the top into a narrow notch in the ridge crest. Climb down slightly onto the other side, then make a horizontal mixed traverse underneath a huge slab to gain the fixed rappel above the Second Col. Rappel 80 feet into the col, being mindful of the huge cornice that forms on the left (west) side.

Cross the col, then climb up 40' of mixed ground on the other side to reach The Slot. Climb out left up The Slot, a difficult chimney followed by an awkward mantle onto a slab (5.8). Continue up around the corner and belay as soon as possible to avoid bad rope drag. Climb steep snow to the ridge crest, and then continue up the long and somewhat corniced ridge for several pitches.

Eventually a second small col and rappel station are reached. It may be possible to down-climb this short descent. Rappel only 40 feet to a small alcove on the climber's right. Climb a short mixed step to a ledge above. Above this a flaky gully heads up and right back toward the ridge crest. Climb this (5.8) and take the right hand exit near the top. This is the last rock climbing step on the route.

Follow the snow or ice arête for three more pitches until forced off the ridge crest to the right by a big boulder. Climb up a steep snow couloir. Exit the couloir either to the left or right, both being about the same difficulty (60 degrees). Climb to the last rock on the ridge crest, below the final ice dome. Climb the 50 to 55-degree ice face for three pitches. The face is only steep for

The Thumb →

Gray Rock →

← S-Couloir

1st Col

← Thin Man's Squeeze

← Flake Gully

about two pitches and then it gradually rolls back to the summit.

Descent:

South Ridge Descent:

From the summit, head east. Immediately, a large bergschrund is encountered. Pass it on the right, then traverse left back to the ridge crest. Follow the low angle ridge east until it starts to steepen considerably. If conditions are good, it is possible to down-climb the entire next section to the rocks low down on the ridge. If down-climbing, climb straight down off the ridge crest on the lowest angle section of snow (45-50 degrees), then start making the long traverse down and right staying 100 to 200 feet below the ridge crest. If down-climbing is not an option, it is possible to rappel using V-thread anchors off available ice bulges nearer to the crest. Make up to 10 traversing rappels toward the rocks low down on the level section of ridge crest (10,100 feet). Locate rappel slings under the first set of rocks encountered. Several rappel lines exist but the general trend is to rappel,

Icefall Hazard

Alternate Descent

Standard Descent

then traverse to the climber's right at the bottom of each rappel to find the next rappel. Stay close to the ridge crest at times, downclimbing on the crest itself. When the ridge crest steepens considerably, rappel straight down and (climber's) right to the glacier below.

From here, carefully consider the following two options:

Option 1: This is the standard descent option, but it is incredibly dangerous. (See Specific Hazards). Head west, straight down the center of the glacier, underneath the huge hanging glacier above. This is a straightforward and fast descent. The objective danger lasts only about 30 minutes. At the base of the glacier, navigate some small crevasses back to base camp.

Option 2: This is a much safer alternative, but much longer as well. After the rappels, climb up to the low point in

the ridge to the south. On the other side, a steep snow couloir leads to the glacier below. Down-climb or rappel this couloir to the West Fork, then go west back up the glacier to base camp.

Descend the Route:

Descending the route is a viable option, especially if you do not make the summit. Many of the rappel stations are fixed from previous attempts. As you get higher, they become less common. Although it has been done, it is not recommended to descend down the south face due to high natural avalanche potential. A major obstacle in descending the route is the Second Col at 10,100 feet. After rappelling into the notch on the descent, it is necessary to ascend the steep wall back out the other side. This requires direct aid and mixed up a steep but short crack system on the right side of the wall.

Other Climbs:

Pt. 6,000, Madera Route and DeClerk/Brueger route

Two short and moderate rock routes are located on the small rock massif just north of Mount Barrill. With easy access from the Mountain House and above average rock for the Gorge, these are great warmup or marginal weather day climbs. Topos are available in the Talkeetna Ranger Station.

Mount Dickey, Snowpatrol

This long route put up, in April of 2004 by Scottish climbers Andy Sharpe and Sam Chinnery, is sure to become a classic. It is probably the first route on the east or south side of Dickey that mortal alpinists may be able to repeat. It is reported to be some 40 pitches of snow, ice, and a little mixed climbing up to WI 5+. Descend the West Face.

Mt Wake, Northeast Ridge

This snow-condition-dependent route has been compared to the (full) West Ridge of the Mooses Tooth. There is a lot of steep and tricky snow terrain as well as free and aid climbing on rock, but the seldom climbed Mount Wake would be a most rewarding experience. Descend the route.

Wisdom Tooth, Base Climbs

A selection of easy and moderate single-pitch climbs exists at the base of the west face of the Wisdom Tooth, just around the corner from the Stump. This is a great spot to do some cragging on a "rest" day. Most of the good-looking cracks are in the 5.7 to 5.10 range. Pick a crack and there is most likely a fixed anchor on top. There is also the opportunity to add more pitches above.

The Stump, Game Boy

Another good-looking route on the Stump is Game Boy. This starts behind the small but prominent tower that stands in front of the Stump to the right of the two dihedral routes. Check the Talkeetna Ranger Station for a good topo.

Sugar Tooth, West Face

In the same cirque as the Eye Tooth is the less impressive Sugar Tooth. Its slabby west wall has an often wet, free, and aid climb that leads to its south ridge. Snow gear must be carried in order to reach the summit. Rappel the route.

London Tower, Northwest Couloir

To the left (north) of the huge west face of London Tower rises a nice looking snow couloir. This would make a great early

season route, comparable to the Japanese Couloir on Mount Barrill. Descend the route.

London Tower, Trailer Park

For those a bit more technically inclined, the Trailer Park (WI 6, M6+), put up in 2000 by Kelly Cordes and Scott DeCapio is a hard test-piece that climbs a couloir that splits up the center of London Tower (to the left of the main summit). Descend off the back side of London Tower, then climb back up to the col south of Hut Tower and descend this couloir back to the Ruth. Check the Talkeetna Ranger Station for an excellent topo.

Rooster Comb, North Buttress

This incredible looking ice line begs to be climbed. Amidst the chaos of the north face of the Rooster Comb, this steep, narrow couloir perfectly splits the massive North Buttress. Start up the lower angled initial couloir and then expect five crux pitches up to M6/AI6 and A2+. At the top of the crux gullies, exit right on an ice ramp to the right ridge crest and then follow this to the summit. Rappel the route.

New Climbs:

Mount Dickey, South Face

There is certainly some bad rock here and there, but there could be a lot of opportunity on this mile-wide big wall.

Mount Bradley, South Face

Reported as being some of the best rock in the Gorge, several lines have been done. Perhaps there is still a bit of potential.

Mount Johnson, East Buttress

Quite possibly the most beautiful unclimbed line in Alaska, this perfect flying buttress is not without attempts. Renee Jackson and Doug Chabot reached a height of 38 pitches and speculated another 15 or so. The route is destined to become climbed, but short of a massive siege attempt it will require some very modern climbing.

Mount Church, North Face

A 4,000-foot couloir splits right up the center of this massive face. Church only has a couple of ascents, and none by a technical route.

Mount Dan Beard, East Face

It's never been done. Maybe for good reason, maybe not.

Peak 11,300, East Face

This is a very complex face composed of numerous steep granite buttresses and dividing couloirs. The face is quite intimidating and there are a few hanging glaciers here and there, but there is certainly lots of opportunity here for new lines.

The East Buttress of Mt. Johnson. Photo by Joe Puryear

Tokositna Glacier

With the exception of Mount Huntington climbers, few people visit the Tokositna Glacier. Sandwiched between the Kahiltna and Ruth Glaciers, the Tokositna isn't as large or far-reaching as its counterparts. Still at 25 miles long it is one of the range's greatest glaciers. Exploration on the Tokositna has been limited because of the difficulty in finding adequate landing spots and the smaller number of accessible major peaks. In addition, there are also no easy routes on the major peaks in the area. The routes on Huntington, Hunter, Thunder, Kahiltna Queen, and the Rooster Comb are all difficult from this side. Two routes on Mount Huntington are highly recommended and are covered here.

Getting There:

Fly into the Northeast Fork of the Tokositna Glacier. Plan for at least a two-week trip into this area. This glacier is a sink for bad weather in the range. It can be sunny and warm everywhere else, but snowing in the "Tok". It is also a difficult spot to land for pilots. Every year at least one plane gets stuck in here. Be prepared to spend a week in here waiting to get out, not to mention a long wait just to get in. Make sure you bring skis or snowshoes to stamp down a runway in the snow. Pilots will need a 30-foot by 1,000-foot strip, with a wider turn-around area at the top. With only two people, this can take days to construct. If it starts snowing, it is best to start work early.

Not all air services will fly into this location. Be sure to ask your service before your trip. The flight takes about 35 minutes one way.

For other routes on Mount Thunder (10,920) and the south side of Hunter, fly to the Southwest Fork of the Tokositna below Mount Thunder's impressive Southeast Face. The same conditions mentioned above apply for this airstrip as well.

Base Camps:

Tokositna Base Camp (8,200 feet): This is the common place where pilots land in the upper Northeast Fork of the Tokositna. It is relatively crevasse-free and safe from avalanches. Set up camp at least a hundred feet from the airstrip to allow planes flexibility in landing. This airstrip services Mount Huntington and Pt. 11,520. Although a difficult eastern bypass to the icefall leading south out of the northern forks of the Tokositna exists, it is not recommended to try to descend out of this basin.

Mount Thunder Base Camp (7,300 feet): Located in the Southwest Fork, this also is a relatively crevasse-free area that is safe from avalanches. Be prepared for heavy snowfall and less plane traffic.

Emergency:

A CB radio is fairly useless on the Tokositna Glacier. There is no one that constantly monitors any channels and most aircraft are not CB-enabled. Occasionally a faint signal can be transmitted to Kahiltna Base Camp but it is unreliable. Having an aircraft radio (for emergencies only) or satellite phone, at least in base camp, is a good idea. Again, a good reasonable method is to stomp a large (10-foot by 30-foot or larger) SOS into the snow. Enough planes frequent the area that it is bound to be seen. Try to get any injured persons to the Tokositna Base Camp. Remember, with the inherent difficulty in accessing this airstrip, rescue may be complicated and time-consuming.

For a map of the Tokositna area, see page 124. See page 45 for a map of the Southwest Fork.

Mount Huntington

This nearly perfect pyramid of rock and ice has captured the imagination of climbers around the world. Mount Huntington (12,240') was named in 1910 by the Brown-Parker expedition. Archer Milton Huntington (1870-1955), who was president of the American Geographical Society, sponsored their trip. The mountain was first climbed in 1964 by a French team led by Lionel Terray, via its Northwest Ridge. Until more modern advances in ice-climbing, this horribly corniced ridge was considered the "easiest" route. Due to the extraordinary objective risk of the north face and the extreme remoteness of the east face, nearly all current attempts are focused on the broad west face. There are no fewer than 10 routes and variations between the French Ridge on the left and the South Ridge on the right. The mountain gets visited several times each season with people lining up to try the West Face Couloir. The nearby Harvard Route also provides an outstanding alpine challenge.

Mt. Huntington from the northwest. Photo by Mike Gauthier

Harvard Route

Difficulty: VI, 5.9, A2, 70-degree ice

Elevation gain: On route: 3,250'. From the airstrip: 4,000'

Total time: 1-2 weeks

Approach time: 1-2 hours

Climbing time: Up: 2-5 days. Down: 10-16 hours

Season: April to mid-June, May is best

The Harvard Route has become almost a lost classic in the Alaska Range. As soon as it was realized that the West Face Couloir, right next to the Harvard, was the easiest route to the summit, climbers began to overlook the more aesthetic lines on this incredible peak. The Harvard is by all means a pleasing and elegant line, characterized by outstanding pure rock, mixed, and steep aid climbing on some of the best granite in the range. This stunning arête that perfectly splits the west face defines the essence of alpine climbing on a peak some maintain is the most beautiful in all of North America.

FA: June 29 to July 30, 1965; summit on July 30; David S. Roberts, Don C. Jensen, Edward M. Bernd, and Matthew Hale, Jr..

History

The first ascent of the central arête of the west face was made by none other than the Harvard Climbing Club. The greatness of the accomplishment was somewhat overshadowed by the death of Ed Bernd on the descent. It was one of those freak and unfortunate accidents that no climber can ever prepare for.

This monumental climb started on June 29, 1965. The team of four was flown into the Northwest Fork of the Tokositna Glacier beneath Mount Hunter. Most parties now fly into the Northeast Fork directly under the peak. They were required to shuttle their gear four miles to the base of the route, which required five long days to do.

As was common of the time, they used expedition style tactics to tackle the climb. More accurately, they did the climb capsule

style – two climbers led and pushed the route forward fixing ropes and gear, while the other two climbers hauled supplies and prepared camps.

They climbed easily to the 8,900-foot col that defined the base of the arête. The initial section that they dubbed the Stegosaur proved very difficult as it was heavily corniced on one side and had steep rock walls on the other. By July 15, they had only managed 15 pitches due to the difficult climbing and the inclement weather. They had not even had a look at the main headwall higher on the route that they knew would contain the crux.

They finally set their first camp below the Alley, a narrow couloir that separated two small hanging snowfields low on the route. On July 20, Jensen and Bernd first attacked the Spiral – the first difficult pitches of the headwall. At last the weather started to improve and the team made faster progress, climbing pitch after pitch of sustained technical terrain. After several difficult pitches, they forged the route to the base of what they called the Nose. This was a prominent roof feature that they had picked out from below as being the probable crux of the route. On July 26, Hale easily aided up the gently overhanging hand crack and over the roof lip to complete the hardest climbing on the route.

Jensen and Bernd then raced up snow and easier mixed ground to reach the final summit ice field. They set up a small bivy at the only rock boulder on the face and waited for Roberts and Hale. As soon as they arrived they agreed to go for the summit and they reached it at 3:30 A.M. on July 30, in the luminescent radiance of the sunrise. Relieved and overjoyed, they celebrated over 30 days of hard work.

The team immediately descended all the way to Nose camp, which they reached after moving for 25 hours straight. The next day, Bernd and Roberts started down first, while Hale and Jensen would come down in a couple days, and clean the remaining fixed lines. The accident happened just one rappel from reaching the bottom of the headwall and easier ground. Just before midnight, while setting up the rappel,

Detail of the Harvard Route on the West face of Mt. Huntington. Photo by Mike Gauthier

Summit Ice Field
Boulder →

ench Ridge

The Cave →

West Face
Couloir

← The Nose

Phantom Wall

The Bastion

The Spiral

Upper Park

→ The Alley

Lower Park

Access Couloir

The Stegosaur

Bernd commented on how good and awake he felt. Moments later as he leaned back to make the rappel something caused his rappel carabineer to fail, and he tumbled down the Spiral and out of sight of Roberts, probably not stopping for some 4,000 feet. Roberts was able to use fixed ropes to safely make it back to the Alley camp. Hale and Jensen finally came down two days later on August 1 and learned of the horrible accident and death of their dear friend. The next day the team of three completed the descent and five days later they flew out with Sheldon.

The second ascent of the route was almost made alpine style by Bruce Wehman and Dean Smith in July of 1975. After fixing ropes on the Stegosaur, they dropped a 600-

Joe Puryear aiding up the gently overhanging Nose Roof. Photo by Mark Westman

foot rope straight down the access couloir, hence were the first ones to climb this popular variation. They climbed the route round-trip in six days after fixing the initial section.

Strategy:

Plan for at least a two-week trip into the Tokositna Glacier. Expect to take a minimum of two entire days on the route and a half day for the descent. Three or four days is a more comfortable schedule. A very fast party can start early in the morning and make the base of the Nose in a day. From there another long day can be spent climbing to the summit and returning to the bivy. It still takes another half day to descend back to the airstrip from there. A slower party will want to make an additional bivy on the Upper Park, and possibly another bivy higher on the route.

Beware there are really no good protected bivouacs on the route. If it starts snowing heavily, the entire west face becomes a torrent of spindrift and sometimes larger avalanches. Even the Nose bivy can get pummeled. Luckily, the route is not too committing as it is only necessary to rappel off from any point to retreat.

Specific Hazards:

Watch for avalanche conditions in the access couloir and on the upper snow fields.

Gear:

Take six or seven cams to three inches with two extra one-inch and 1.5-inch sizes. Take one set of stoppers, a selection of four to six thin and medium pins, six to eight ice screws, and two pickets. Take two 200-foot ropes. Consider bringing a lead line and a haul line since some pitches will necessitate jumaring. Take one set of etriers each and ascenders. Bring two ice tools per person.

Camps:

Advanced Base Camp (8,900 feet): Some climbers may wish to get a closer look at the route and camp in the upper basin. Don't be tempted to camp directly underneath the West Face. In April of 1998, a massive slab avalanche came off from below the

West Face Couloir and wiped out a team's old camp and cache in the basin below. The climbers were fortunate only to lose their snowshoes and their radio. A better place to camp is near the 8,950-foot col at the base of the Stegosaur at the south end of the basin.

Upper Park (10,200 feet): Anywhere on the Upper Park would make suitable bivy. At the top there is a large boulder with a fixed pin. This is probably the best spot to dig a platform. If trying to weather out a storm, this spot is not safe from avalanches.

The Nose (c. 11,000 feet): The biggest and best bivy on the route is underneath the Nose roof. There is an odd arrangement of old bolts on the wall above providing a good anchor. Don't be fooled into thinking this is a very sheltered spot though. Spindrift still funnels in here.

The Cave (c. 11,400 feet): If you continue above the Nose with bivy gear, good campsites are difficult to find. The large cave on the traverse could be dug into for a very small bivy or brew stop.

Off-route Bivy (c. 11,500 feet): Above the cave, there is a steep snow ramp that leads up and left to a decent bivy site. This looks like it might actually be the way to go, but the wall above is steep and difficult. Making this the high camp will necessitate rappelling down the couloir back to the route, then climbing back up to camp on the descent.

Summit Ice-field Boulder (c. 11,800 feet): This was the high camp of the first ascent party. Although the boulder provides a good anchor, it would be time-consuming to chop a ledge under it, especially when you are so close to the summit.

Approach:

From the airstrip, head up toward the base, passing the small icefall on the left, and into the basin above (8,900 feet). Cross the basin to the south and head for the access couloir that leads up to the Harvard ridge. This six-pitch couloir bypasses the original start, The Stegosaur, which is rarely climbed

Mark Westman leading the Spiral in snowy conditions. Photo by Joe Puryear

anymore. If the bergschrund proves to difficult to pass here, a couloir further right can be used to access the Stegosaur at a lower point.

Route:

Access Couloir:

Cross the bergschrund at the left side of the couloir and head to the base of a short but steep ice step (75 degrees). Climb this then continue up the 55-degree couloir using snow and ice pro and fixed anchors on the left side of the couloir. The top of the couloir breaks out into the top of the Lower Park. It's possible to bivouac here but a better one is to be found a few pitches higher.

The Alley and Upper Park:

Climb up and right into the above gully with a short mixed step at its top. This leads to the Upper Park. There is a two-pin fixed anchor on the only boulder protruding from the snow here. Depending on the amount of snow, the anchor could be buried. From here, climb up the moderate snow for two pitches to a larger boulder on the crest of the arête with a single fixed pin. This makes a great bivy or you could bivy almost anywhere on the Upper Park.

The Spiral:

This is where the real climbing begins. Climb up and right on snow, heading toward the prominent dihedral at the snow's apex. This is the Spiral. Climb the pure rock dihedral (5.9) and belay at a fixed piton anchor on top. For the second pitch of the Spiral, climb out left on ice for fifty feet then up steep mixed ground. Climb a short bit of A2 up a thin seam, or climb mixed terrain around. Continue straight up easier mixed ground and sling a boulder for the belay.

The Bastion:

From here there are three route options. The best option is to climb up and right 30 feet then make a 60-foot horizontal traverse right to gain a fixed anchor at the bottom of a huge right curving chimney/dihedral. Climb the chimney (5.9) and exit right. Instead of climbing the chimney, the second option is to climb the narrow couloir that exits up and right from the belay. Stand atop a huge horn and aid up a crack 50 feet (A1). Either way will lead to a main gully system in the center of the face. The third and least favorable option is to climb straight up from the top of the Spiral on snow and easy mixed ground to the base of the Bastion, the huge granite buttress looming above. Here you should find an old bolt anchor on the wall. Climb a dihedral up and right (M5 A2+) to a ledge with a slung horn. Do a short traverse right (5.7) back into the main gully system.

Climb this snow or ice gully for three pitches (up to 60 degrees). When it ends at a wall above, traverse out left then back up for a pitch and this will deposit you at the base of the Nose.

The Nose:

This is the best bivy you'll get on the upper section of the route. From here it's possible to go to the summit and back in a push if conditions are good. The next pitch climbs the beautiful Nose roof. Traverse 50 feet left from the bivy and locate a shallow dihedral with a thin crack, underneath the imposing black roof with a diagonal hand crack. Aid up the crack (A2), step left, then aid the slightly overhanging crack up and right. Eventually take a thin crack to overcome the lip of the roof and aid back up and left to a belay on a pedestal. From here traverse left on slabby mixed ground for 30 feet then head up the main ramp system for three pitches of snow (50 degrees) to meet the intersection with the West Face Couloir.

Upper Slopes:

From here route-finding can be a bit tricky. Generally you want to keep heading up and right but not go up too soon to gain the Summit Ice Field. After two pitches, you will see a big cave and a steep ice ramp heading up and left. There is a good bivy atop this ramp, but it is the wrong way to continue up. Keep trending up and right for two more pitches, overcoming a couple short steep mixed steps. Eventually the rock band above narrows and it will be easy to break through it via a short mixed pitch. Another option is to continue traversing right until able to skirt the rocks completely and then traverse back left. Once on the ice field, climb straight up 50 degree ice for four pitches until you intersect the French Ridge. After two pitches, you will reach the summit ice field boulder which has a fixed anchor. Follow the ridge several rope lengths to the summit. There is a steep snow fluting to overcome and the ridge is very corniced and crevassed. Just beyond the summit is a quite large area that would accommodate an outstanding, if not risky, bivy site.

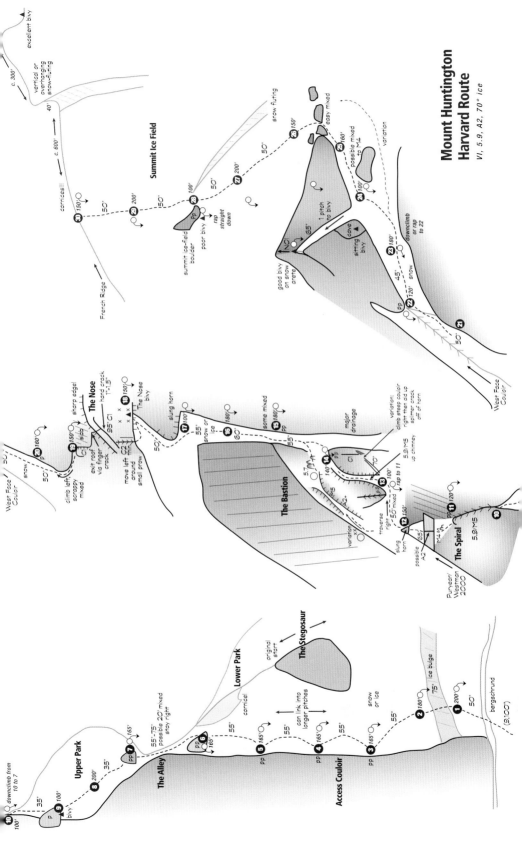

Mount Huntington
Harvard Route
VI, 5.9, A2, 70° ice

Descent:

Climb back down the ridge, then rappel or down-climb to the ice field boulder. Instead of retracing your ascent route, it is possible to rappel straight down and slightly to the climber's left. Find fixed anchors on rock out-croppings below and rappel back to the line of ascent. Then make two traversing raps off rock back to the Harvard and West Face Couloir confluence. If you didn't leave any gear on the Harvard you could rap down the West Face Couloir. Otherwise, continue down the Harvard. Most of the raps are fixed on rock. After reaching the Upper Park, down-climb to the boulder atop Pitch 7, then continue rappelling off fixed anchors. A V-thread or two may be required in the lower gully. In total, it is about 24 rappels plus some down-climbing.

The Bastion

The Spiral

Upper Park

Detail of the Spiral and the Bastion from the Upper Park. The middle line is the preferred variation. Photo by Joe Puryear.

West Face Couloir

Difficulty: **V, 85-degree ice**

Elevation gain: **On route: 3,250'. From airstrip: 4,000'**

Total time: **1-2 weeks**

Approach time: **1-2 hours**

Climbing time: **Up: 12-24 hours. Down: 8-14 hours**

Season: **April to mid-June, May is best**

Upon seeing Mount Huntington for the first time, it's hard to imagine there to be any easy way to access its perfect pyramidal summit. The north face is dominated by massive hanging glaciers and huge seracs. The eastern face is a complicated façade of steep buttresses above impassable glaciers. And the west face, the most often photographed, is a steep and seemingly impenetrable fortress of rock and ice. On this wall, however, there exists a hidden ice couloir that splits the striated rock to allow a cunning passage to the summit of this stately mountain. The West Face Couloir is a straightforward ice climb with easy access, a short approach, and an uncomplicated descent. Although not as inspiring a line as the neighboring Harvard Route, this is the line that will get you to the summit.

FA: To within 200 feet of the summit ridge: April 1978; John Evans and Denny Hogan; To the summit ridge (intersecting the French Ridge route): June 1978; Steve and Ron Matous and Bruce Adams. To the summit: May 24, 1989; Dave Nettle and James Quirk.

History

Similar to the North Buttress of Mount Hunter, the West Face Couloir is festooned with controversy over its first ascent. Denny Hogan, Vic Walsh, and John Evans first climbed the West Face Couloir in April of 1978. They made a camp at the top of the snow face leading to the couloir. After fixing three pitches of difficult ice, they made a single push attempt but retreated in the face of severe spindrift. Hogan and Evans made a second effort, climbing nine pitches of ice to the intersection with the Harvard. They decided to push directly to the summit, but ended up traversing back

left to the summit snow field boulder as darkness came. They bivied at the boulder and made one final attempt for the summit. They reached a point just below the French Ridge, but retreated as a storm approached. This was an outstanding effort as they completed all the new terrain of the West Face Couloir, but weren't able to tag the summit.

In June of the same year, Steve and Ron Matous and Bruce Adams climbed the same route and were able to complete the West Face to the French Ridge, just a couple hundred feet below the summit. There was a least one more early-on attempt that climbed the couloir to the confluence of the Harvard Route.

In May of 1989, Dave Nettle and James Quirk climbed the route to the summit of Mount Huntington and in a front section article in the 1990 AAJ, claimed the first ascent.

In 2002, Mount Huntington received its first solo by the West Face Couloir. Alaskan hardman Chris Turiano free-soloed the route in 17 hours round-trip.

Strategy:

The route is excellent for alpinists to test their light and fast skills. The route is straightforward and so is the descent. One of the most successful strategies of recent times is for teams to leave behind bivy gear and bring good down jackets, a shovel, and a stove. Instead of a full-fledged bivy, an extended brew and rest stop allows climbers to not have to worry about digging an adequate bivy site. And lighter packs allow climbers to focus more on the enjoyable climbing.

Specific Hazards:

Watch avalanche conditions on the initial snow face and the upper ice slopes. Although rockfall is not common in the couloir, it is not unheard of.

Gear:

Take four to five cams to two inches, one set of stoppers, eight to 10 ice screws, and two pickets. Take two 200-foot ropes. Bring two ice-tools per person.

West Face Couloir

Harvard Route

Camps:

Advanced Base Camp (8,900 feet):
Some climbers may wish to get a closer
look at the route and camp in the
upper basin. Don't be tempted to camp
directly underneath the West Face. In
April of 1998, a massive slab avalanche
came off from below the West Face
Couloir and wiped out a climber's old
camp and cache in the basin below.
The climber's were fortunate only to
lose their snowshoes and their radio. A
better place to camp is near the 8,950-
foot col at the base of the Stegosaur at
the south end of the basin.

**The Nose (Harvard Route) (c.11,000
feet):** It is a mistake to believe that it
is easy to get to the Nose bivy on the
Harvard Route from the confluence of
the two routes. This bivy takes three
full length rappels to reach, and the last
one must be fixed over the Nose Roof.
This would necessitate using ascenders
and etriers to re-climb; gear that would
not normally be taken on this route.
It would also involve re-climbing the
awkward mixed pitch above the Nose, then
another 300 feet of snow or ice back to the
confluence. This option for bivying is not
recommended.

The Cave (c. 11,400 feet): The large cave
on the traverse could be dug into for a very
small bivy or brew stop.

Off-route Bivy (c. 11,500 feet): Above
the cave, there is a steep snow ramp that
leads up and left to a decent bivy site. This
looks like it might actually be the way to
go, but the wall above is steep and difficult.
Making this the high-camp will necessitate
rappelling down the couloir back to the
route, then climbing back up to camp on
the descent.

Summit Ice-Field Boulder (c. 11,800 feet):
This was the high-camp of the first ascent
party. Although the boulder provides a
good anchor, it would be time-consuming
to chop a ledge under it, especially when
you are so close to the summit.

Georgie Stanley leading the opening crux pitch of the couloir.
Photo by Dave Anderson

Approach:

From the airstrip, head up toward the
base, passing the small icefall on the left,
and into the basin above. Locate the West
Face Couloir above and the large snow face
below it. Look for the best place to cross
the bergschrund and climb toward the
couloir.

Route:

Ascend the initial 45 to 55-degree 700-foot
snow face toward the couloir. At the top of
the face, skirt right around a rock outcrop
and then traverse back left and up to the
base of the wall on the left (north) side
of the couloir. Here lies the crux of the
route, two steep ice or mixed pitches up to
85 degrees. Depending on the time of the
year, these pitches can be straightforward
ice or thinner and more mixed. Continue
up the huge ramp for 10 more pitches of 55
to 60-degree ice. At the top of the couloir

the route merges with the Harvard Route. Check the Harvard Route topo for more detail.

From here route-finding can be a bit tricky. Generally you want to keep heading up and right but not go up too soon to gain the upper ice field. After two pitches, you will see a big cave and a steep ice ramp heading up and left. There is a good bivy atop this ramp, but it is the wrong way to continue up. Keep trending up and right for two more pitches, overcoming a couple short steep mixed steps. Eventually the rock band above narrows and it will be easy to break through it via a short mixed pitch. Another option is to continue traversing right until able to skirt the rocks completely, and then traverse back left. Once on the ice field, climb straight up 50-degree ice for four pitches until you intersect the French Ridge. After two pitches, you will reach the summit ice field boulder which has a fixed anchor. Follow the ridge several rope lengths to the summit. There is a steep snow fluting to overcome and the ridge is very corniced and crevassed.

Descent:

Down-climb back down the ridge, then rappel or down-climb to the ice field boulder. Instead of retracing your ascent route, it is possible to rappel straight down and slightly to the climber's left. Find fixed anchors on rock out-croppings below and rappel back to the line of ascent. Then make two traversing raps off rock back to the Harvard and West Face Couloir confluence. Continue down the couloir using V-threads. Down-climb the final snow slope to the glacier.

Andy Johnson leading on the mid-section of the couloir. Photo by Roy Leggett

Other Climbs:

Mount Huntington

Mount Huntington's West Face has probably received more attention per square foot than any other face in the range. From the French (Northwest) Ridge on the left, to the South Ridge on the right, there are at least 10 routes and variations. Some worth considering are:

Colton-Leach: Similar to the West Face Couloir but more difficult and less direct, this ice and mixed route climbs the major gully system to the left of the large central buttress (Count Zero Buttress) on the left of the West Face Couloir. The climbing is great up to the point where you must traverse right several pitches and gain the upper French Ridge. Descend the Harvard Route or West Face Couloir.

Phantom Wall: This wall to the south of the Harvard Route is huge and intimidating but looks to be one of the best routes in the range. It is still unrepeated after Jay Smith and Paul Teare made their impressive ascent in May 1991. Approach by descending on the left (east) side of the main icefall heading out of the Northeast Fork. Descend the Harvard Route or West Face Couloir.

Pt. 11,520, North Face

This sub-peak of Mount Hunter's East Ridge sits halfway up the Northwest Fork of the Tokositna and is easily accessible from the Huntington airstrip. A route was climbed in May of 2002 via an ice and mixed route on its North Face by climbers Anna Keeling and Karen McNeill. The line is direct and certainly looks worth repeating. Descend the route.

Kahiltna Queen, South Face

Kahiltna Queen sits at the head of the Northwest Fork of the Tokositna, just opposite Mount Hunter and about four miles from the Huntington airstrip. Its south face has a moderate couloir used by the first ascensionists of the peak. Two harder routes were climbed in 2003 up weaknesses in the huge wall to the right of the couloir. Descend the route.

Thunder Mountain, Southeast Face

While not accessible from the same landing strip as Huntington, the 3,300-foot Southeast Face of Thunder Mountain holds enough climbing for an entire trip. Several gigantic granite buttresses rise in perfect proportion while steep ice and mixed gullies split between them. A few routes have been climbed and several more exist.

Mount Hunter

Several rarely-climbed Mount Hunter routes are accessed via the Tokositna. Climbs such as the South Ridge (location of the Happy Cowboys Traverse) and the difficult Southeast Spur are accessed from the Southwest Fork. Several other routes await second ascents.

New Climbs:

East Fork of the Tokositna (Diamond Arête Cirque)

Only one pilot in the range may or may not land you here, but if you could get in here several huge granite buttresses await potential alpine rock enthusiasts.

Southwest Fork of the Tokositna

Besides new route possibilities on Mt. Thunder, Mount Providence (11,200 feet), the next peak to the northeast, has only one ascent by its south face. There are certainly more routes available. Also several very small and sharp unclimbed peaks line the east side of the Tokositna across from the airstrip.

Little Switzerland

While not nearly as grandiose as the Ruth Gorge or the Kichatnas, Little Switzerland sports a fine array of quality granite rock routes. In early season there are ample possibilities for snow, ice, and mixed climbing as well. Vaguely similar to some of the real Swiss Alps, Little Switzerland, named by glacier pilot Don Sheldon, refers to a grouping of small peaks and glaciers 35 miles south of Denali. The main glacier is the Pika Glacier, a small southeastern arm of the greater Kahiltna Glacier. Most climbers focus their attention here because the routes are bigger, more solid, and easier to get to. Other glaciers in the group include the Crown, Hidden, and Granite, all of which are rarely visited. Little Switzerland is a fun alternative to the major peaks in the range and a week or two spent here rock climbing after a big expedition is a great way to finish off the season. It has also become very popular with guide services offering instructional courses in rock climbing and ski touring.

Getting There:

There are two options for getting to Little Switzerland:

1. Nearly all parties fly with a licensed air service out of Talkeetna. The main landing area is on the Pika Glacier and several different air services will land on this straightforward airstrip. If wanting to land on other glaciers in the area, be sure to discuss this with your air service before your trip. The flight takes about 35 minutes one way.

2. A walk-in approach is possible, but I'll leave most of the adventure of that up to you. Here's the general idea: At the town of Trapper Creek on the George

Climber on the Royal Tower with the Trolls behind. Photo by Brian McCullough

Parks Highway (mile 114.5), turn left on Petersville Road. Drive this rough road to a parking area at about mile 33. Go up Peters Creek and over a pass into Bear Creek. Go up Bear Creek then up Wildhorse Creek. Go over the pass and down into Granite Creek. Go up the creek and onto the Granite Glacier. Travel up the glacier taking its West Fork. Go northwest to the 5,850-foot pass separating the Granite and Pika Glaciers. This is called Exit Pass. Go southwest down the glacier and onto the main Pika Glacier. Allow 3-4 days for the trip.

Base Camps:

Pika Base Camp (5,600 feet): The airstrip changes slightly with the time of year and season, it is usually near the head of the glacier. Most parties find it sufficient to set up their base camp near where the plane drops them off. From here all of the climbs are very accessible. The farther you drag your equipment from the plane, the less noisy it will be.

Emergency:

A CB radio is ineffective in Little Switzerland. A cell phone may work from the ridges and summits of peaks on the east side of the Pika Glacier, but not from the Pika Glacier itself or even the low cols of the Pika. An aircraft radio (for emergencies only) or satellite phone is a good bet for emergency situations. A good reasonable method is to stomp a large (10-foot by 30-foot or larger) SOS into the snow. Enough planes frequent the area that it is bound to be seen. Self-rescue to the Pika airstrip is always the best option if possible.

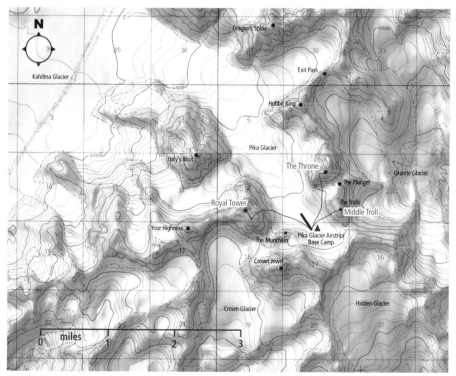

Map: Talkeetna C-3

Middle Troll, South Face

Difficulty: **III, 5.8, 45-degree snow**

Elevation gain: **1,300'**

Total time: **1-2 weeks**

Approach time: **10 minutes**

Climbing time: **Up: 2-5 hours. Down: 1-3 hours**

Season: **Mid-May to August**

The three Trolls stand guard on the eastern rim of the upper Pika Glacier. They provide the easiest access of all the peaks in the area, being a mere ten minutes from the airstrip. The rock tends to be some of the best in Little Switzerland and many quality routes can be explored among the formations. In particular, the South Face of the Middle Troll (6,900 feet) is a fine objective on excellent rock and can either be a quick warmup for harder routes, or a fun goal for less experienced parties. The climb actually faces more southwest, but is commonly referred to as the South Face. As with all of the climbs in the area, the crux of the climb may be crossing the ever-changing moats and bergschrunds below the rock.

FA: June 1984; Pete Pollard and John Rich.

History

In June of 1984, Reese Martin, Pete Pollard, and John Rich spent a very successful 17 days in Little Switzerland. The trio made a 23-hour round trip push of a new route on the southwest buttress of the Throne. They went on to make a 30-hour climb of a new route on the southwest face of the Dragon's Spine. Pollard and Martin then made the probable first ascent of the Munchkin (6,200 feet), the small satellite peak immediately southeast of Royal Tower. Finally, Pollard and Rich climbed what they called the South Face of the Middle Troll. They reported the climb as a new route variation on clean rock. It is unknown if there were prior attempts on this formation.

Strategy:

Earlier in the season much of the rock on the lower face will be covered in snow, making the gully start more attractive. As the rock melts out, it is favorable to climb as much rock as possible by starting near its toe. Much of the lower route is quite easy in grade and could be simul-climbed. It's best to leave your snow gear at the point that you access the rock.

**Middle Troll
South Face**

III, 5.8, 45° snow

(6,900')

huge
overhanging
fin

7 200'

80'

3rd class

6 150'
100'

5.7 face
to anchor

5.8

5.7

50'

5 170'
60'

chimney

South Troll

left
crest

5.5   5.8

5.6

100'

broken
5.5-5.6

ramps

slabs

70'

4 160'

5.4

60'

5.4

100'

3 100'

4th
class

downclimb 30'

4th
class

4th
class

ROCK
FALL!!

2 200'

90'

3rd
class

100'

50°

snow
gully

5.6

broken

1 200'

covered in
snow early
season

3rd and 4th
class

loose

200'
over bergschrund

variation

bergschrund (6,000')

start

Specific Hazards:

There is often rock fall down the gully separating the South and Middle Troll.

Gear:

Take one set of cams to three inches, one set of stoppers, slings and draws. One or two pickets may help protect the bergschrund crossing and the lower snow sections. One 200-foot rope is all that is necessary on the route, but an extra 200-foot rope left at the base of the rock will help facilitate the descent down the snow. Take ice axe and crampons to the base of the rock.

The South Face of the Middle Troll. Photo by Joe Puryear

Camps:

Camp at the Pika Base Camp.

Approach:

From the airstrip, hike directly to the base of the Middle Troll. Find a good bergschrund crossing, and then climb straight to the right side of the base of the formation.

Route:

From the base of the rock there are two options. The rock climbing can be started from the lowest point, which provides fun low 5th class climbing, or you can continue up the gully between the South and Middle Troll for several more hundred feet, then cut into the route up higher, finishing with the three last pitches. Check the topo for specific route details.

On the summit is the most amazing leaning block that provides an excellent photo opportunity for those willing to scoot out towards its edge. From the air it has the shape of a grizzly bear, keeping a watchful eye over the Pika.

Descent:

Rappel the route. The route is set up to be rappelled with one 200-foot rope. Several of the rappels are purposely short to avoid rope drag and snagging. However, later in the season as the route melts out it is possible to rappel over the bergschrund with two 200-foot ropes from the lowest rocks on the face.

The Throne,
The Lost Marsupial

Difficulty: **III, 5.8**

Elevation gain: **On route: 1,300'. From the Airstrip: 1,800'**

Total time: **1-2 weeks**

Approach time: **30 minutes**

Climbing time: **Up: 4-8 hours. Down: 3-6 hours**

Season: **Late-May to August**

Directly across the Pika Glacier from the Royal Tower lies the hulking mass of The Throne (7,390 feet). This appealing peak quite possibly has the best rock in the area. It offers a variety of routes from the vertical west wall, to the more broken south face, to lesser known routes on its north and east faces. From the summit, the views of Foraker, Denali, and Hunter are nothing short of spectacular. The peak consists of two bulky masses separated by a deep cleft up its south face. To the left of this cleft a rounded but distinct ridge provides a fun and safe route up to the main east-west trending ridge crest. If snow conditions (or lack thereof) allow, this interesting knife-edge ridge makes a magnificent finish to the top summit block. This route, The Lost Marsupial, is one of many great routes that climbers enjoy on The Throne's south face.

FA: July 15, 1996; Campbell Mercer and Matt Walsh.

History:

In July of 1996, an Australian team of four arrived in Alaska and ran a tour de force in Little Switzerland. The climbers were Campbell Mercer, Rob Pease, Matt Walsh, and Mike Woolridge. While Pease and Woolridge made the first ascent of the Northeast Ridge of the North Troll, Mercer and Walsh repeated the Plunger (which they named Fish Tail Spire) and climbed a short new route on the South Face of The Throne called Half Way Hotel. On July 15, Mercer and Walsh ascended The Lost Marsupial on The Throne's South Face. The pair reached the summit ridge, but did not continue to the summit, probably due to terrible snow

conditions. They rappelled straight down their line of ascent. The four of them went on to do two new routes on the Royal Tower's east face: Di's Surprise by Pease and Woolridge and Boomerang Buttress by Mercer and Walsh. They also climbed many short rock routes on The Munchkin, which they entitled Little Arapiles.

Strategy:

The route can be climbed in one day round trip from camp. Snow gear can generally be left at the base after crossing the bergschrund, unless planning to complete the climb up the summit ridge under snowy conditions. The summit ridge generally melts out by late July or early August, allowing much easier passage to the top.

Michelle Puryear cruising up solid granite just below the summit ridge. Photo by Joe Puryear

Specific Hazards:

The gully to the right of the route has considerable rockfall that spills down the snow cone used to access the route.

Gear:

Take one set of cams to three inches, one set of stoppers, draws, and slings. A picket might be useful to protect the bergschrund

crossing. Take one 200-foot rope. Bring an ice axe for the snow leading up to the base.

Camps:

Camp at the Pika Base Camp.

Approach:

From the Pika Base Camp, go north toward The Throne. Stay close to the North Troll and climb a short snow slope to the flat crevassed area below the south face of The Throne. Climb the snow cone that comes out of the central couloir of the South Face and look for an adequate bergschrund crossing. Because the bottom part of the route is ledgy, the bergschrund can be crossed in several places along the side of the snow cone, then moderate rock leads up to the base of the ridge.

Route:

Once over the bergschrund, follow the topo to the summit.

Descent:

The route is equipped to be rappelled with one 200-foot rope, although two ropes could expedite a few of the rappels. Down-climb from the summit back along the sharp west ridge to the top of the route. Rappel the line of ascent.

The Lost Marsupial on the south face of the Throne. Photo by Joe Puryear

The Throne
The Lost Marsupial
III, 5.8

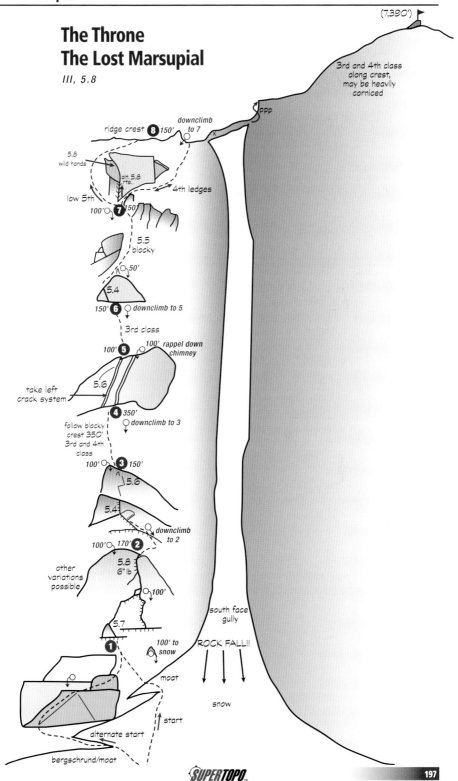

(7,390')

3rd and 4th class
along crest,
may be heavily
corniced

ppp

downclimb
to 7

ridge crest **8** 150'

x

5.8
wild hands

alt. 5.8
rte.

4th ledges

low 5th

100' **7** 150'

5.5
blocky

5.4

150' **6** downclimb to 5

3rd class

100' **5** 100' rappel down
chimney

take left
crack system

5.6

4 350'
downclimb to 3

follow blocky
crest 350'
3rd and 4th
class

100' **3** 150'

5.6

5.4

downclimb
to 2

100' 170' **2**

5.8
6" lb

other
variations
possible

100'

5.7

1

100' to
snow

south face
gully

ROCK FALL!!

moat

snow

start

alternate start

bergschrund/moat

The Royal Tower, Gargoyle Buttress

Difficulty: **IV, 5.10a**

Elevation gain: **2,500'**

Total time: **1-2 weeks**

Approach time: **20 minutes**

Climbing time: **Up: 7-16 hours. Down: 3-7 hours**

Season: **June to August**

The Royal Tower (8,130 feet) is the tallest and most prominent peak in Little Switzerland. With its twin summits and amazing flying buttresses into the Pika, it is this peak that defines the essence of the region's namesake. To the left of the major gully that divides the east face is a sweeping ridge of granite of near perfect proportions. This, the Gargoyle Buttress, is by far the most striking and obvious line out of the Pika Glacier. While most parties will be content to just complete the rock climbing portion of the route, it is the complete package that makes it one of the finest alpine climbs in the region. Although the natural line finishes at the slightly lower South Summit, to stand on either summit of this grand massif is a notable accomplishment. First ascensionist Dave Anderson recalls that the "featured rock and great moderate crack systems as well as the breath-taking positions encountered along the route are incredible."

FA: June 26, 1999; Dave Anderson and Rob Feeney.

History

In late-June of 1997, Kristian Sieling and Doug Munoz climbed a direct route up the left side of the buttress dubbed The Chase (IV, 5.10, A2). The Gargoyle Buttress intersects this route one pitch from the top of the rock. Prior to 1999, there were several mostly undocumented attempts on this right-hand route that probably reached no higher than pitch 6. On June 20, 1999 Dave Anderson and Rob Feeney flew into the Pika Glacier. They warmed up by climbing the South Face of the Middle Troll. On June 26, they started up the Royal Tower at 5:00 A.M. with unstable weather. Anderson remarks, "The climbing was moderate and we passed many rap anchors, some that where composed of three camming units that were left by either really rich climbers or climbers that got really hammered by the AK weather." This might have been a hint as to what was to come. While half way up Pitch 8 or 9 it started dumping snow. They retreated to a small ledge and pulled out their ultra-lightweight bivy gear—two large garbage bags. After a few hours, the snow fortunately stopped and the rock dried out and they continued to the top of the rock section, arriving nine hours after they left. They named the route Gargoyle Buttress, referring to the distinct rock formation that looms on top of the buttress.

Anderson and Feeney later on that trip managed to free climb the Plunger, a small rock spire next to The Throne, at 5.12a/b.

Strategy:

Most parties will be able to complete the climb in one long day. Since all of the anchors and rappels are fixed, there is a low commitment factor and you can bail off from any point on the climb. Remember, with the long Alaskan days you can sometimes climb comfortably throughout the darkest hours.

Many parties that attempt the route find it only necessary to climb to the top of the rock and then descend. If this is the case, only basic rock gear and light day packs need to be carried. Planning on summiting the Royal Tower adds an entirely different element to the climb. With 500 feet of snow above the rock, it is necessary to carry boots and an ice axe to complete the climb.

Specific Hazards:

The bottom three pitches are seriously threatened by snow and rock avalanches. The bottom of the route is disconcertingly close to the gully on the right. Avalanches come off the wall on the right side of the gully and occasionally spill over the route.

Gear:

Take a double set of cams to two inches, one three-inch piece, and one four-inch piece. Take a set of stoppers, draws, and

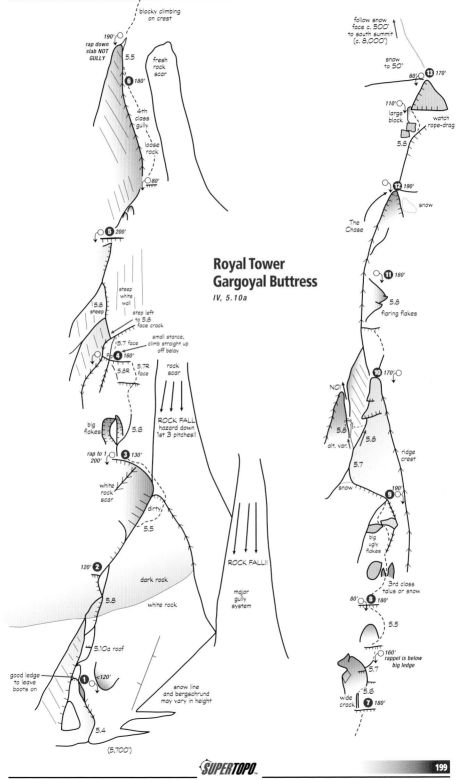

follow snow
face c. 500'
to south summit
(c. 8,000')

blocky climbing
on crest

190'
rap down
slab NOT
GULLY

5.5

fresh
rock
scar

6 180'

4th
class
gully

loose
rock

80'

5 200'

snow
to 50'

60' 13 170'

110'
large
block

watch
rope-drag

5.8

12 190'

snow

The
Chase

**Royal Tower
Gargoyal Buttress**
IV, 5.10a

steep
white
wall

5.8
steep

step left
to 5.8
face crack

5.7 face

5.8R
5.7R
face

small stance,
climb straight up
off belay

4 160'

rock
scar

big
flakes

5.6

rap to 1
200'

3 130'

white
rock
scar

dirty

5.5

120' 2

dark rock

5.8

white rock

5.10a roof

good ledge
to leave
boots on

1 <120'

5.4

(5,700')

ROCK FALL
hazard down
1st 3 pitches!!

ROCK FALL!!

major
gully
system

snow line
and bergschrund
may vary in height

11 180'

5.8
flaring flakes

10 170'

NO!

5.8
alt. var.

5.8

5.7

snow

ridge
crest

190'
9

big
ugly
flakes

3rd class
talus or snow

80' 8 180'

5.5

160'
rappel is below
big ledge

5.7

wide
crack

5.6

7 180'

slings. Take two 200-foot ropes. Take an ice axe and snow boots if continuing to the summit, otherwise leave these at the bergschrund.

Camps:

Camp at the Pika Base Camp.

There are several good places for an emergency bivy between the top of Pitch 5 and the top of Pitch 9 should the need arise.

Approach:

From the landing strip the buttress is plainly visible down glacier on the left about .5 miles away. Go over the gentle glacier to the route's base.

Route:

The route starts half way up the left side of the snow cone coming out of the major gully splitting the South and North summits. Look for a right-trending crack system with a pillar at its base. Getting over to the crack can be difficult due to a rather large moat. Be creative in looking for ways to cross the moat which changes immensely over the course of the season. Be wary of crossing hollow snow bridges that promise easy access to the rock. It may be better to down-climb into the moat and onto jumbled snow blocks to start. If needed, there is a good ledge to leave your boots on top of the first pitch. Follow the topo from here.

Descent:

From the summit, downclimb the snowfields to the top of the rock buttress. Make about 15 full length rappels down the route. All of the rappel anchors are currently fixed. On the lower angled blocky sections in the middle of the climb, it is common for the rappel rope to become stuck. The bottom rappels generally have smooth pulls.

The Gargoyle Buttress on the Royal Tower from the east. Photo by Joe Puryear

Other Climbs:

South Troll, West Pillar

Two side-by-side routes on the West Pillar are reported as being very high quality on excellent rock. Start up the couloir between the South and Middle Troll and then cut right up a steep snow gully to access the climbs. Check the Talkeetna Ranger Station for a topo. The rappels are fixed down the left-hand route.

South Troll, South Ridge

A good moderate route up an aesthetic ridge. Climb up a snow couloir between the South Troll and the tiny sub-peak just north of the major col. Follow the crest of the ridge until a major gendarme blocks the way. Take the easy route to the left, then climb back to the ridge crest or tackle the gendarme directly. Descent can be made via the West Pillar or by rappelling the North Face and traversing to the Middle Troll, South Face route to continue that descent.

The Throne, South Face

To the right of The Lost Marsupial lies a plethora of routes up the broken and ledgy face. Several variations on the central steep cliff band have been climbed but not well documented. Pick a line that looks good and go for it.

The Throne, West Face

The West Face is perhaps the steepest of all faces in Little Switzerland, but it is disappointingly short for a big wall. Several routes and attempts exist across the face and exact details are hard to come by. The rock is reported to be very good.

The Plunger

A cool feature just south of the Throne, this thin spire apparently has two routes up it. One goes at 5.6, A1 or 5.10a, while another goes at 5.12a/b.

Royal Tower, Arizona Highways

Put up in 2000 by John Burcham, John Mattson, and Josh Zimmerman, this climb has 1,000 feet of excellent rock climbing up to 5.10, followed by mixed snow and rock to the summit. The climb starts on the left side of the east face, where there are two splitter crack systems (The Jester and the Blade) in an area of white rock. Continue up the buttress above. Descend the route.

The Munchkin

This south face of this small peak has seen a lot of attention for good "rest day" cragging.

Your Highness, West Face

This is the peak (c. 7,800 feet) directly west of Royal Tower and is not visible from base camp. Travel down the Pika, then up the side glacier just north of Royal Tower. This accesses the West Face which can be climbed in four pitches up excellent granite.

Dragon's Spine, Various Routes

The massive Dragon's Spine (7,490 feet) at the lower northern end of the Pika has endless possibilities. Large tilted planes and sharp ridges define this complex and peculiar peak.

New Climbs:

Certainly there is potential for new climbs in the area, but because of such poor documentation of climbs over the years, it is hard to discern what has been done and what hasn't. By no means has the area been climbed out, and hopefully the area's history will be fully pieced together in the near future.

Michelle Puryear takes in the views from the summit ridge of the Throne. Mt. Foraker in the distance. Photo by Joe Puryear

The North Side

The north side of the Alaska Range has substantially different character than the south. Because it has the only vehicle access point to Denali National Park, it is where most tourists congregate to see what the park has to offer. The 89-mile Park Road (not to be confused with the George Parks Highway) offers visitors a chance to enter deep into the park and discover its vast openness and beauty. Expansive tundra, huge rivers, abundant wildlife, glaciers, and incredible mountain scenery await. For climbers, the north side offers a huge selection of easy and moderate alpine climbs that require a full array of wilderness skills. Because the north side of the Alaska Range is predominately composed of black schist rock, most of the climbing sticks to snow and ice routes.

Getting There:

Because the land area north of the crest of the Central Alaska Range is in Denali National Park Wilderness boundaries, there is no airplane service to the north side glaciers. All of the routes in this section must be accessed via an overland approach from Wonder Lake. There are three options for reaching the Wonder Lake Trailhead.

1. At any time during the season, climbers can charter a plane to Kantishna—a small old mining town 8 miles north of the park. Planes can be taken from either Talkeetna or Denali Park. This is a great early season option when the Park Road is snowed in. From the airstrip, follow the Park Road south eight miles to Wonder Lake.

2. For the full Alaskan experience, ski in to Wonder Lake from the George Parks Highway before the Park Road is open. Parking is available at the Park Headquarters. Follow the Park Road 85 miles to Wonder Lake. Allow at least an extra week each direction for this adventure.

3. Weather permitting, the Park Road usually opens by early June, but the trip to Wonder Lake is closed to private vehicles. Instead, Park shuttle buses run between Denali Park and Wonder Lake. The six-hour ride is worth doing by itself. In addition to riding past much of the Alaska Range, there is ample wildlife viewing—often times in the middle of the road. In 2005, fares for a roundtrip ticket to Wonder Lake were $32.50. Reservations can be made by calling 800.622.7275 or 907.272.7275, or visiting www.reservedenali.com

Denali Park:

The main entrance of **Denali National Park and Preserve and Park Headquarters** is located at mile marker 238 on the George Parks Highway (Alaska Route 3); 238 miles north of Anchorage, 138 miles north of the Talkeetna Spur Road cut-off, and 125 miles south of Fairbanks. Several shuttle companies run from Anchorage or Fairbanks (see appendix). The **Alaska Railway** runs from Anchorage or Fairbanks.

Inside the main entrance there is a visitor center, a couple of campgrounds, and the railroad station. Just north of the park entrance there are several seasonal businesses, which operate from mid May to early September to accommodate summer tourism. Groceries, laundry, internet access, and showers can be found at the **Riley Creek Mercantile** a half mile north of the park entrance. Do not expect to find much in the way of expedition food or supplies in Denali Park. Check out http://www. nps.gov/dena/home/visitorinfo/services/ for more information. Remember, all expeditions climbing Denali must check-in in person at the **Talkeetna Ranger Station** prior to the climb. If not climbing Denali, climbers must register for a backcountry camping permit with one of the ranger stations. Anyone entering the park on the north side must also pay the standard park entrance fee.

Mark Westman enjoying a clear March day on the north side tundra. Photo by Joe Puryear

The communities of Healy and Cantwell lie 30 miles to the north and south of the park entrance. These year-round communities also offer limited services.

Campgrounds:

Riley Creek Campground

1/4 mile west of the George Parks Highway. For RV's and tents. Reservations are recommended. In 2005, the nightly cost was $19.00 per site.

Wonder Lake Campground

Available for tent camping only. Reservations are recommended. In 2005, the nightly cost was $16.00 per site.

Approach:

Distances

Wonder Lake Trailhead to McKinley River: 2.25 miles
McKinley River: to Turtle Hill: 3.25 miles
Turtle Hill to Clearwater Creek: 2.9 miles
Clearwater Creek to Cache Creek Camp: 2.6 miles
Cache Creek Camp to Oastler Creek: 4.65 miles
Oastler Creek to McGonagall Pass: 2.5 miles
Oastler Creek to Oastler Pass: 2.8 miles

All of the routes in this section use the same overland approach from Wonder Lake, with the variation of choosing McGonagall Pass or Oastler Pass at the end.

Wonder Lake Campground is located on the southern end of the lake and the trailhead (2,100 feet) is almost a half-mile east of here. With lots of snow cover this may be difficult to find but generally there are plenty of dog-sled tracks to lead you in the right direction. The trail travels south through black spruce forest to the north side of the McKinley River in 2.25 miles.

Here is the first major obstacle of the route and to some parties the most difficult. The McKinley River has been the source of many accidents and deaths over the years and has turned around several parties. Here the river is at its widest with numerous braids and channels. The river varies and changes with the season and the year. In early season (up to mid April) it may be possible to ski right across without even seeing water. As the season progresses, the channels melt out and by June there may be as many as 30 crossings, some narrow, some wide, some benign and shallow, and some swift and deep. Pick a good path and be careful. It may be helpful to probe or toss rocks into a channel to gauge depth. Crossing in a group with arms locked together is a good method.

In the distance, the largest bump on the close set of rolling hills is Turtle Hill (2,807 feet). A route directly to Turtle Hill is not recommended; it is best to approach it from the northeast. Head slightly southeast as you cross the river toward a small stand of spruce trees on the south bank. Climb to the top of Turtle Hill. From here, locate the best path down to Clearwater Creek. This is a good place to locate McGonagall Pass, Oastler Pass, and get your bearings. Continue south across the open tundra toward the Clearwater Bluff, a 90-foot high, steep grassy bank. Descend the bluff and cross Clearwater Creek (2,300 feet). This is just past the halfway point from Wonder Lake—about 10 miles from the lake, 9 miles to the pass. After crossing, go west, down-river. In about a half mile, turn south again and go 1.2 miles up the Cache Creek valley heading toward another prominent bluff. Cross Cache Creek and follow it southeast for a little over a mile to a nice campsite at 2,600 feet. After another 1.5 miles, cross Cache Creek again and follow its east bank for about three miles. At this point choose between going up Oastler or McGonagall Pass. If heading up Oastler Pass (5,540 feet), turn left up the Oastler Creek and follow it about 2.5 miles to the pass. If heading toward McGonagall Pass (5,720 feet), stay right, crossing Oastler Creek and possibly crossing Cache Creek once more, and continue about 2.5 miles up the steepening grade to the pass.

For meticulously detailed information about the approach and the Muldrow Glacier, check out the 40-page *Muldrow Glacier Guide* by Bradford Washburn, available in the Talkeetna Ranger Station.

Dog Freighting:

Many parties use the dog freighting service to haul loads across the tundra. This helps ease the load bearing on the long approach and is especially useful for teams trying the Muldrow Glacier. This century-old tradition has been used since the early pioneers ventured around Denali's north side and over McGonagall Pass. The work is a grueling process of leap-frogging your gear from point to point across a frigid

landscape. Each piece of freight is handled nearly 15 times and the mushers are often off the sled pushing it. The hard work pays little for the amount of effort and logistics involved and it is mainly done out of the passion to keep the tradition alive.

Denali Dog Freight Expeditions is the only concessioned dog freighter in the park. They need to have your reservation as far in advance as possible and no later than December 31. Expeditions with over 500 pounds. of gear need to make reservations by August 1 of the year preceding the climb. The gear then needs to be packaged and flown to Kantishna no later than February 20. Contact the dog freighter for rates, packaging requirements, and other considerations (see appendix).

Approach Camps

Numerous camping locations exist on the approach as your tent can be set up just about anywhere on the tundra.

Approach Hazards:

Besides crossing the McKinley River, the only other major hazard is posed by bears. Both black bears and grizzly bears reside in Denali National Park. Take responsibility to learn about avoiding and managing bear encounters. Precautions can be taken to protect both you and the bears. For more information, refer to the NPS website: http://www.nps.gov/dena/home/visitorinfo/backcountry/bearsafety.htm

More of an annoyance than a hazard, mosquitoes are prevalent during the summer months. Be sure to come prepared with head-nets and bug-juice. Especially don't forget these items if you are traversing over the mountain from the West Buttress and hiking out to Wonder Lake.

Emergency:

Cell phones are useless on the north side of the park. CB radios have limited functionality. Aircraft are less frequent so an aircraft radio is less reliable, as are signals stamped into the snow. Your best bet in an emergency is a satellite phone or self-rescue back to Wonder Lake or Kantishna.

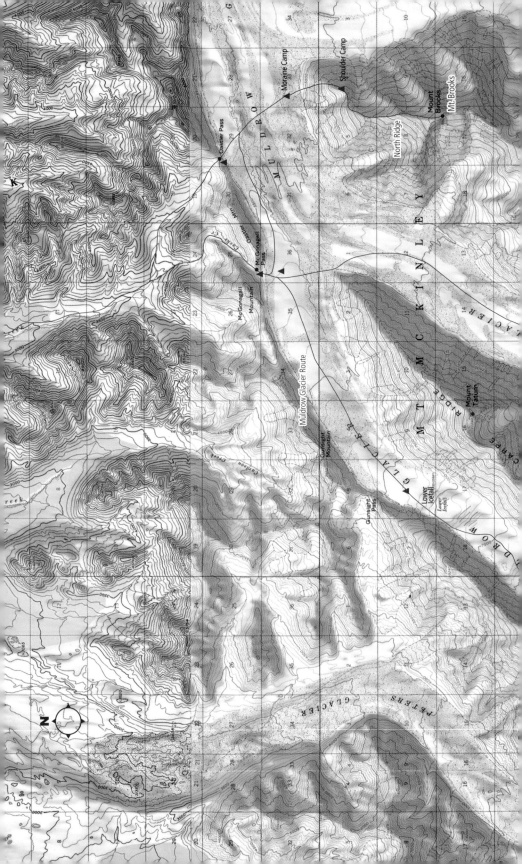

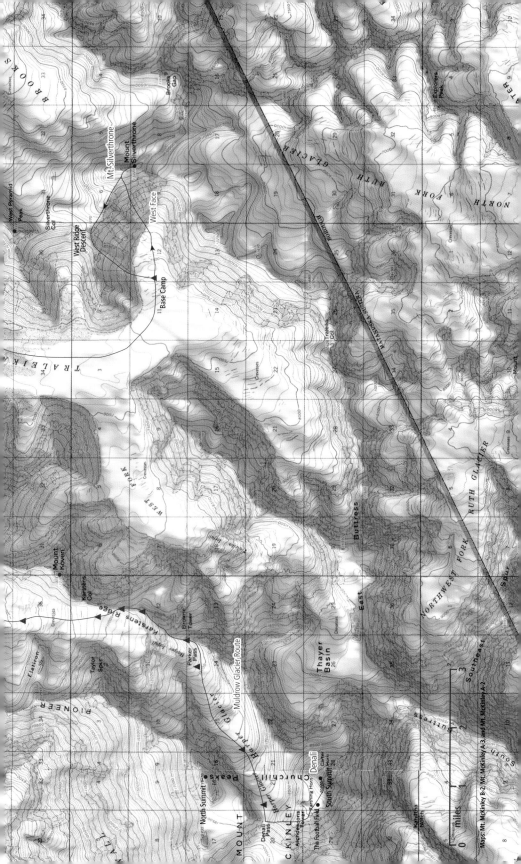

Denali and the Muldrow Glacier in late season. Photo by Joe Puryeal

Denali, Muldrow Glacier

Difficulty: **Alaska Grade 2, 40-degree snow**

Elevation gain: **From Wonder Lake: 18,200'. From McGonagall Pass: 14,600'**

Total time: **16-28 days round-trip**

Approach time: **From Wonder Lake to McGonagall Pass: 2-6 days**

Climbing time: **Up: 10-14 days. Down: via route: 3-5 days; via West Buttress: 2 days**

Season: **April to early-July; June is best**

The Muldrow Glacier is the largest and longest north side glacier, extending some 34 miles to its terminus that nearly reaches the Park Road. The Muldrow and Harper Glaciers are part of the same glacial system, separated by the enormous Harper Icefall. Historically, the Muldrow route is probably the most important in the Central Alaska Range. It was the first major route climbed in the range as well as the scene of many early attempts and tragedies. Due to its gentle nature and lack of technical difficulties, it is often reputed as being the "easiest" route up Denali, but that can be

seriously misleading. The route is remote, the approach is long, the elevation gain is huge, and the glacier travel dangerous. There are far fewer people to route-find, break trail, and establish campsites. The Muldrow glacier itself is one of the world's most dangerous glaciers. Intense crevassing and glacier movement combined with a lack of freeze-thaw conditions, make journeying up or down it a complicated and sometimes tedious task. In addition, the route involves serious objective danger where heavily broken icefalls force climbers to the glacier's edge and underneath hanging glaciers. But this aside, the ascent is one of the grandest and most scenic in the range. A popular trip is to traverse the mountain either from or to the West Buttress route, providing a unique full-on Alaskan adventure.

FA: June 7, 1913: Hudson Stuck, Walter Harper, Harry P. Karstens, Robert G. Tatum.

History:

The Muldrow was named after topographer Robert H. Muldrow. Along with George H. Eldridge in 1898, made the first scientific determination of the height of Denali,

Climbers ascending Karstens Ridge in April. Photo by Mark Westman

measuring it to be 20,464 feet. The route was established in 1910 by the so-called Sourdoughs, a group of tough but modest gold miners that worked in Kantishna. Their expedition allegedly ascended up the Muldrow Glacier to the lower North Peak of Denali—the summit visible from Fairbanks. The team was led by Thomas Lloyd, along with Charles McGonagall, Peter Anderson, and William Taylor. The climb came on the heels of the much more controversial Frederick Cook's claim to have ascended Denali from the south. The team left in December, using dogs and horses to make progress on the frozen rivers and tundra. By mid-March, they had worked their way up and over McPhee Pass (later McGonagall Pass), up the Wall Street Glacier (later Muldrow Glacier), and established an 11,000-foot high camp at the base of Karstens Ridge. The next several days were spent preparing the route up a steep knife-edge ridge (Karstens Ridge) to around 14,600 feet, using a coal shovel to cut steps.

Up to this point, the almost four-month expedition was well documented and photographed. What happened next was poorlydocumented and unfortunately embellished by team leader Lloyd. McGonagall, Anderson, and Taylor claimed to have left their camp at 11,000 feet on April 3, hauling a 14-foot limbed spruce tree. They ascended the knife-edge ridge, and then crossed the Harper Glacier to a steep 2,200-foot ice couloir. They ascended the 50 to 55-degree Sourdough Couloir in creepers (an instep crampon that fit only on the insole of their flimsy boots) chopping steps occasionally, with their long alpine poles, still dragging the 14-foot spruce pole. After planting the pole in some rocks a couple hundred feet from the North Summit, the unacclimatized team strolled to the top, spent two hours on the summit, then returned to camp in a mere 18 hours round trip.

The Sourdough's climb was highly controversial at the time and was eventually called a hoax. It was discovered that Lloyd lied about not only accompanying the party to the summit (later it was admitted that

he was not even on the summit push), but he claimed to have climbed both the North and South Summits. They had no evidence of their climb and no photographs were taken above 11,000 feet. It wasn't until three years later, during the first successful ascent of the South Peak, that Walter Harper and Hudson Stuck's team claimed to have seen the spruce pole from over a mile away. The pole was not seen on prior attempts, nor was it ever seen again. It's hard to imagine what they actually saw, but if it was the pole, then the Sourdough's ascent was one of the greatest mountaineering achievements ever.

No one has ever tried to repeat this "amazing" feat, but for comparison it may be worth taking a look at the speed-climbing trend on the West Buttress. Aside from a slight elevation difference, the distance from 11,000 feet on the West Buttress to the summit is similar to the distance from 11,000 feet on the Muldrow to the summit, over similar terrain. The fastest recorded time on the West Buttress on this segment is 18 hours and 30 minutes round trip, accomplished in 2004. This was by an extremely fit and acclimatized modern athlete going solo and carrying very little personal gear (and no spruce trees). In addition to using the latest high-tech equipment, the athlete had the advantage of a broken trail all the way to the summit and fixed lines up the steep ice sections. Although some historians accept the Sourdough's claim as legitimate, a logical analysis of the ascent has caused many climbers to be a bit skeptical.

Another near-successful attempt on the Muldrow occurred in 1912. Herschel Parker, Belmore Browne, and Merl LaVoy made a valiant effort on the South Summit, coming within 300 feet of the top before being turned around by a tremendous storm. Too tired to make another try, they retreated only to have an earthquake completely devastate the Muldrow Glacier and Karstens Ridge just a few days later.

An Episcopal missionary and Archdeacon of the Yukon, Hudson Stuck assembled a team of four enthusiastic Alaskans in 1913 to make the first successful ascent to the actual South Summit. Stuck once exclaimed, "I would rather climb that mountain than discover the richest gold-mine in Alaska." Stuck had some prior mountaineering experience, having climbed in Colorado and the Canadian Rockies, and he had made a successful ascent of Mount Rainier. Stuck first chose Harry Karstens, a skilled wilderness adventurer who some five years earlier guided naturalist Charles Sheldon around the north side of Denali. Two younger team members were Walter Harper and Robert Tatum, both twenty-one. Harper was a skilled dog team-driver and Tatum, who was staying at the Nenana Mission, was to be the expedition cook. None of them had any true mountaineering experience, but they were strong Alaskan survivalists and experts in winter travel.

Stuck outfitted the entire expedition for less than a thousand dollars, considerably less than previous and subsequent attempts. The meticulously organized expedition left Nenana on March 17 with over one ton of weight and reached the Muldrow Glacier by mid-May. They found the glacier to be very crevassed but were able to mush the dogs as far as 11,000 feet. At one point a dog fell into a crevasse and had to be rescued.

Upon arriving at what had been described as a perfect knife-edge ridge, the climbers were surprised to find that the entire northeast ridge was wrecked by the previous year's earthquake. It was a jumbled chaos of ice blocks and they spent three difficult weeks chopping out a staircase in the ice.

By May 27 the team reached the top of Karstens Ridge. Then they traversed into the Grand Basin and placed camp at 16,000 feet. It was bitter cold at night but very hot during the day. The climb was going great. After reaching a camp at 16,600 feet, the team had over two weeks of supplies left. On June 7, they made their final ascent in clear but cold weather. Harper was the first person to step foot on the actual summit, followed by Stuck. Stuck later wrote of the summit in his book Ascent of Denali, "The snow-covered tops of the remoter peaks, dwindling and fading, rose to our view as though floating in thin air when their bases were hidden by the haze, and the beautiful crescent curve of the whole Alaskan range exhibited itself from Denali to the sea." They took a few pictures and from a mercurial barometer they determined the elevation to be 20,300 feet. The descent was uneventful. There was little doubt that these four determined men had finally stood on the highest summit in North America.

Strategy:

The Muldrow Glacier route is a major expedition undertaking. Many parties use the dog freighting service to shuttle loads across the tundra. Check the North Side Introduction for more details on dog freighting. Parties not using this service generally double-carry loads the entire way on the approach and up the mountain. If the ascent is made in early season, a sled will come in handy on most of the approach and on the Muldrow Glacier.

Skis or snowshoes should be considered mandatory for the climb. While skis are much safer for travel on the Muldrow Glacier, they can be cumbersome to carry up Karstens Ridge and carry down the upper West Buttress if descending that way. Be aware that for ascents from late April to mid June, the tundra can change considerably from the approach to the return as rapid snow melt and river break-up occurs.

Make sure each campsite is well fortifed and protected from the elements, especially when climbing above Karstens Ridge. The Harper glacier is a raw and unforgiving place as storms from the southwest funnel over Denali Pass and down this trough. Snow caves can be difficult to make due to icy conditions, and igloos are probably better bets. Seracs can also be used for protection against severe storms.

Gear:

Take standard glacier travel gear. Be sure to include many wands.

Specific Hazards:

The Muldrow is one of the most heavily crevassed glaciers in the world. Crevasse falls are common and extra prudence should be used when traveling on this glacier. Avalanche danger from both sides of the Muldrow valley can be severe. Beware of both serac fall and snow loading after storms.

Camps:

Both the Muldrow and the Harper Glacier provide a multitude of camping options. The following locations have been historically used and are relatively safe with fewer crevasses. It is necessary at every camp to diligently probe the area to search for crevasses.

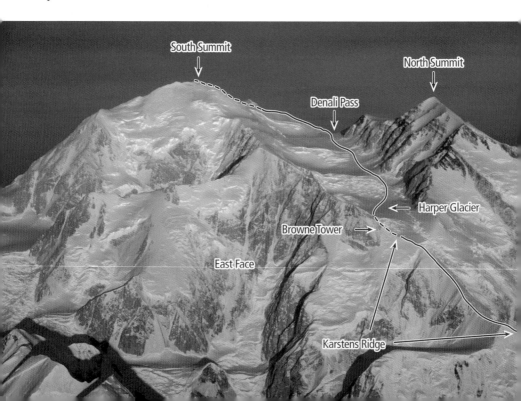

McGonagall Pass (5,720 feet): Over the years, this area has become polluted with human waste, but does allow climbers to camp on rock later in the season. It may be more desirable to camp on the Muldrow glacier just below the pass.

Muldrow Glacier (5,700 to 10,800 feet):

5,700 feet: Camp in middle of the glacier just below the pass.

6,600 feet: This is a good location before tackling the Lower Icefall. Camp toward the right side away from Mount Tatum.

8,100 - 8,600 feet: Camp nearer the right side of the glacier on the level section above The Hill of Cracks.

9,700 feet: After passing the Great Icefall, camp on the right side below the Flatiron.

10,800 feet: Camp in the basin at the base of Karstens Ridge. Be aware of heavy snowfall at this location. Mark any caches left here well.

Karstens Ridge Camps (11,575 and 12,100 feet): Before the narrow Coxcomb there are two good camp locations on the crest of the ridge.

Browne Tower Camp (14,600 feet): At the top of Karstens Ridge is an exposed campsite just below the imposing Browne Tower.

Lower Harper (14,900 feet): Be careful when camping in this exposed, windswept basin. It is best to try to dig into available seracs or build an igloo or other snow structure.

Middle Harper (16,800 feet): Another exposed spot. Dig into seracs below a small icefall. This is the high camp for many parties. A summit attempt can be made from here.

Below Denali Pass (18,000 to 18,200 feet): A risky spot to camp but one used by Washburn on his ascent. This makes for an easier summit day and puts you in a good position if you are traversing down the West Buttress.

Route:

Distances

McGonagall Pass to the Great Icefall: 7.85 miles
Great Icefall to Karstens Notch: 3.0 miles
Karstens Notch to Browne Tower: 2.2 miles
Browne Tower to Denali Pass: 3.5 miles
Denali Pass to South Peak: 1.5 miles
Denali Pass to North Peak: 1.5 miles

Muldrow Glacier

From McGonagall Pass, descend 100 feet onto the Muldrow Glacier. The first five miles to the Lower Icefall feel practically level, gaining just over 1,000 feet. There is little crevasse or avalanche danger on this section. The fern line typically reaches the base of the Lower Icefall. Over the next six miles there are numerous crevasses and significant avalanche danger. The Lower Icefall is the first major crux and is passed on either the far left or far right margin. Either way is exposed to avalanche danger from hanging glaciers on the valley walls. Scout the best way from below and move quickly to another level section above 7,500 feet. The next obstacle is the Hill of Cracks, between 7,700 feet and 8,100 feet. A central bulge in the glacier is criss-crossed with an array of crevasses. This can be passed either by a depression on the left, or a less crevassed area on the right. Continue up the center of the glacier to the base of the Great Icefall (8,600 feet). The Great Icefall (8,700 feet to 9,700 feet) is generally passed via a less-crevassed area in the middle or by skirting the icefall on its far left side (exposed to avalanche danger). Continue up glacier (south) to a good campsite at 10,800 feet at the base of Karstens Ridge.

Karstens Ridge

Karstens Ridge is the long slender ridge on the left (east) side of the Muldrow Glacier that gains access to the Harper Glacier, bypassing the monstrous Harper Icefall. Snowfall in this area can be copious. Some parties may elect to camp on the more exposed ridge (11,575 feet or 12,100 feet) to avoid getting completely buried. Two options allow access onto the ridge. One is to climb to Karstens Notch (10,930 feet) or the slope just right of it to gain the ridge crest. The easier option is to take a natural ramp that leads up right to left and accesses the ridge at 11,575 feet. Once on the ridge crest, follow it to the base of Browne Tower (14,600 feet). The ridge has a maximum steepness of 40 degrees and is quite narrow on the Coxcomb between 12,100 feet and 14,600 feet.

Harper Glacier

From the Browne Tower Camp, make a level traverse onto the Harper Glacier. Go up the glacier heading for the right side of the prominent icefall between 15,600 feet and 16,400 feet. As you climb into the upper basin, there are a few different options for reaching the summit. From 16,400 the 1912 expedition headed southeast across the Harper and climbed a snow slope to the Northeast Ridge. The 1913 party took a similar variation but continued to 17,400 feet on the Harper before traversing across. Most parties will probably find it easiest to continue up to Denali Pass (18,200 feet) and finish on the standard West Buttress route. This also allows climbers to check for incoming weather. Turn south at the pass and climb the right side of the 40-degree slope on the left (east) side of the crest. When the slope

becomes less steep, continue up the near the ridge crest, heading for the right side of Archdeacon's Tower. A small descent leads to the Football Field at 19,500 feet. Traverse southeast across this flat expanse to the final slope heading up to the summit ridge. Climb this short slope to Kahiltna Horn (20,120 feet). Continue east along the sharp and exposed summit ridge to the top.

For those who are bold and adventurous, a trip to the North Peak is very worthwhile. From Denali Pass, climb up toward the black rock to the north. A prominent diagonal rocky ledge extends up through the rocks. Follow this up with a short 50-degree section. From the top of the cliffs it is necessary to descend 270 feet down a broad slope before making the final climb to the summit. Go northeast over a mile to the North Summit. Don't forget the 270 feet you need to re-climb on the descent!

Descent:

If traversing the mountain, descend the West Buttress route. Otherwise, retrace the route of ascent back to McGonagall Pass and out to Wonder Lake.

Climbers descending Karstens Ridge after a successful traverse from the West Buttress. Photo by Brian McCullough

Tash Summit on her way up the lower Muldrow Glacier. Photo by Ben Summit

Mt. Brooks from the northeast. Photo by Joe Puryear

Mount Brooks, North Ridge

Difficulty: **III, 65-degree snow or ice**

Elevation gain: **On route: 6,600'. From Wonder Lake: 9,840'**

Total time: **6-10 days**

Approach time: **From Wonder Lake to Oastler Pass: 2-6 days**

Climbing time: **Up: 1-2 days, or 7-14 hours. Down: 4-8 hours**

Season: **March to August**

Because of its beauty and prominence from Wonder Lake, Mount Brooks (11,940') has long been a focus of photography, art, and climbing activity. The peak holds an awesome position at the confluence of three of the major north side glaciers—the Muldrow, Traleika, and Brooks. The gentle North Ridge is the logical and most direct route. The climb makes for a great week-long trip that is a true Alaskan adventure, combining river crossings, tundra, mosquitoes, glaciers, and ultimately a spectacular summit.

FA: July 5, 1952; Thayer Scudder, Winslow Briggs, John S. Humphreys, and David Bernays.

History

In July of 1952, Mount Brooks not only got its first ascent, but second and third as well, all as part of the 1952 Brooks-Mather Expedition from the Harvard Mountaineering Club. Described by Thayer Scudder in his 1953 AAJ account as being a group of "embryonic scientists," the team was under the direction of Bradford Washburn to help in surveying for his mapping project as well as study flowers on the tundra. In addition to chief surveyor Scudder, this motley group consisted of Winslow Briggs, a first year graduate student and team botanist, John S. Humphreys, a surveying assistant, and David Bernays an MIT grad who was a bit of a logistics manager. The team drove a rehabilitated hearse up the Alaskan Highway to Denali Park and on to Wonder Lake. They left Wonder Lake on June 26 and after packing many loads by way of McGonagall Pass, reached their Brooks Base Camp on July 4. The next day the weather was good, so the four of them decided to go for it leaving at 8:00 A.M. Scudder mused at how "this beautiful peak, so prominent to all who reach McGonagall Pass, had

Climbers ascending the North Ridge with the Muldrow Glacier below. Oastler Pass is in the center of the hills behind. Photo by John Burcham

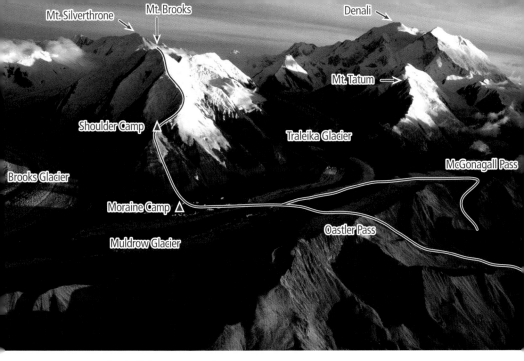

Mt. Silverthrone — Mt. Brooks — Denali — Mt. Tatum — Shoulder Camp — Traleika Glacier — McGonagall Pass — Brooks Glacier — Moraine Camp — Muldrow Glacier — Oastler Pass

remained unclimbed for so long." They climbed up the lower Northeast spur and upon reaching the greater North Ridge, Scudder remarked that the way ahead appeared to be "some vast highway of the gods." The climbing was never too difficult and the views of Denali and the Muldrow were stupendous. The party of four reached the summit just after 4:00 P.M. After a few summit shots, they quickly descended back to base camp.

After an extended stint of bad weather, during which they did some minor survey and botanical work, it was time to re-ascend Brooks with the necessary surveying equipment to do their principal surveying. After establishing a high camp at 9,800 feet, Humphreys and Scudder summited on July 10, but the weather was too bad for any work. The next day the entire team summited again and they dug a snow cave on the summit and spent the night. They were able to complete all of their necessary surveying. After a brief incident with the stove the next afternoon, which blackened the inside of the cave with soot, they descended the ridge back to the base.

The team went on to make the first ascent of Mount Mather on July 20 and 21 as before making the long and wet trip back to Wonder Lake.

Mount Brooks was named after Alfred H. Brooks—an explorer and geologist who crossed the Alaska Range in 1902.

Strategy:

Allow six to 10 days round trip for a climb of Mount Brooks. Add more time if attempting other peaks in the area. Mount Brooks can be climbed from March to August. All months can be good and present different challenges and opportunities.

The climb can be made in a one day round trip from the Muldrow Glacier. If breaking it up, take a day to move camp to the 7,520 foot shoulder. This will allow good acclimatization and make for an easier summit push.

Gear:

Take standard glacier travel gear.

Camps:

McGonagall Pass (5,720 feet): Over the years, this area has become polluted with human waste, but does allow climbers to camp on rock later in the season. It may be more desirable to camp on the Muldrow glacier just below the pass or continue to the base of the ridge.

Oastler Pass (5,540 feet): Camp amongs the rocks on the pass. This pass is less used so established campsites are harder to come by.

Moraine Camp (5,300 feet): Camp near the base of the ridge after crossing the Muldrow. This is the final camp for many parties.

Shoulder Camp (7,520+ feet): This is the first good camp spot on the route. Camping here makes for a much easier summit day.

Upper Ridge (9,400 to 11,000 feet): Several camping options exist all along the ridge, but they are very exposed to weather. Pick a spot wisely.

Approach:

The best access is from Oastler Pass, although McGonagall Pass can be used as well. From Oastler Pass, descend loose talus down the south side. Head southeast toward the toe of the northeast spur of the North Ridge that forms the divide between the Brooks and Muldrow Glaciers (5,300 feet). Crossing the glacier can be quite complex due to the merging of the Muldrow and Traleika Glaciers. Several moraines and streams must be crossed to reach the base and the best path changes yearly.

Route:

Climb up the broad ridge on talus or seasonal snow slopes. A central snow couloir can be followed to avoid rock outcroppings. Beware of rock-fall and avalanche potential. At around 6,700 feet the ridge becomes more defined. Just past Pt. 7,520 is the first good campsite on the ridge. Continue along the beautiful ridge to where the northeast spur intersects the North Ridge proper at 8,900 feet. Here a steep (up to 65 degrees) but short (about 100 feet) slope is encountered. Continue up the moderately angled ridge. Watch for crevasses crossing and parallel to the ridge crest. Several camp sites can be found between 9,400 and 11,000 feet, but they are very exposed to the elements. There is a final steep slope above 11,000 feet, then a short traverse to the summit. A small amount of black schist rock can be found here.

Descent:

Retrace the line of ascent.

Mount Silverthrone, West Face

Difficulty: **III, 60-degree snow or ice**

Elevation gain: **From Base Camp: 5,600 feet. From Wonder Lake: 12,120 feet**

Total time: **8-14 days**

Approach time: **From Wonder Lake to McGonagall Pass: 2-6 days**

Climbing time: **Up: 1-2 days or 8-14 hours. Down: 4-7 hours.**

Season: **Mid-March to June**

Mount Silverthrone (13,220') is the fifth highest peak in the Alaska Range. It holds a significant position, being at the head of both the Ruth and Brooks Glaciers, as well as facing the Traleika. Remarkably, for being such a large peak it doesn't lend itself to very many routes, there being only four major ones climbed. Bradford Washburn gave the peak this descriptive name when viewing the peak from the Brooks Glacier. He and his team first climbed the peak in April of 1945 from the north. The North Ridge has long been a popular skiing objective. The South Ridge from the Ruth Glacier, until recently, also provided an easy way up. Now with the break-up of the main icefall in the North Fork of the Ruth Glacier, this is no longer an easy or recommended route. The only aspect of the mountain that holds any interest for a steeply inclined mountaineer is the western. A series of gullies and rock spurs are tightly contained in the cirque formed by the mountain's west and southwest ridges. Unfortunately the rock here is the non-climber-friendly black schist that is commonly found on the range's north side. The couloirs of the West Face, however, provide a unique and direct route to a much acclaimed summit.

FA: April 2, 1997; Joseph Puryear and Mark Westman.

History

Mark Westman and I first saw the West Face while attempting Silverthrone from the south in 1995. Gazing across at it from a

col between the Ruth and Traleika, we both knew that we would see this big remote face again. Viewing it later while climbing the South Buttress of Denali the next year confirmed our mutual desire to climb it. In March of 1997 we found ourselves flying to Kantishna on the north side. Over the next week we made slow progress toward its base, enduring night after night of -25 to -30-degree F temperatures.

The weather had been holding so the day after we arrived at base camp we decided to do a reconnaissance onto the face to preview our proposed route. The objective danger proved considerable as we watched avalanches from either side run across our tracks. We rested a day during a storm and then on March 31 we made our first attempt on a narrow gully that split directly up the center of the face. Halfway up, the weather moved in and we were forced into a speedy retreat. After two more storm days, we left camp at 6 A.M. on April 2. Mark

Approaching the face up the Traleika Glacier. Photo by Joe Puryear

Sunrise on Mt. Brooks from near McGonagall Pass. The North Ridge is the left skyline. Photo by Brian McCullough

was in the lead and I was following exactly in his footsteps. Within 100 feet of camp, I suddenly started falling amidst a flurry of powder snow. I had taken a crevasse fall and hit a small ledge 20 feet down. Mark, not feeling the rope go tight, just heard a small scream and turned around just in time to see nothing. I was able to climb out unhurt, but it was a hell of a way to start the day.

After running through the death-zone avalanche area twice previously, we finally came to our senses and picked the easier and much safer left couloir for our ascent line. We started up the couloir, finding much unconsolidated snow. This eventually led way to a short bit of steeper serac ice, then rotten snow and ice to the ridge crest. The weather had been changing for the worse all day, so here we were faced with a big dilemma. With only down jackets and a stove, facing cold Alaskan temps on the north side in the middle of nowhere with an unknown descent and quickly changing weather, the summit seemed almost an unnecessary risk. But we had come a long way. We went for it and for a few short moments, we stood in bliss on the pointy summit. We ran down the West Ridge, knowing that complete darkness was only a few hours away. We located our proposed descent couloir and the down-climbing began. We finally reached our base camp at 7 P.M. that night. We returned to Kantishna 15 days after our journey began.

Specific Hazards:

There is considerable avalanche and serac danger on the approach to the climb from the cliffs on the right (south). Other lines farther right on the face are severely threatened by avalanches from three directions. Natural rock fall is a possibility especially later in the season.

Gear:

Take three to four ice screws and two or three pickets. Take one 165 or 200-foot rope. Bring two ice tools per person.

Strategy:

Allow eight to 14 days round trip for a climb of Mt. Silverthrone. Add more time

if attempting other peaks in the area. The climb is straightforward and can be accomplished in one day from base camp. If breaking it up, a camp can be made at the top of the couloir.

Camps:

McGonagall Pass (5,720 feet): Over the years, this area has become polluted with human waste, but does allow climbers to camp on rock later in the season. It may be more desirable to camp on the Muldrow glacier just below the pass.

Muldrow (5,700 feet): Camp anywhere on the flat glacier.

Main Traleika (5,800 to 7,000 feet): Camp anywhere on the flat and smooth glacier. Beware of exposure to winds.

West Face Base Camp (7,300 feet): Camp near the entrance of the Southwest Fork of the Traleika. The upper valley is threatened by seracs.

Route: No recommended bivies are available in the couloir. After joining the ridge crest, a good camp could be dug almost anywhere.

Approach:

From McGonagall Pass, go south and slightly east across the Muldrow toward the toe of the Northeast Ridge of Mount Tatum. Getting onto the Traleika is a complicated task. The intersecting glaciers create a maze of moraines, moulins, and rivers. The best path is generally found nearer Mount Tatum. Pick your way through then onto the smooth Traleika (5,750 feet). Follow the Traleika for about eight miles until reaching the Southeast Fork (7,050 feet). Turn east and head up to about 7,200 feet, just over the first rise. Above and directly to the north is the descent couloir. Directly east is the start of the route.

Route:

Go east up glacier toward the West Face. The face has five major gully systems. The middle three are all threatened by hanging glaciers. The right was the couloir used

Joe Puryear approaching the top of the couloir on the first ascent. Photo by Mark Westman

Descent detail of the southwest facing couloir off the west ridge. Photo by Joe Puryear

right, and center. Start up the northeast trending couloir at 8,100 feet. Climb 40 to 45-degree snow slopes up the couloir. Later in the season some rock scrambling may be encountered here if it is melted out. Continue up, staying on the couloir's right side. A steeper section is encountered at around 10,500 feet (up to 60 degrees). Keep the rocks on the upper part of the couloir to your left and intersect the broad crest of the West Ridge near 12,300 feet. Head southeast and climb up the low angle snow slope toward Mount Silverthrone's North Ridge. Once on the ridge go south and climb up the last couple hundred feet to the summit.

Descent:

Under good conditions it would be possible to descend the ascent route, but a shorter and lower angle couloir exists a ways down the West Ridge. Climb back down to the top of the West Face Couloir and then go west and slightly north to Point 11,270. Climb down the sharper ridge crest to the top of the triangular-shaped, southwest-trending couloir that tops out at 10,200 feet. Down-climb this 40 to 45-degree couloir to its base (7,400 feet) and cross the glacier back to camp.

on the first attempt of the face. The larger left gully was the route used on the first ascent and described here. As you ascend into the basin beneath the face there may be considerable objective danger. Climbing the left couloir keeps this danger to a minimum. Any other routes on the face are threatened by multiple hangers to the left,

Other Climbs:

Mount Silverthrone, North Ridge

As a classic mountaineering outing, the ease of this route is offset by the long approach. It is best done as an early season ascent when skis can be used for the approach and ascent. The peak is quite popular for skiing on this side. Approach via McGonagall or Oastler Pass, cross the Muldrow and then go up the Brooks Glacier. Ascend to Silverthrone Col and climb the gentle ridge to the summit.

Mount Tripyramid, Normal Route

A long ridge of small summits extends between Mount Brooks and Silverthrone Col. The ridge trends northeast to southwest and the three highest central points are named East, Central, and West Tripyramid. They can be climbed via numerous routes. The most common is to climb to the Silverthrone Col via the Brooks Glacier, then ascend the ridge to the north.

Mount Brooks, Northwest Ridge

This great looking ridge, which rises out of the junction of the Traleika and Muldrow Glaciers, is a slightly more technical alternative to the North Ridge. Descend the easier North Ridge. First climbed by Randy Waitman et al in 1992, the ridge was soloed by Alaskan great Jeff Benowitz in 1997.

Mount Brooks to Mount Silverthrone Traverse

An outstanding alpine adventure is the grand traverse of the Mount Brooks and Mount Silverthrone massifs. Start by climbing the North Ridge of Mount Brooks and continue along the crest over the three Trypyramids. Descend to Silverthrone Col and then ascend the North Ridge of Mount Silverthrone. Descend by way of the Brooks Glacier back to the Muldrow. Allow several days and enjoy the views.

Mount Tatum, Northeast Ridge

This long elegant ridge defines the southern border of the Muldrow Glacier above its junction with the Traleika. The ridge ultimately connects the summits of Mount Tatum, Mount Carpe, and Mount Koven, then goes on to include Karsten's Ridge, culminating with Browne Tower. Though nothing more than a long ridge slog to the summit of Mt. Tatum, the ridge certainly provides breathtaking views of Mount Brooks, the Muldrow, and the East Face of Denali. Approach via McGonagall Pass, then cross the Muldrow straight to its base.

Mount Koven and Mount Carpe

These are two rarely visited summits. Both can be ascended up moderate ridges on their south and east sides. In the winter of 1996, Randy Waitman and Mike Litzow climbed Koven by climbing up to the col between Karstens Ridge and Koven from the south, then climbing the Southwest Ridge of Mount Koven to its summit.

Mount Mather, North Ridge

This large peak east of Mount Brooks holds a similar climbing objective. Approach can be made via McGonagall or Oastler Pass, then down the Muldrow. From the south side of the Muldrow, climb into a small cirque directly to the base of the ridge. Climb the aesthetic ridge with maximum difficulties of 50-degree snow and ice. Descend the route.

New Climbs:

Mount Silverthrone, West Face

This face certainly holds the possibility for another line. The narrow couloir to the right of the original route attempted by the first ascensionists is a more direct, albeit more dangerous, route.

Denali, East Face

Is this the last great unclimbed problem on Denali? So says Bradford Washburn, who once again put out a grand proposal to the climbing community to conquer this massive face. Dangerous is an understatement, but someday it will get climbed. Approach up the West Fork of the Traleika for a dose of reality.

Traverse from Mount Tatum to Browne Tower

This is probably the longest continuous unclimbed ridge in the range. It would be an absolutely epic traverse combined with a summit of Denali and descent via the West Buttress.

Far West

To the west of Mount Foraker lie a vast number of largely unexplored smaller peaks. Halfway between Mount Foraker and the pristine granite spires of the Kichatnas even farther west, one solitary summit towers above the rest. Mount Russell is the highest peak in the far western part of the Central Alaska Range and the chance to climb to its beautiful summit is worth a climbing trip to itself. The peak is plainly visible from Talkeetna—the lone pointy summit far to the left of the big three.

Getting There:

Fly into the Upper Yentna Glacier to the high glacial basin, northeast of the North Ridge, with a licensed air service out of Talkeetna. The flight takes about 50 minutes one way. Even though your climb may only take two days, plan for at least a 10 day trip. Because of the areas remoteness, pilots may not check on you until your due-date. They may be also less likely to try to pick you up unless the weather is perfect. Make sure you bring skis or snowshoes to stamp down a runway in the snow. Pilots will need a 30-foot by 1,000-foot strip, with a wider turn-around area at the top. With only two people, this can take days to construct. If it starts snowing it is best to start work early.

Not all air services will fly into here—make sure yours does.

Base Camps:

Yenta Base Camp (8,200 feet): Set up camp next to the airstrip. Be sure to mark your camp or cache with an extra long wand. It can snow heavily here.

Emergency:

The Yenta is an exceptionally remote location and communication with the outside world can be difficult. CBs, cell phones, and aircraft radio usage is extremely limited. The climb is not under any normal flight path so airplane traffic is almost non-existent. A satellite phone is your only reliable source of communication short of waiting for your scheduled pick-up date. Be extra-prepared for emergency situations.

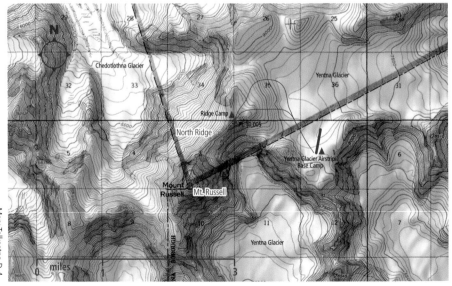

Map: Talkeetna D-4

Mount Russell, North Ridge

Difficulty: **III, 65-degree snow and ice**

Elevation gain: **3,500'**

Total time: **2-10 days**

Approach time: **30 minutes**

Climbing time: **Up: 1-2 days. Down: 8-14 hours**

Season: **March to June; April and May are best**

Mount Russell (11,670 feet) has captured the imagination of climbers for years. From certain aspects it has been likened to K2 in appearance, although it sits nearly 17,000 feet lower. Mount Russell receives the brunt of the weather systems approaching the Alaska Range. That, coupled with its extreme remoteness, makes an attempt on this attractive peak a challenging endevor.

The North Ridge of Mount Russell is splendid outing up a beautiful glaciated ridge. It is made easier by an airplane landing area just northeast of the peak. With only six recorded ascents, it is likely you will have this peak to yourself.

FA: July 4 to July 13, 1972; Thomas Kensler, Peter Brown, John Hauck, Dick Jablonowski, and Dan Osborne

History

The mountain has only been climbed by three routes. Its first ascent was in May of 1962 by a team led by Hellmut Raithel. They started on the north side, traveled up the Chedotlothna Glacier, and traversed beneath the mountain's great West Face to the South Ridge. They finished the route on the upper South Ridge to the summit.

The second ascent of the mountain was made by the now popular North Ridge, which they referred to as its Northeast Ridge. Thomas Kensler, Peter Brown, John Hauck, Dick Jablonowski, and Dan Osborne flew to the upper Yenta Glacier in July of 1972. From their account of the route, it appears as if the ridge was much more jumbled up than it is now. Their climb required much route-finding through a maze of crevasses, blocks, and ice chimneys. Kensler describes one part of the route in his 1973 AAJ account as being "very airy, frothy, rimey, and well-corniced." Higher up he exclaimed, "Now we were in the ice-cube tray—a mass of tumbled ice blocks and holes." The team overcame all of the difficulties and pulled onto the summit on July 13 after 10 days of climbing.

In true Alaska style the team walked down the treacherous Yentna Icefall and out to Wonder Lake. Here they encountered the "standard fare of oppressive swarms of mosquitos, swamps, endless willow thickets, circuitous detours around grizzlies, and

Pt. 10,005

Airstrip

Upper Yentna Glacier

five glacial rivers brimming with excessive
summer melt."

Strategy:

Plan on spending at least a week for this
climb and take food for 10 days. Don't be
fooled by its easy access. Mount Russell is
very isolated compared to the other peaks
covered here. Due to variable weather
and a long distance from the regular flying
routes, your actually pickup date may be a
week past your scheduled one.

   The climb could be completed in a
long day round trip from base camp on
the Yentna, but most parties will want to
make an intermediate camp. This allows
more time for the upper ridge, should
snow conditions or route-finding problems
become a factor. Make sure to mark your
base camp well. It can quickly dump
numerous feet of snow at this location.

Specific Hazards:

The traverse around the bergschrund at
10,300 feet leads on to the avalanche-prone
northern slopes. Be sure to assess avalanche
conditions carefully.

Gear:

Take four ice screws and two or three
pickets. Take one 165 to 200-foot rope.
Bring two ice tools per person.

Camps:

Camp at the Yentna Base Camp.

Ridge Camp (9,800 feet): A good camp can
be dug anywhere on the plateau near Pt.
10,005.

Route:

There are two ways to access the ridge crest.

Option 1:

From the airstrip, go west toward a long
snow and ice slope between 8,300 and 9,600
feet. This slope climbs directly up to the
plateau beneath Pt. 10,005. Leave your
skis or snowshoes at the base and cross the
bergschrund in the best location. Ascend
the 45 to 55-degree slope.

Kieth Nyitray on the North Ridge. Photo by Brian McCullough

Option 2:

From the airstrip, go northwest around
to the north side of the ridge to an icefall.
Ascend the lower angled slopes through
crevasses to the south up to the plateau
beneath Pt. 10,005.

   From the plateau, climb south along
the ridge. The ridge descends nearly 400
feet and becomes sharp and fluted with
several rimed bumps along the way. Try
to stay along the ridge crest as much as
possible and not drop off the right side. As
the ridge approaches the steeper section at
9,700 feet, a bergschrund cutting across it
(around 10,300 feet) becomes evident. It is
generally necessary to drop off the ridge to
the right (west) on 50 to 60-degree slopes
and traverse out right onto the northwest
face to bypass this obstacle. Traverse

Overview of Mt. Russell from the northeast. Photo by Joe Puryear

Detail of route showing the traverse around the bergschrund near 10,300 feet. Photo by Mike Gauthier

Once back on the ridge crest, continue straight up, surmounting several interesting obstacles as they appear. The ridge seems to change year to year and several short ice-bulges and crevasses can require intricate route-finding skills. There is generally always a good path; just keep poking around until you find it. As you ascend higher on the ridge it tends to become easier, ranging from 30 to 45-degree snow slopes, until reaching the small summit.

back left to the ridge crest above it. The bergschrund could be climbed directly with difficult snow, ice, and/or aid climbing. As you are going up, try to gauge a good place to rappel back over the bergschrund for the descent.

Descent:

Descend the route, rappelling where necessary. Rappel over the bergschrund instead of climbing around it.

Lisa Roderick and Joe Puryear ascending the ice slope below Pt. 10,005. Photo by Mark Westman

Mt. Russell from the northeast. Photo by Joe Puryear

Other Climbs:

Once on the upper Yentna, there are no other major peaks that are accessible by foot travel. The basin is difficult at best to leave; the icefall to the east is extremely broken. There are a few other small snow peaks in the basin that would provide some additional climbing and great views.

New Climbs:

Mount Russell, West Face

Mount Russell only has three routes to its summit. The North Ridge, the South Ridge, which was the first ascent route, and the East Face, a steep horror show that the first ascensionists parapeted off essentially because there was no other good way back to base camp. There may certainly be more potential on the East Face, but it is the West Face that is completely unclimbed. This huge face has an obvious line up the center that begs to be climbed. There may be access to the face from the upper Yentna basin by crossing over low on the North Ridge, otherwise an overland approach from the North Side up the Chedolatna Glacier will have to be made.

The Chedolatna Glacier is not landable by airplane because it lacks snowfall and is very rocky.

Mount Laurens (c. 10,000 feet)

With only one ascent, this large mountain south of Mount Foraker has a huge amount of potential. Early season landing can be made on the Yentna Glacier, west of the mountain.

Transportation Services

Air Services:

Doug Geeting Aviation
PO Box 42
Talkeetna, AK 99676
907.733.2366
800.770.2366
airtours@alaska.net
www.talkeetnaalaska.com

Fly Denali
P.O. Box 1152
Talkeetna, AK 99676
907.733.7768
866.733.7768
info@flydenali.net
www.flydenali.com

Hudson Air Service
PO Box 648
Talkeetna, AK 99676
907.733.2321
800.478.2321
hudson@mtaonline.net
www.hudsonair.com

K2 Aviation
P.O. Box 545
Talkeetna, AK 99676
907.733.2291
800.764.2291
info@flyk2.com
www.flyk2.com

Talkeetna Air Taxi
P.O. Box 73
Talkeetna, AK 99676
907.733.2218
800.533.2219
info@talkeetnaair.com
www.talkeetnaair.com

Shuttle Services:

Alaska Backpackers Shuttle
P.O. Box 232493
Anchorage, AK 99523
800.266.8625
907.344.8775
abst@juno.com

Alaska Trails
P.O. Box 84608
Fairbanks, Alaska 99708
888.770.7275
info@alaskashuttle.com
www.alaskashuttle.com

Denali Overland Transportation
P.O. Box 330
Talkeetna, AK 99676
907.773.2384
800.651.5221
info@denalioverland.com
www.denalioverland.com

Talkeetna Shuttle Service
PO Box 468
Talkeetna, AK 99676
888.288.6008
907.733.1725
tshuttle@alaska.net
www.denalicentral.com

Dog Sled Support:

Denali Dog Freight Expeditions
Jeff and Lori Yanuchi
P.O. Box 482
Healy, Alaska 99743
907.683.1008
stampede@mtaonline.net

Other:

Alaska Marine Highway System
Reservations:
6858 Glacier Highway
Juneau, AK 99801-7909
800.642.0066
www.ferryalaska.com

Alaska Railroad Corporation
Passenger Service Department
PO Box 107500
Anchorage, AK 99510-7500
800.544.0552
907.265.2494
reservation@akrr.com
www.akrr.com

   Anchorage Ticket Office/Depot:
   411 West First Avenue

   Talkeetna Ticket Office/Depot
   Mile 13.5 Talkeetna Spur Road

   Fairbanks Ticket Office/Depot
   280 N. Cushman
   907.458.6025

The People Mover Bus
3650 A E. Tudor Rd.
Anchorage, Alaska 99507-1252
907.343.4536
www.peoplemover.org
wwtd@ci.anchorage.ak.us

Equipment and Supplies

Equipment Sales and Rentals:

Alaska Mountaineering and Hiking
2633 Spenard Road
Anchorage, Alaska 99503
907.272.1811
amh@alaska.net
www.alaskamountaineering.com

Alaska Mountaineering School
PO BOX 566
3rd Street
Talkeetna, AK 99676 USA
907.733.1016
info@climbalaska.org
www.climbalaska.org
Rentals only.

Recreational Equipment, Inc.
1200 W Northern Lights Blvd
Ste A
Anchorage, AK 99503
907.272.4565
www.rei.com

Groceries:

Costco
330 West Dimond Blvd
Anchorage, Alaska 99515
907.349.2335
www.costco.com

Fred Meyer
1000 E Northern Lights Blvd
Anchorage, AK 99508
907.279.8651
www.fredmeyer.com

Nagley's General Store
P.O. Box 608
Talkeetna, AK 99676
907.733.3663
dennis@nagleysgeneralstore.com

Natural Pantry
3801 Old Seward Hwy
601 E. Dimond Blvd
Anchorage, AK 99503
907.770.1444
www.natural-pantry.com

New Segaya's Midtown Market
3700 Old Seward Highway
Anchorage, AK 99503
907.561.5173
800.764.1001
www.newsagaya.com

Riley Creek Mercantile
Denali Park, AK 99755
907.683.9246

Talkeetna Natural Foods
P.O. Box 986
Talkeetna, AK 99676
907.733.3882
vincecooks@yahoo.com
www.talkeetnanaturalfoods.com

Tanner's Trading Post
P.O. Box 646
Main Street
Talkeetna, AK 99676
907.733.2621

Showers and Laundry:

Tanner's Trading Post
Main Street
Talkeetna, Alaska 99676
907.733.2621

Film Processing:

PhotoWright Labs
927 West Fireweed Lane
Anchorage, Alaska. 99503
907.277.0518
www.photowright.com

Climbing Guides

Authorized guides for Denali, Foraker, and the Central Alaska Range:

Alaska Mountaineering School, LLC
P.O. Box 566
3rd Street
Talkeetna, AK 99676
907.733.1016
info@climbalaska.org
www.climbalaska.org

Alpine Ascents International, Inc.
121 Mercer Street
Seattle, WA 98109
206.378.1927
climb@alpineascents.com
www.alpineascents.com

American Alpine Institute, Ltd.
1515 12th Street
Bellingham, WA 98825
360.671.1505
info@aai.cc
www.mtnguide.com

National Outdoor Leadership School
284 Lincoln Street
Lander, WY 82520
307.332.5300
800.710.6657
admissions@nols.edu
www.nols.edu

Mountain Trip International, LLC
P.O. Box 658
Ophir, Colorado 81426
907.369.1153
866.886.8747
info@mountaintrip.com
www.mountaintrip.com

Rainier Mountaineering, Inc.
P.O. Box Q
360.569.2227
888.892.5462
info@rmiguides.com
www.rmiguides.com

Other authorized guides for the Central Alaska Range:

Alpine Skills International
11400 Donner Pass Road
Truckee, CA 96161
530.582.9170
asi@alpineskills.com
www.alpineskills.com

Colorado Mountain School
341 Moraine Ave
Estes Park, CO 80517
888.267.7783
970.586.5758
cmschool@cmschool.com
www.cmschool.com

Mountain Link, LLC
164 NW Greenwood Ave
Bend, OR 97701
800.408.8949
541.312.8766
info@mountain-link.com
www.mountain-link.com

San Juan Mountain Guides, LLC
PO Box 1214
Ouray, CO 81427
866.525.4925
970.325.4925
info@ourayclimbing.com
www.ourayclimbing.com

Sierra Mountain Center, LLC
174 West Line Street
Bishop, CA 93514
760.873.8526
office@sierramountaincenter.com
www.sierramountaincenter.com

St. Elias Alpine Guides, LLC
PO Box 92129
Anchorage, AK 99509
888.933.5427
907.554.4445
info@steliasguides.com

Lodging, Food, Resources:

Talkeetna:

Denali Fairview Inn
P.O. Box 1109
Talkeetna, AK 99676
907.733.2423
info@denali-fairview.com
www.denali-fairview.com

Latitude 62 Lodge / Motel / Restaurant
P.O. Box 478
Talkeetna, AK 99676
907.733.2262
www.latitude62.com
info@latitude62.com

Mountain High Pizza Pie
P.O. Box 733
Talkeetna, AK 99676
907.733.1234
www.mhpp.biz

The Mountain House
Roberta Sheldon
Alaska Retreat
P.O .Box 292
Talkeetna, AK 99676
907.733.2414.

Sparky's
Main Street
Talkeetna, AK 99676
907.733.4363

Swiss Alaska Inn
P.O. Box 565
Talkeetna, AK 99676
907.733.2424
vern@swissalaska.com
www.swissalaska.com

Talkeetna Hostel International
P.O. Box 952, I Street
Talkeetna, AK 99676
907.733.4678
hezim@gci.net
www.talkeetnahostel.com

Talkeetna Roadhouse
Lodging, Meals, Bakery
P.O. Box 604
Talkeetna, AK 99676
907.733.1351
info@talkeetnaroadhouse.com
www.talkeetnaroadhouse.com

West Rib Pub and Grill
100 Main Street
Talkeetna, AK 99676
907.733.3663

Anchorage:

Bear Tooth Theatrepub & Grill
1239 W 27th Ave
Anchorage, AK 99503
907.276.4200
www.beartooththeatre.net/index2.html

Earth Bed and Breakfast
1001 W. 12th Avenue
Anchorage, Alaska 99501
907.279.9907
www.earthbb.com
info@earthbb.com

The Middle Way Café
1200 W Northern Lights Blvd
Anchorage, AK 99676
907.272.6433

Moose's Tooth Pub and Pizzeria
3300 Old Seward Hwy
Anchorage, AK 99503
907.258.2537
www.moosestooth.net/index2.htm

Organic Oasis
2610 Spenard Road
Anchorage, AK 99676
907.277.7882
www.organicoasis.com

Other Addresses:

Denali National Park:

Denali National Park and Preserve
P.O. Box 9
Denali Park, AK 99755
907.683.2294
denali_information@nps.gov
www.nps.gov/dena

Denali Visitor Center
Mile 1 Park Road
907.683.1266
Open: May 15 to May 27, 8 A.M. to 5 P.M.
May 28 to Sept 16, 7A.M. to 8 P.M.
Sept 17 to Sept 25, 10 A.M. to 4 P.M.

Denali Park Shuttle Bus and Campground
Reservations
800.622.7275
907.272.7275
Doyon/ARAMARK
241 West Ship Creek Ave.
Anchorage, AK 99501
www.reservedenali.com

Talkeetna Ranger Station
B Street
P.O. Box 588
Talkeetna, AK 99676
907.733.2231
DENA_Talkeetna_Office@nps.gov
Open:
Mid-April to Labor Day, 8 A.M. to 6 P.M.
Remainder of year, 8 A.M. to 4:30 P.M.,
M-F

Resources / Organizations:

Alaska Alpine Club
1736 Farmers Loop
Fairbanks, AK 99709
907.479.2149
climb@alaskanalpineclub.org
www.alaskanalpineclub.org

The Alaska Mountain Forum
Alaskan Climbers' Bulletin Board
www.alaskamountianforum.com

The Milepost magazine
www.themilepost.com

Mountaineering Club of Alaska
PO Box 102037
Anchorage, AK 99510
www.mcak.org

National Weather Service
Alaska Region Headquarters
222 West 7th Ave., #23
Anchorage, AK 99513-7575
907.271.5088
Alaska Weather Line:
800.472.0391
www.arh.noaa.gov

International Climbers Websites:

Travel documentation requirements:
http://www.customs.ustreas.gov/xp/cgov/
travel/vacation/kbyg/documentary_req.xml

Information on traveling with food and
specialty items:
http://www.aphis.usda.gov/travel/travel.
html

Equipment List

This is a comprehensive list of items that are useful and/or necessary for climbing in the Alaska Range. Not all items may be carried on any one climb. Pick the gear off this list that will work for you based on the season, your chosen route, and your style of climbing.

Personal Gear

Clothing:

Plastic double-boots or insulated leather boots (for summer rock routes)
Overboots
Super-gaiters
Thick wool or synthetic socks
Thin liner socks
Synthetic briefs or boxers
Light-weight synthetic long underwear tops and bottoms
Expedition-weight synthetic long underwear tops and bottoms
Fleece or synthetic pullover or jacket
Fleece or synthetic pants
Shell jacket
Shell pants
Large down or synthetic parka with hood
Large down or synthetic pants
Thick wool or synthetic stocking cap
Balaclava or face mask
Sun hat
Bandanas
Sun glasses
Ski goggles
Expedition-style double-layer mittens
Thinner multi-purpose shell gloves with liners
Fleece gloves
Synthetic liner gloves

Camping:

Backpack
Sled bag w/ extra webbing or straps
Sleeping bag
Sleeping pads
Bivy sack
Headlamp (for early season)
Wide-mouth water bottles
Insulated water bottle parkas
Drinking cup and spoon
Pee bottle (clearly marked!)
Sunscreen, lip protection (SPF 30+)
Ear plugs
Knife
Hand warmers
Toothbrush, paste, toilet paper, and other personal effects
Altimeter watch
Camera, film
Journal and pencil
Personal radio/mini-disc/MP3 player
Books
Extra batteries

Group Gear:

Tent
Stove
Stove board
Fuel bottles, fuel
Lighters
Pot set
Dipper cup
Frying pan, spatula
Route guide, topo, and map
Compass, GPS
Communication device (CB, sat. phone, aircraft radio, etc.)
Monocular or binoculars

Shovels
Snowsaw
Wands
Repair Kit
Medical Kit
Clean Mountain Cans
Latrine bags
Garbage bags
Food

Climbing Gear:

Snowshoes
Skis and skins
Ski poles
Sleds
Ropes
Ice axe
Ice tools, extra picks
Crampons
Rock shoes
Chalk bag
Helmet
Harness
Chest harness
Locking and non-locking carabiners
Belay/rappel device
Ascenders, prussiks
Etriers, daisy chains
Extra runners, draws, and slings
Rescue Pulleys
V-thread device
Nut tool
Pickets
Ice screws
Rock protection: stoppers, cams, pitons
Hooks

About the Author:

Joseph Puryear has spent the last 15 years exploring the peaks of the Central Alaska Range. He has also climbed extensively throughout the United States and Canada and particularly enjoys the Cascade Range of Washington State. Other climbing adventures have taken him to Argentina, Chile, China, Mexico, Nepal, Peru, Switzerland, and Thailand. Joseph is an avid photographer. More of his photography can be viewed at his website www.cascadeimages.com. In 2004 he married Talkeetna, Alaska local Michelle O'Neil on the Pika Glacier near Denali. When not enjoying their small cabin in Talkeetna, Joe and Michelle make their home in Leavenworth, Washington.

About the Contributors:

Dr. Jim Litch

Dr. Jim Litch is a mountain and travel medicine physician, climber and mountain guide from Seattle. He is a former NPS mountaineering ranger on Denali (Mt. McKinley) and Mt. Rainier, and has been involved in rescue and mountain safety efforts on 5 continents, including Antarctica. He has climbed and guided several 8000 meter peaks, including Mt Everest via the North Ridge, and is a veteran of 22 expeditions worldwide. Jim has published widely on high altitude and travel medicine, and is currently clinical assistant professor at the University of Washington.

Joe Reichert

Joe Reichert is one of Denali National Park's nine mountaineering rangers. After climbing Denali in April 1992, he decided that he wanted to make his living on the mountain. In 1994 he was a SCA volunteer for Denali National Park and signed on as a seasonal ranger the following summer. Expedition climbing is Joe's preferred style of outdoor adventure. Over 10 expeditions in Alaska and a couple to the big walls of Patagonia have allowed him to visit spectacular corners of the planet. Work has taken him from the fishing boats of Prince William Sound to the South Pole. His BS in Forest Biology from UVM is being put to the test searching for those elusive glacier trees!